Calming the Bipolar Storm

Calming the Bipolar Storm

A Guide for Patients and Their Families

Robert G. Fawcett, MD

ROWMAN & LITTLEFIELD
Lanham · Boulder · New York · London

Published by Rowman & Littlefield
An imprint of The Rowman & Littlefield Publishing Group, Inc.
4501 Forbes Boulevard, Suite 200, Lanham, Maryland 20706
www.rowman.com

6 Tinworth Street, London SE11 5AL, United Kingdom

British Library Cataloguing in Publication Information Available

Library of Congress Cataloging-in-Publication Data

Names: Fawcett, Robert G., 1946– author.
Title: Calming the bipolar storm : a guide for patients and their families
 / Robert G. Fawcett.
Description: Lanham : Rowman & Littlefield, 2021. | Includes
 bibliographical references and index. | Summary: "Calming the Bipolar
 Storm describes the symptoms and subtypes of bipolar disorder, its
 causes, and the role of the social and biologic environment in affecting
 its course. It also emphasizes positive health-promoting behaviors and
 describes treatments, including psychotherapy and medications for mania
 and depression and for relapse prevention" — Provided by publisher.
Identifiers: LCCN 2020046473 (print) | LCCN 2020046474 (ebook) | ISBN
 9781538145647 (cloth) | ISBN 9781538145654 (epub)
Subjects: LCSH: Manic-depressive illness—Treatment. | Psychotherapy. |
 Manic-depressive illness—Prevention.
Classification: LCC RC516 .F42 2021 (print) | LCC RC516 (ebook) | DDC
 616.89/5—dc23
LC record available at https://lccn.loc.gov/2020046473
LC ebook record available at https://lccn.loc.gov/2020046474

This book is dedicated to my wife Letty,
my daughters Carrie and Susan,
and my granddaughter Amelia,
who make everything worthwhile.

Author's Note

This book does not constitute a treatment relationship with any of its readers, nor is it a substitute for professional care. It is very important to coordinate one's personal medical and mental health care with one's providers, especially when dealing with a serious disorder such as bipolar mood disorder.

Contents

Introduction

$\mathcal{E}$rnest Hemingway, a preeminent figure among twentieth-century writers, and Nobel Prize winner for literature, suffered from bipolar mood disorder. He described his depressions in a letter to fellow writer John Dos Passos, "I felt that gigantic bloody emptiness and nothingness." He said he could not fight, write, or have sex, and was "all set for death."[1] One biographer wrote that "the pendulum in his nervous system swung periodically through the full arc from megalomania to melancholy."[2] As a youth he would stay up all night drinking and reading poetry aloud. His first wife described his elated period thus: "sky high, emotionally intense, and ready to explode."[3] He wrote prolifically during these high spells, completing seven short stories during a high spell in 1924.

Hemingway described his episodes of mixed mania and depression: "Had a spell where I was pretty gloomy . . . and didn't sleep for about three weeks. Took to . . . going out to the little house to work until daylight because when you're writing on a book and can't sleep your brain races at night and you write all the stuff in your head and in the morning it is gone and you are pooped."[4]

Hemingway avoided treatment until late in his life, instead self-medicating with alcohol. His enthusiastic pursuit of hunting and fishing perhaps channeled some of his intense emotions. He told Ava Gardner, "Even though I am not a believer in the Analysis, I spend a hell of a lot of time killing animals and fish so I won't kill myself."[5]

Later in life his disease worsened. He had delusions that the FBI was watching him and that his friends were plotting to kill him. He entered the Mayo Clinic for seven weeks in 1960. His blood pressure medication, reserpine, now known to sometimes cause depression, and his barbiturate sleep aids were stopped. He received electroconvulsive treatments (ECT), a treatment for depression that preceded our current arsenal of psychotropic medications. The treatment was successful. He wrote *A Moveable Feast* in that post-hospital period. But his depression returned with a vengeance, so severe that he was unable to write. He became desperately suicidal. His wife found him as he was loading a shotgun. He was hospitalized in Ketchum, Idaho, then transferred back to the Mayo Clinic. On the trip there, while changing planes at an airport, he strode toward the whirling blades of an airplane propeller. The pilot stopped the engine in time to avert disaster.[6]

At Mayo he once again received ECT during his two-month hospitalization. Despite his outward appearance of improvement, he remained terminally depressed. Within a week of discharge, he slipped away from his sleeping wife and shot himself in the head with both barrels of his shotgun. His suicide in 1961 was a close reenactment of his father's suicide in 1928. This family tendency toward suicide claimed the lives of his younger brother Leicester, younger sister Ursula, and his niece Margaux.

Genetics plays the primary role in causation of bipolar disorder. His father, who had several prolonged "rest cures" for his depression and was prone to periods of high irritability, was probably bipolar. His mother had problems with depression. Alcohol abuse, which plagued Ernest, is common in bipolar disorder and tends to aggravate its course, with more hospitalizations and suicide attempts. Nevertheless, many persons with bipolar disorder drink to calm their racing thoughts and insomnia.

Hemingway's childhood included abusive events that may have enhanced his risk both for drinking and for suicide. His father, prone to fits of anger, used a razor strop to whip Ernest. When he was a young boy his mother dressed him like a girl to an age that surpassed the usual practice in those Victorian times. Ernest harbored a strong sense of hatred toward her. This cross-dressing may have stimulated a reaction toward the hypermasculine pursuits of big game hunting, fishing, and placing himself in dangerous fronts during the World Wars.[7]

His impulsivity and recklessness, fueled by both his bipolar disorder and alcoholism, led him into situations where he sustained at least five concussions during his life, in auto and airplane accidents and drunken falls on a boat. Such cerebral trauma may have worsened his mood disorder. Although lithium, with its mood stabilizing and anti-suicidal effects, was being used in Europe during the 1950s, it was not available in the States until 1970. Perhaps with the biological and psychotherapeutic treatments now available Ernest Hemingway might have lived several more decades and added more volumes to his literary treasure trove.

Calming the Bipolar Storm gives readers an understanding of the disorder, its symptoms, its multiple forms, and its course. The book discusses the "self-medication hypothesis" among other explanations for the high rates of substance use disorders among bipolar persons, and describes how adverse childhood experiences worsen the course of bipolar disorder.

In recent decades bipolar disorder has emerged from the shadows and become more visible in society and in the popular media. Characters with bipolar disorder are frequently depicted in movies such as *Silver Linings Playbook*, television series such as *Homeland*, and in popular novels and songs. Actress Patty Duke and newscaster Jane Pauley both wrote autobiographies that detail their struggles with bipolar disorder. Many of these efforts have reduced the stigma of bipolar disorder and made it more acceptable to seek help. This book is an attempt to enlarge the public's understanding of bipolar mood disorder.

It is estimated that between 1 and 2 percent of the population will be afflicted by bipolar I disorder in their lifetime, and an equal number by bipolar II. Bipolar disorder has a very significant impact on them and those close to them, on the health care system, and on our national economy. *Calming the Bipolar Storm* informs readers about the disorder and its treatment, adding to the coping skills of patients and family members.

The book starts with an overview of what constitutes bipolar mood disorder. The disorder presents in many different ways. Perhaps you wonder whether you or a loved one has bipolar disorder, or whether the emotional difficulty is simply a form of depression or another disorder such as schizophrenia, attention deficit disorder, or borderline personality disorder. This book will help educate you on the fundamental features of bipolar disorder and what makes it different from other disorders with overlapping features.

We will explore the landscape of bipolar disorder itself. How does bipolar I disorder differ from bipolar II? What is bipolar spectrum disorder? What is cyclothymic disorder? We shall look back at the history of bipolar disorder and how the concept has matured and developed through decades of medical research and study.

Naturally people are curious about the causes of bipolar disorder and whether it is passed along to one's children and grandchildren. We shall discuss the genetics and inheritance of bipolar disorder. Do childhood traumas, psychological stressors in adult life, drugs, and medical illnesses affect the development of bipolar disorder and its course? We shall look at those questions.

Explaining the pros and cons of various drugs and therapies for bipolar disorder, both traditional and emerging, takes up a sizable section of the book. We shall look at how bipolar disorder interacts with other psychiatric, substance abuse, and medical disorders and look at the concept of secondary mania (when mania is caused by medical factors). We shall focus on some special areas such as pregnancy, suicide, and bipolar youth, and list some resources for further education and study.

You do not have to read the entire book, but can use selected chapters to explore particular areas. However, unless you are knowledgeable about bipolar disorder it is best to read the first three chapters. Some facts and issues are mentioned in several chapters (e.g., the influence of substance abuse on the course of bipolar disorder). The book is based on both my own extensive studies of the scientific literature and my experience treating hundreds of patients with bipolar mood disorder through more than forty years of practice. Some relevant and interesting cases are presented to illustrate concepts in a more lively and poignant way. Certain details may be left out or changed to disguise a person's identity in those cases. If you do read the entire book you should gain a solid, up-to-date understanding of bipolar mood disorder.

This book does not constitute a treatment relationship with any of its readers. It is very important to coordinate one's personal medical and mental health care with one's providers, especially when dealing with a serious disorder such as bipolar mood disorder.

What Is Bipolar Disorder?

$\mathcal{N}$orm had trouble with depression in his teens, seeing a counselor and struggling sometimes with suicidal thoughts. His chaotic homelife did not help. His father leaving when he was just ten was a mixed blessing. He drank heavily and was physically abusive to Norm's mother and verbally abusive to Norm.

In his twenties Norm continued to have stretches of depression lasting sometimes for many weeks. At times he could not force himself out of bed and lost some jobs because of it. He also had periods where he had a great deal of energy and felt adventuresome. He felt happy and carefree, but noticed his temper was short. He would drive to a different town, get a motel, drink or do drugs if he could find them, have sex with women he would meet, and sleep very little. Sometimes he wrote bad checks to bankroll his adventures. After several days or a few weeks on such a high, he would awaken one morning depressed, guilty, and regretful about his behavior. Then he slept excessively, his appetite was poor, and he could not focus or concentrate. After a few more weeks his mood normalized for a while. His family doctor tried Norm on some Prozac. At first he thought it helped, but then another high mood followed by a depression would occur. He was not surprised when a psychiatrist diagnosed him with a bipolar II mood disorder.

Bipolar disorder is an illness characterized by abnormal swings in mood and in energy levels. The classical bipolar patient displays mood swings between the opposite poles of manic elation and depressive lows. How did we come to our present-day concept of bipolar disorder?

From the time of the renowned Greek physician Hippocrates around 300 BCE, clinicians have described episodes of mania and depression. The Greeks described mania as a form of excitement and agitation that would include not only today's bipolar mania, but organic brain disorders such as states of confusion and delirium. Depression was termed *melancholia* and presumed to result from an excess of black bile as the term *melancholia* implies. Mania was thought to be the result of too much yellow bile or a mixture of yellow and black bile. These ideas were spelled out in the Greek humoral theories of disease wherein health depended on the proper balance of four bodily humors or substances.[1]

Around 100 AD Soranus of Ephesus described mania as an impairment of reason with continual wakefulness, delusions, and fluctuating states of merriment and anger. He described the melancholic as downcast, never cheerful or relaxed, dejected, weeping for no reason, and sometimes longing for death. Galen of Pergamon (131–201 CE) wrote that mania could be primary or secondary to other diseases, foreshadowing the modern concept of *secondary mania*.

In the second-century AD Aretaeus of Cappadocia proposed that mania was an end stage of melancholia. Indeed, we sometimes see patients who have had multiple episodes of depression for decades ultimately exhibiting a manic episode.[2]

In 1378 CE, after the death of Pope Gregory, the college of cardinals elected Pope Urban, a Roman cardinal described as "learned, modest, and devout." Presumably under the influence of a bipolar mood disorder, Pope Urban's behavior changed radically after his ordination. In volatile angry diatribes he berated cardinals, individually and as a group. He got into brawls with visitors, and made grandiose statements (e.g., that he could depose emperors and kings). Despite the pleadings of the cardinals he refused to step down as pope, leading to the Great Schism of the Catholic church from 1378 to 1418, when two men claimed the title of pope.[3]

Another prominent leader afflicted with mood disorder was King Ferdinand VI of Spain, whose personal physician Andrés Piquer diagnosed him with "melancholic-manic affect" and concluded that melancholia and mania were part of the same illness.[4]

In 1854 two Parisian psychiatrists argued publicly about who was first to describe what we now regard as bipolar disorder. Jules Baillarger wrote, "There exists a special type of insanity characterized by two regular periods, the one of depression and the other of excitement." He called this disorder *folie à double form*, which translates to "insanity in dual form." His rival, Dr. Jean-Pierre Falret, dubbed the disorder he described *folie circulaire* or "circular insanity." The feuding Frenchmen both described the illness as showing alternating episodes of depression and mania that could occur one immediately after the other or be separated by years. The frequency of episodes could vary widely from patient to patient. Their terminology did not seem to catch on, however, or to exert much influence over the clinical practice of the time, unlike the giant of the era, German psychiatrist Emil Kraepelin, who followed them.[5]

Kraepelin coined the term *manic-depressive disorder* in 1899 for the sixth edition of his psychiatric textbook, and it differs a bit from our current concept of bipolar disorder.[6] In a time when the "splitters" were ascribing numerous different diagnoses to mental disorders based on their symptom picture, Kraepelin was a "lumper." He divided the realm of major nonorganic mental illness into manic-depressive illness and dementia praecox (similar to what is now called schizophrenia). Manic-depressive illness was an illness of episodic recurrences of abnormal mood. Some such patients had episodes of mania and of depression, but he also included highly recurrent depression under manic-depressive illness. This was not the kind of reactive depression one might see in people who have suffered a major loss, such as the death of a spouse or a divorce. Such an episode of reactive depression is often triggered by external factors, and once it lifts the depression may not recur. Kraepelin was including the recurrent form of depression that may strike a person three, four, or a dozen times throughout life, often with no clear precipitating factors, and results in moderate to severe symptoms. He also favored using the term *depression* instead of the term *melancholia*, which bespoke its own erroneous theory of causation by "black bile." Kraepelin's textbooks, widely read in Europe, and with translation in the English-speaking countries, fostered wide acceptance of his concepts of mental illness.

In 1957 another German psychiatrist, Karl Leonhard, proposed the term *bipolar disorder* along with monopolar depression as a way to subdivide manic-depressive illness.[7] This terminology caught on and was incorporated in 1980 into the *Diagnostic and Statistical Manual* (*DSM*), a book sanctioned by the American Psychiatric Association to be used as a diagnostic manual in clinical and research settings. Let's look more closely at psychiatric diagnosis.

For many years psychiatric disorders have been defined as patterns of symptoms and signs. Symptoms are complaints voiced by the patient or others. A decreased need for sleep is an example. Signs are observations made during an evaluation, for example, speech being rapid and loud. If enough of these symptoms and signs fit the prescribed definition of disorder Z and the patient does not have another similar disorder, we can describe the patient as having disorder Z. For example, if the patient has three symptoms from the list "A, B, C, D, and E" and two from the list "F, G, and H," and she does not have disorder X, she fits the diagnosis. This has been whimsically referred to as the Chinese restaurant style of diagnosis. There are other possible ways to try to define a disorder. For example, one could assess measurements on a variety of scales (e.g., depression, anxiety, or psychosis scales) and define a disorder based on the patient's scores on all the scales. Or one could describe a prototypical bipolar patient or schizophrenic patient and say that whichever prototypical pattern the patient most closely resembled determined her diagnosis. Perhaps someday we shall have biologic markers for psychiatric disorders, much as we now have for other diseases. For example, one might suspect a deficiency of vitamin B12 if a patient has the sign of an anemia with oversized red blood cells and symptoms of numbness and tingling in the feet from neuropathy, but the clincher is measuring a low B12 level in the blood.

The *Diagnostic and Statistical Manual V* or *DSM-5*[8] is the current diagnostic scheme used by North American psychiatrists to describe a patient's disorder for research and clinical purposes. As the fifth iteration of this manual, which has been used since the mid-1900s, it has gone through many changes. Some diagnoses, such as involutional melancholia, have been eliminated. Others, such as bipolar disorder, have been refined into more specific categories. Most of these changes are made by committees of experts reaching consensus, often informed by research studies regarding these diagnoses. The *DSM* is a work in progress that will undoubtedly have further changes in *DSM-6*.

Across the globe many clinicians use the *International Classification of Diseases* (*ICD-10*), which differs a bit from *DSM-5*. In May 2019 member countries from the World Health Organization approved *ICD-11*, which will be in common use by January 2022, replacing *ICD-10*. *ICD-11* uses most of the terms and definitions from *DSM-5*.

The majority of psychiatric diagnoses, including bipolar disorder, are based on clusters of symptoms and signs. A few, such as vascular dementia, make use of laboratory findings, for example, a CT scan or MRI of the brain to correlate an area of cerebral infarct or stroke with the dementia presenting clinically. A diagnosis of rapid eye movement sleep behavior disorder might rely on sleep recordings to reach a valid diagnosis. But most diagnoses rely on symptoms described by the patient or others and behavioral signs the clinician can observe.

We want diagnoses to be both reliable and valid. A reliable diagnosis means that many clinicians will reach the same diagnosis when evaluating the patient's symptoms. For example, if nineteen out of twenty psychiatrists diagnose patient A as having bipolar I disorder, manic phase, and one psychiatrist diagnoses the patient with major depression with mixed symptoms, then the diagnosis of that patient would be 95 percent reliable within that group of doctors.

Predictive validity means a diagnosis tells us something useful about the patient's condition: what forms of treatment are likely to be helpful, what course the patient's illness is likely to take in the future, how likely other close relatives are to share this or similar disorders, what associated medical and psychiatric disorders the patient is prone to. Bipolar disorder can be diagnosed with good reliability and validity, but sometimes the assessments of clinicians differ when the diagnosis is unclear.

The hallmark of bipolar disorder is the presence of a manic episode or episodes. Most bipolar patients have depressive episodes as well. In fact, most have many more days spent in a depressive mode than in a manic one. However, rarely do we see someone who has manic spells but no depressions. Studies range between 5 percent and 28 percent of bipolar patients having mania but no depression.[9]

A manic episode shows increased goal-directed activity. In contrast, persons with an agitated depression tend to have more purposeless, repetitive movements. A manic person talks more than usual. Often, he speaks more loudly and rapidly. Thoughts seem to flow more quickly and creatively, so that the speech of a manic person may show a "flight of ideas." His thoughts rapidly slip from one topic to another in a manner than may befuddle the listener. Often the manic person experiences a sense of racing thoughts. Some patients with anxiety disorders describe a similar, but still discernably different, flow of worrisome thoughts, frequently when trying to sleep.

Mood during a manic phase changes classically to euphoria—a happy, outgoing optimistic glow. But also, irritability or aggressiveness may be the predominant mood. Often a euphoric mood changes quickly to anger or irritability when the demands of the manic patient are not met. The patient may show grandiose thinking, such as believing she has a fantastic money-making business plan and withdrawing all her savings to invest in it. Sometimes these grandiose trends reach delusional proportions. A manic patient once approached me in the hospital and said, "Excuse me, Doctor, I just wanted to let you know that I am the Messiah." Another manic patient told me that he had invented a perpetual motion machine.

Some bipolar patients will show a predominantly paranoid mood in the manic phase, believing themselves to be persecuted and feeling suspicious of others. Sometimes paranoid delusions occur (e.g., that the government is after them, tapping their phones and computers, or that aliens from space are broadcasting messages to them).

At times, hallucinations may occur. Most often these are auditory, in the form of a voice commenting to or commanding the patient, but sometimes visual, tactile, or olfactory hallucinations occur.

Mania revs one up, so that even physical movements are faster and in greater abundance. Literally hundreds of bipolar patients have told me they cleaned the house during the middle of the night, because impaired sleep is another hallmark of mania. Usually it is a lessened need for sleep, so patients stay alert in the daytime despite their reduced sleeping hours. But sometimes the severe sleep deprivation leads to episodes of daytime drowsiness or naps.

The increase in goal-directed activities is often directed to goals different from and riskier than usual. Excessive spending of money is typical and may include overly generous gifts to others. Patients may impulsively buy things they really do not need and can ill afford, such as an Alaskan vacation, a motorcycle, or a rickshaw. Other risk-taking behaviors occur such as gambling, speeding in an automobile, or uncharacteristic use of drugs.

Libido is usually increased during mania and impulse control is slackened. This combination can lead to sexual behaviors and indiscretions that are foreign to the patient's usual behavior. More than a few marriages have been jeopardized or ruined because of a partner's sexual escapades when manic. The manic patient may choose a sexual partner who differs in gender from her usual choice or experiment with a different form of sexual activity.

In 1881 Mendel described *hypomania* as "a form of mania which typically shows itself only in the milder stages, abortively, so to speak."[10] What we now call bipolar II disorder was described in the late 1880s by Hecker as alternating periods of depression and a milder form of exuberance that often escaped the notice of family, physicians, and even the patient himself.[11] Still today many persons with bipolar II disorder are treated for depression with their hypomanic periods passing under the radar.

The distinction between hypomania and mania hinges on the severity of impairment in social and occupational functioning. To be characterized as manic, the impairment must be marked, for example, rendering the patient unable to function at a job or to care for children at home. Some patients with hypomania may continue to function in their roles, often causing more distress to those around them because of irritability or other symptoms, but unless the impairment is marked, the episode is one of hypomania. In addition, if a patient is hospitalized, usually because of some level of dangerousness to themselves or others, or has psychotic symptoms, such as hallucinations or delusions, she is classified as manic, and not hypomanic.

In addition, the manic symptom picture should not be the result of some other biologic stimulus, such as hyperthyroidism or abuse of stimulant drugs. Those instances, which we shall look at later in this book, are termed *secondary mania*.

To meet the criteria for a manic or hypomanic state the mood has to be a significant change from the patient's baseline and present throughout most of the day nearly every day. For mania the hyperactive spell must last at least a week, and for hypomania at least four days. It is important to recognize that we as scientific observers do our best to parcel up what nature offers into coherent packages like mania and hypomania. But the rules we impose are somewhat arbitrary and nature does not abide by them. Thus, it is common to see patients who exhibit symptoms that do not quite fit all the criteria for a full-blown manic or hypomanic episode. Perhaps their abnormal mood lasted only three days or they met only two instead of the needed three ancillary symptoms of mania. Such patients are described by the term *bipolar spectrum disorder*. In fact, researchers found that most hypomanic episodes lasted from one to three days, thus falling short of the definition for bipolar II disorder, which requires four days of hypomania.[12] Textbox 2.1 presents the criteria for a manic episode.

MANIC EPISODE

A. A distinct period of abnormally and persistently elevated, expansive, or irritable mood and abnormally and persistently increased goal-directed activity or energy, lasting at least one week and present most of the day, nearly every day (or any duration if hospitalization is necessary).
B. During the period of mood disturbance and increased energy or activity, three (or more) of the following symptoms (four if the mood is only irritable) are present to a significant degree and represent a noticeable change from usual behavior.

1. Inflated self-esteem or grandiosity.
2. Decreased need for sleep (e.g., feels rested after only 3 hours of sleep).
3. More talkative than usual or pressure to keep talking.
4. Flight of ideas or subjective experience that thoughts are racing.
5. Distractibility (i.e., attention too easily drawn to unimportant or irrelevant external stimuli), as reported or observed.
6. Increase in goal-directed activity (either socially, at work or school, or sexually) or psychomotor agitation (i.e., purposeless non-goal-directed activity).
7. Excessive involvement in activities that have a high potential for painful consequences (e.g., engaging in unrestrained buying sprees, sexual indiscretions, or foolish business investments).

C. The mood of the disturbance is sufficiently severe to cause marked impairment in social or occupational functioning or to necessitate hospitalization to prevent harm to self or others, or there are psychotic features.
D. The episode is not attributable to the physiological effects of a substance (e.g., a drug of abuse, medication, other treatment) or to another medical condition.

Note: A full manic episode that emerges during antidepressant treatment (e.g., medication, electroconvulsive therapy) but persists at a fully syndromal level beyond the physiological effect of that treatment is sufficient evidence for a manic episode and, therefore, a bipolar I diagnosis.

Note: Criteria A–D constitute a manic episode. At least one lifetime manic episode is required for a diagnosis of bipolar I disorder.

Reprinted with permission from the *Diagnostic and Statistical Manual of Mental Disorders*, 5th ed. (Arlington, VA: American Psychiatric Association, 2013).

The other pole referred to in bipolar disorder is, of course, depression. Although most people have some understanding of this widespread syndrome, let's look at the criteria for a major depressive episode. Patients must show a persisting depressed mood most of the day, nearly every day for at least two weeks or a pervasive *anhedonia* or loss of the ability to experience pleasure or interest in activities during that time. Whereas in the past a visit from the grandchildren would bring a sense of excitement and delight, in the midst of a depression the patient may feel no emotional boost at all and wish to retreat from them.

Appetite is often disturbed during depression, usually diminished, but occasionally enhanced. A pervasive change in appetite is a symptom of depression and a significant change in weight a sign of depression. Food often tastes bland or uninteresting.

Sleep is also disturbed in depression, with insomnia or excessive sleep nearly every day a common symptom. Insomnia may occur in the early, middle, or end portion of the sleep period.

Fatigue and loss of energy is a common symptom of depression. Sarah found when she cycled into depression that she could not get out of bed to go to work and often had to call in sick. Even showering and getting dressed was a struggle, so she often stayed in bed for long hours. This fatigue of depression is different from the fatigue of medical disorders like heart disease. The patient with congestive heart failure may want to perform activities, but climbing a flight of stairs or walking a block leads to fatigue (and often shortness of breath as well) so the patient needs to rest. The fatigue of depression saps the patient's energy before she even begins a task, and the drive or motivation itself is low.

This slowing down of functions may be visible to family and friends. The depressed patient moves and talks more slowly. She may talk much less than usual. Often facial features appear depressed, sad, or fatigued. An *omega sign* is the name for the two vertical wrinkles appearing above the bridge of the nose when frowning. It is often present in depression. Occasionally we see instead of the slow-motion picture of *psychomotor retardation* a frenzied agitation in which the patient is pacing, wringing her hands, and rocking to soothe herself. About half of depressed patients have significant anxiety.

Thinking and concentration are impaired in depression. Attention span is poor. Decisions often seem overwhelming. I have had severely depressed patients waver for hours trying to decide to sign into a hospital or agree to take a medication, while their family and I did our best to encourage them to decide. Each time the patient picked up a pen and put it to paper she would then express doubt and put the pen down again. Such behavior can be very frustrating for family and providers, trying their patience severely.

Thoughts about death or suicide are common in depression. These can range from brief feelings of hopelessness with the fleeting thought of suicide immediately rejected, to persisting hopeless feelings that lead to suicidal planning and attempts. The lifetime rate of suicide among bipolar persons may be as high as 20 percent, ten to thirty times the rate of the general population.[13] Suicide will be discussed in more depth in a later chapter.

Feelings of excessive worthlessness and guilt are another of the diagnostic criteria for a major depressive episode. Often these are very irrational, for example, a person who is very effective and successful in her job and family life, loved by many friends and family, may still feel unworthy according to some internal standard. Sometimes successful celebrities such as Robin Williams with fame, money, and success commit suicide, leaving fans to wonder how he could do that with all he had going for him.

To count as a *major depressive episode*, this period of depression needs to last at least two weeks, cause significant impairment in social or occupational functioning, and not be clearly caused by a medical condition or other physiologic cause. Just as we see *secondary mania* so we can see *secondary depression*. Common causes can include hypothyroidism or medication effects. My local papers carried the story of a suicide committed by the son of one of our Michigan congresspeople. The young man, with no history of depression, had been taking isotretinoin for acne. This is among the drugs that have been associated with depression, and it now carries a warning label from the U.S. Food and Drug Administration (FDA).

Criteria for a major depressive episode are listed in textbox 2.2.

MAJOR DEPRESSIVE EPISODE

A. Five (or more) of the following symptoms have been present during the same 2-week period and represent a change from previous functioning; at least one of the symptoms is either (1) depressed mood or (2) loss of interest or pleasure.

Note: Do not include symptoms that are clearly attributable to another medical condition.

1. Depressed mood most of the day, nearly every day, as indicated by either subjective report (e.g., feels sad, empty, or hopeless) or observation made by others (e.g., appears tearful). (Note: In children and adolescents, can be irritable mood.)
2. Markedly diminished interest or pleasure in all, or almost all, activities most of the day, nearly every day (as indicated by either subjective account or observation).
3. Significant weight loss when not dieting or weight gain (e.g., a change of more than 5% of body weight in a month), or decrease or increase in appetite nearly every day. (Note: in children, consider failure to make expected weight gain.)
4. Insomnia or hypersomnia nearly every day.
5. Psychomotor agitation or retardation nearly every day (observable by others; not merely subjective feelings of restlessness or being slowed down).
6. Fatigue or loss of energy nearly every day.
7. Feelings of worthlessness or excessive or inappropriate guilt (which may be delusional) nearly every day (not merely self-reproach or guilt about being sick).

8. Diminished ability to think or concentrate, or indecisiveness, nearly every day (either by subjective account or as observed by others).

9. Recurrent thoughts of death (not just fear of dying), recurrent suicidal ideation without a specific plan, or a suicide attempt or a specific plan for committing suicide.

B. The symptoms cause clinically significant distress or impairment in social, occupational, or other important areas of functioning.

C. The episode is not attributable to the physiological effects of a substance or another medical condition.

Note: Criteria A–C constitute a major depressive episode. Major depressive episodes are common in bipolar I disorder but are not required for the diagnosis of bipolar I disorder.

Note: Responses to a significant loss (e.g., bereavement, financial ruin, losses from a natural disaster, a serious medical illness or disability) may include the feelings of intense sadness, rumination about the loss, insomnia, poor appetite, and weight loss noted in Criterion A, which may resemble a depressive episode. Although such symptoms may be understandable or considered appropriate to the loss, the presence of a major depressive episode in addition to the normal response to a significant loss should also be carefully considered. This decision inevitably requires the exercise of clinical judgment based on the individual's history and the cultural norms for the expression of distress in the context of loss.

Reprinted with permission from the *Diagnostic and Statistical Manual of Mental Disorders*, 5th ed. (Arlington, VA: American Psychiatric Association, 2013).

Not uncommonly, patients show mixed features with elements simultaneously of both mania and depression. For example, a manic patient with high energy, irritability, rapid speech, and little need for sleep might also show a very unhappy dysphoric mood, feelings of worthlessness, and prominent suicidal thoughts. This would constitute a manic episode with mixed features. An episode of mania or depression must show at least three nonoverlapping symptoms of the other mood pole to be classified in *DSM-5* as having mixed features. Symptoms such as insomnia or restlessness are overlapping; they commonly occur in both mania and depression.[14] *ICD-11* retains the diagnosis of a mixed bipolar episode, while *DSM-5* refers to a *primary mood syndrome* (manic or depressed) with mixed features.

Bipolar I disorder includes patients who have experienced a full-blown manic episode at some time in their lives. Even if later episodes of high mood only rise to the level of hypomania, they still are classified as bipolar I. Rarely bipolar I patients may vary between normal and high moods without depression. Most patients, however, experience more depressed days than manic days. Textbox 2.3 describes criteria for bipolar I disorder.

BIPOLAR I DISORDER

A. Criteria have been met for at least one manic episode (Criteria A–D under "Manic Episode" above).
B. The occurrence of the manic and major depressive episode(s) is not better explained by schizoaffective disorder, schizophrenia, schizophreniform disorder, delusional disorder, or other specified or unspecified schizophrenia spectrum and other psychotic disorder.

Reprinted with permission from the *Diagnostic and Statistical Manual of Mental Disorders*, 5th ed. (Arlington, VA: American Psychiatric Association, 2013).

Bipolar II disorder is defined by the presence of at least one episode of hypomania (but no full manic episodes), and at least one episode of major depression. The diagnosis of a bipolar disorder is very significant because bipolar tends to be a lifelong disorder. With treatments that we shall discuss it can go into prolonged remission, but persons remain vulnerable to recurrence of a mood episode. After an episode of mania chances are about 90 percent that a person will have a recurrence of mania or depression.[15]

Cyclothymic disorder describes patients who have both some hypomanic symptoms and some depressive symptoms intermittently over a period of at least two years, but the severity of their episodes never rises to the level of full-blown hypomania or of a major depressive episode. Bipolar spectrum disorder refers to the group of patients who have various bipolar symptoms, but either the length of time of their episodes is too short or the severity is not sufficient to be classed as bipolar I or II.

ICD-10 does not subclassify bipolar disorder into bipolar I and bipolar II forms, and also requires two or more abnormal mood episodes before a bipolar diagnosis is rendered. Research has confirmed the usefulness of identifying bipolar I and II forms, so *ICD-11* (to be in use after 2022) follows *DSM-5* in describing bipolar I and II forms and in classifying someone with only one episode of mania as bipolar I.[16]

Ruth was a wife and mother who sought treatment for depression, sometimes improving after starting an antidepressant drug, but then relapsing after a few weeks. A careful history revealed that for two days before her depressive relapse she was full of energy, up all night cleaning house, calling friends all day, very talkative and bubbly. Her energy spurts were short-lived; she woke up the next day feeling sad and fatigued, with low energy and poor appetite, and wracked by guilt. Her bipolar spectrum disorder diagnosis led to her successful treatment with a mood stabilizing medication. Bipolar spectrum disorder refers to patterns that do not meet criteria for bipolar I or II or cyclothymic disorder but show some hypomanic and depressed periods.

Thus, we see that the day-to-day picture for bipolar patients differs widely among individuals. Some patients have a severe episode of mania, are hospitalized with delusional thinking, recover, and live largely free of mood symptoms. More often bipolar patients experience some depressive symptoms short of a full-blown major depression for long stretches of time, punctuated by episodes of mania or hypomania or full-blown major depression. Treatment seeks to turn those uncomfortable days full of symptoms to more comfortable symptom-free days, so the patient can enjoy a more fulfilling life.

Each person is unique and so is her pattern of symptoms. We impose our somewhat arbitrary classifications of disease to improve our communication and our ability to predict and to treat. But many patients "fall through the cracks" of our diagnostic criteria with complex and sometimes subtle symptoms. Symptom pictures may change over time with patients originally diagnosed with a bipolar spectrum disorder because they show a lower level of symptoms later manifesting a full picture of bipolar I or bipolar II disorder. This happens in about one-third of those bipolar spectrum cases.[17]

Alice experienced several hospitalizations with full-blown mania, having grandiose and paranoid delusions, even believing she was the "Messiah." Later in life, when on mood stabilizers, she had a rapid cycling pattern alternating every few weeks between hypomania and depression. Because of the earlier psychotic episodes, she was still classed as having a bipolar I disorder. Patients with bipolar II or bipolar disorder, unspecified sometimes convert to bipolar I when they exhibit a manic episode. But once correctly classified as bipolar I patients retain that diagnosis, even if they are later having only depressive and hypomanic episodes.

The course of bipolar disorder is variable. Most often people experience severe symptoms in their late teens or early adult life, but a minority show no severe mood problems until middle age or later. A first episode of depression is the most common onset, but sometimes an episode of mania first occurs. An initial manic episode happens more often in males than in females.[18] Bipolar disorder is well recognized in teens and even in younger children.

One often-cited study found that bipolar patients were treated on average for eight years before the correct (bipolar) diagnosis was made.[19] Most often bipolar disorder is mistaken for unipolar depression, that is, recurring episodes of depression without mania.[20] Certainly bipolar disorder may start that way and be indistinguishable from recurrent depression. But often close scrutiny will uncover the brief high periods that distinguish bipolar disorder. Bipolar depressive episodes may come on more quickly than those of unipolar depression and "out of the blue" without a clear stressor as cause.

Often the first episode of bipolar depression or mania has some apparent trigger of physical or psychological stress, but subsequent episodes occur without apparent stressors, in response to some internal mechanism of mood cycling. The postpartum period is a common time for bipolar disorder to present with either postpartum depression or mania. Emil Kraepelin, who authored *Manic Depressive Insanity and Paranoia* in 1899, described the typical longitudinal course as worsening as the patient grew older.[21] That is, episodes became more severe and more frequent. But certainly not all patients followed that path. Today with appropriate treatment most patients can avoid such a pattern of gradually worsening symptoms.

Other disorders besides depression can be confused with bipolar. Schizophrenia often has an onset in late teens and early adult life. Sometimes a young person experiences a psychotic episode with a picture of insomnia, agitation, hallucinations, and delusions and it is not clear whether this represents a first episode of bipolar mania or of schizophrenia. Classically, patients with schizophrenia show more persisting difficulties with socializing and with functioning in school or the workplace after their psychosis resolves. Some patients with schizophrenia have persisting hallucinations or delusional thinking or show a derailment of thought we refer to as *thought disorder*. Schizophrenic patients may show negative symptoms of loss of enthusiasm and diminished ability to experience pleasure, slipping into a withdrawn, apathetic pattern. The bipolar patient is more able to bounce back toward his original level of functioning in those arenas. An unclear diagnosis often becomes clear with time. *Schizoaffective disorder* describes patients who show mood swings with manic or depressive features but retain some persisting symptoms of schizophrenia chronically.

Attention deficit–hyperactivity disorder (ADHD) can sometimes look like hypomania. Both disorders may show shifting attention, trouble focusing and concentrating, rapid speech and movements, difficulty sleeping, anxiety, irritability, impulsivity, and emotional lability. ADHD tends to be a chronic disorder, usually apparent in childhood years. About half the people with childhood ADHD will show significant symptoms as adults. In contrast, bipolar disorder shows an episodic pattern of symptoms with mood and energy levels shifting markedly as the patient experiences the depressed, neutral, or manic phase of the disorder. A good history and observation over time clarifies the diagnosis, but to complicate matters, some folks have both ADHD and bipolar disorder.

Substance use disorders can sometimes trigger or resemble bipolar episodes. Stimulant drugs such as cocaine, methamphetamine, MDMA, and many others can create an excited, agitated, sleepless state, sometimes with hallucinations and delusions, that clinically looks like a manic episode. Abusing large doses of stimulants such as methylphenidate (Ritalin and others) and amphetamines (Adderall, Vyvanse, and others) that are used therapeutically for ADHD can give similar results. Long-term abusers of stimulants may develop a chronic paranoid state that may be permanent.[22] Testing the blood or urine and getting a careful history from the patient and from others who know the patient well helps to determine whether a manic episode is drug-induced or is a bipolar phenomenon. Many patients, when manic, lose inhibitions for many risky behaviors and are more prone to abuse alcohol and drugs. Patients coming down from extensive abuse of stimulants may experience a lethargic, depressed state often accompanied by guilt about their spree of drug use or about behaviors they engaged in when high. This could easily be mistaken for a bipolar mood shift from mania to depression.

Borderline personality disorder might sometimes be misdiagnosed as bipolar disorder and vice versa. A personality disorder is a more enduring pattern of relating to oneself and to the world in a fashion that leads to dysfunction. Borderline personality disorder is characterized by dysphoric or depressed moods. Often in borderline personality disorder this dysphoria is brought on by anger at important others, often by the perception of abandonment or rejection. Often anger may be the predominant emotion. Threats or acts of self-harm are sometimes carried out to try to prevent abandonment. Sixty to seventy percent of borderlines engage in some form of self-harm, such as cutting or burning. Often this self-harm gives a temporary relief from distressing emotions.

Impulsivity is another diagnostic criterion for borderline personality disorder. Impulsivity can take the form of gambling, sexual encounters, eating disorders, substance abuse, or other manifestations. Bipolar patients when hypomanic or manic may show similar impulsive behaviors, but the impulsivity decreases when their mood normalizes. Borderline patients often have an unstable self-image or sense of self. Feelings of self-worth may fluctuate wildly, often depending on the nature of personal relationships, just as other people are idealized or devalued. Thus, interpersonal relationships are intense, but unstable. The intense affective instability of borderlines (angry, depressed, anxious, irritable) is most often in reaction to interpersonal situations and often lasts hours to a few days. The mood states in bipolar disorder, especially depressed moods, are often of much longer duration. Inappropriate intense anger in borderlines is part of their enduring personality style, while in bipolar patients it may be episodic, in the midst of a manic or depressed episode. Chronic feelings of emptiness are another diagnostic feature in borderlines. Transient paranoid symptoms or dissociative symptoms (flashbacks, amnesia) are another borderline diagnostic criterion. Bipolar patients may have paranoid features during mood episodes, but usually no dissociative features, which might include having gaps of memory or amnesia or reenacting past traumas.

Other features such as family history of bipolar disorder or the absence of childhood abuse or trauma may help differentiate the bipolar patient from the borderline. A majority of borderline patients report some type of child abuse. In bipolar patients the 20–30 percent incidence of childhood abuse is much lower, but higher than the 10–20 percent in the general public.[23] One can see that differentiating the two disorders is sometimes difficult. Often the nature of the problem becomes clear over time: in the borderline patient understanding her intrapsychic life and interpersonal world helps make sense of the flareups. The bipolar patient shows mood changes sometimes far out of synch with her interpersonal life.

Is bipolar disorder disabling? Sometimes, but not necessarily. Patients span a wide range of functioning levels. I have treated bipolar patients who were physicians, nurses, attorneys, teachers, and clergymen, as well as people in skilled trades, business, and factory jobs. Many are able to continue successful careers in their chosen area. However, many persons with bipolar disorder are significantly hampered by the frequent mood swings and the cognitive (memory, concentration, attention) and motivational symptoms that are part of bipolar disorder. Several nurses with bipolar disorder whom I treated had to scale back to working part-time or move to a less demanding occupation. Some patients have mood swings or residual symptoms that are severe enough that they become disabled. I have treated many persons with bipolar disorder who had to give up full-time work and receive private disability or Social Security Disability payments. Some needed to live in adult foster care homes because their symptoms were so severe or frequent that they could not manage their own day-to-day activities of living, or they needed close supervision to take their medications, maintain reasonable nutrition, and make scheduled appointments. Patients who accept that they have an illness and form a solid partnership with their treating professionals have a much better chance to maintain higher functioning levels of career, personal relationships, and fulfillment of their life goals.

Long-term outcomes can be divided roughly into thirds.[24] One-third recover well from episodes with good functioning in job and social realms. One-third have some chronic impairment that affects social and workplace functioning, but get by fairly well. Another third are severely affected by bipolar disorder with significant disability.

A recent review of bipolar epidemiologic studies, which look at the frequency of disorders in large populations, surveyed data from twenty-five worldwide studies finding a lifetime prevalence (the frequency of carrying this diagnosis at some point in life) of about 1.1 percent for bipolar I disorder and 1.6 percent for bipolar II.[25] A different review found the prevalence of bipolar I and bipolar II disorder in North America to be about 1.5 percent.[26] When other bipolar subtypes, such as cyclothymic disorder and bipolar spectrum disorder, were included, a total prevalence for bipolar disorders of about 2.9 percent was found. Although bipolar disorder occurs throughout the world, the rates in Asia and Africa are reported at about half that frequency, while Europe and the Middle East fall between those two. South American rates are close to those for North America. The reason for these discrepancies in prevalence is not clear.

Now with a good grasp of its symptomatic picture let's turn in the next chapter to the question of what causes bipolar disorder.

· 3 ·

What Causes Bipolar Disorder?

*W*hat do we know about the causes of bipolar disorder? What gives rise to the drastic mood swings that define the disorder? How do the brains of bipolar individuals differ from the brains of the average man (or woman) on the street? And how do these differences bring about the symptoms of bipolar disorder? We have only partial answers to these questions because we are far from having a comprehensive understanding of the biology of bipolar disorder. But we can look at some of the fascinating research findings.

The structure and function of the brain can be studied from many perspectives including postmortem brain assessments; imaging studies with CT scans; MRIs and more sophisticated research tools such as functional MRI (magnetic resonance imaging), MRS (magnetic resonance spectroscopy), SPECT (single-photon emission computed tomography), and PET (positron emission tomography); electrical measurements such as electroencephalography (EEG); and measurement of direct current potentials. All these methods and more have been used to study bipolar brains.

Various studies have found a slight decrease of gray matter (composed of nerve cell bodies) and a decrease of nerve cell activity in several brain regions in bipolar patients.[1] These changes are seen even when patients are in remission, not just in the midst of a manic or depressive mood episode. Decreased gray matter has been found in parts of the prefrontal cortex, which is important in memory functions, attention, and in the regulation and control of behavior. One consequence of injury to the frontal lobes is a disinhibition of behavior, leading to reckless or socially inappropriate behaviors. Shulman pointed out the similarities between manic behavior and frontal lobe disinhibition syndromes.[2] The frontal lobe is also a focus of electromagnetic treatments for depression, such as transcranial magnetic stimulation.

Another brain region with decreased gray matter in bipolar persons is the ventral striatum, which lies beneath the cortex and controls reward anticipation and prediction. Some impairment in this area could lead, for example, to overestimating the rewards in making a risky investment or in gambling.

The limbic system is a brain region that processes emotion and that shows abnormalities in bipolar brains. Limbic means "border" and it lies on the border between the thalamus and the cortex of the brain (see figure 3.1). One famous limbic system component, the amygdala, named from the Greek word for almond because it is shaped like one, supports automatic processing of the emotions and emotional learning and memory. Another limbic structure, the hippocampus (which looks like a seahorse) is crucial in episodic memory, that is, the recording of the "who, when, and where" of daily experiences. It also helps integrate information into relational associations. Both the amygdala and hippocampus show reduced gray matter in bipolar patients. The cingulate cortex is another limbic region with abnormal reduction of gray matter in some studies. See figure 3.1.

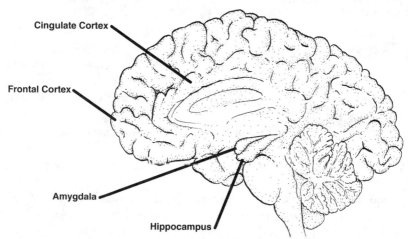

Figure 3.1. Some brain structures that are important in bipolar disorder. *Source:* Robert G. Fawcett, MD, and Susan E. Fawcett, PhD.

Many of the long white matter tracts, which carry neural information from one brain region to another along the nerve axons, the output channels of nerves, are also affected. Bipolar individuals have more white matter hyperintensities on MRI, believed to reflect some level of damage to these white matter connecting tracts.[3]

Along with these slight reductions in gray and white matter areas, there is a slight enlargement of the lateral ventricles, a space in the middle of the brain filled with cerebrospinal fluid.

These structural brain abnormalities are subtle differences that can be teased out between normal control groups and bipolar groups. But they are not large enough that we can do a brain imaging scan and say with confidence that this is the brain of a bipolar person.[4] There is too much overlap with normal brains. At this point these structural differences remain in the realm of research, but the time may come when many brain measurements looked at in combination may help us diagnose bipolar disorder or target treatment to selected areas of the brain.

Along with these subtle shifts in the structure and metabolic functioning of the brain, we can also look at the microscopic world within our brains for clues to the causes of bipolar disorder. Our entire nervous system, including the brain, contains nerve cells that communicate with one another. The cell bodies, which form the gray matter of the brain, have thousands of receptors on their surface and on the dendrites, which are extensions from the cell body. Nerve cells secrete neurotransmitters into the synapse, which is the space between the end of the axon of the communicating cell and the cell body or dendrite of the receiving cell. When enough of these neurotransmitters act on the cell to depolarize it, it sends an electrical signal, called an action potential, down its one axonal appendage. That action potential triggers the release of packets of a neurotransmitter from the far end of the axon.

Each nerve cell has only one axon, while it may have thousands of dendrites and receptors. The axon may synapse with other nerve cells or a different type of cell, for example, a muscle cell. Nerve cell bodies in our spinal cord send out axons that extend several feet, terminating in muscles of our upper and lower limbs and controlling their muscular movements. Each nerve cell produces only one type of neurotransmitter, which is stored in small bubbles or vesicles for release at the synapse. See figure 3.2.

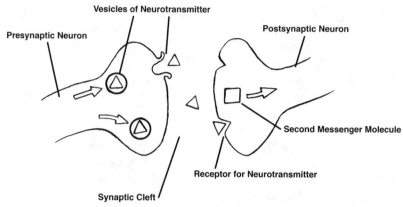

Figure 3.2.   Schematic diagram of a synapse. *Source:* **Robert G. Fawcett, MD, and Susan E. Fawcett, PhD.**

Many lines of research have studied neurotransmitters, which affect our moods and emotions, our sleep, appetite, and activity levels. Norepinephrine, NE, is present in the frontal lobes and in the limbic system discussed above. Higher levels and more rapid turnover of norepinephrine occur when bipolar patients are manic and lower levels occur when they are depressed. The same is true for dopamine, a neurotransmitter famous for acting on the reward systems in the brain located in the nucleus accumbens. Acetylcholine is a neurotransmitter that shows an opposite variation: higher in depression and lower in mania.[5]

But the situation is far more complex than this. Once a neurotransmitter crosses the synapse it acts on a receptor located in the postsynaptic membrane, on the surface of the receiving cell. That receptor in turn activates a *second messenger system* (the neurotransmitter is considered the first messenger). These second messenger molecules affect various enzyme systems within the cell. A series of biochemical events may, among other tasks, trigger transcription factors (complex proteins) that enter the cell nucleus and turn on or turn off genes within the cell's DNA or RNA. This cascade of intracellular events may ultimately affect synaptic plasticity—growing new synapses or nerve fibers or pruning synapses or even causing cell death.

Bipolar persons show differences from those with no mood disorders in the levels or properties of these intracellular chemicals, including second messengers, transcription factors, or other intermediary substances in these complex biochemical cascades. Of great interest is the fact that the mood stabilizers lithium and valproate both exert significant effects on this intracellular cascade of events. One difficulty in studying all these intercellular and intracellular events is knowing what is a primary change caused directly by a person's bipolar status, what is a change that may be a downstream effect, or what may even be a compensatory effect by the body to an abnormal biochemical state.[6]

To trace bipolar abnormalities to their source it is logical to look for biochemical differences between bipolar persons and controls in the blueprints for the developing brain—in the genes. The following case illustrates the strong familial patterns of bipolar disorder.

Karl came to see me in his mid-forties for ongoing maintenance treatment of his bipolar I disorder. He had been working part-time and was happily married to his second wife. He had been fairly stable for years on 5 mg per day of olanzapine, a second-generation antipsychotic, and occasional use of zolpidem, a sleep aid. Decades before, I had treated his mother with lithium for her bipolar disorder, but Karl could not tolerate lithium side effects. I had treated Karl's son during one of his many hospitalizations with bipolar I disorder. His son would become loud, aggressive, and rambling in his thoughts with delusions during his episodes. He often had poor compliance with his medications and lapsed into drinking and drugging. When he eventually saw the benefit of taking his meds and avoiding alcohol, his son became more stable, living in a home supervised by community mental health. He was not able to return to work and received disability payments. Karl's daughter, who was not my patient, committed suicide, which led to prolonged grief in Karl.

For centuries people have observed that many emotional disorders run in families. I have treated several sets of bipolar patients spanning three generations: grandparent, parent, and child. Genetic research in the early and mid twentieth century looked at the prevalence of bipolar disorder in affected families compared to the general population. Adoption studies looked at how often children of a bipolar parent adopted out at birth would develop bipolar disorder. These adoption studies were small and inconclusive.[7]

However, twin studies were more productive. Monozygotic (identical) twins, who share the same genes, were compared with dizygotic (fraternal) twins who, like other siblings, share about 50 percent of their genes. In three large studies summarized by Barnett and Smoller,[8] the dizygotic twins were concordant (both had the disorder) 4.5–5.6 percent of the time, while the monozygotic twins were concordant 38.5–43 percent of the time.

Thus, researchers have found that bipolar disorder tends to be very strongly inherited, more so than other psychiatric disorders such as depression, panic disorder, or schizophrenia, and even more so than many medical disorders, such as breast cancer. In the general population the lifetime prevalence of bipolar I disorder is about 1 percent, bipolar II disorder about 1.1 percent, and other forms of bipolar disorder that do not meet full criteria about 2.4 percent.[9] But if one parent has bipolar disorder each child has a risk of about 9 percent of developing bipolar disorder during his or her lifetime. The risk for that child developing a unipolar major depressive disorder is even higher at about 15 percent. The risk for a child of a bipolar parent to develop some mood disorder, either bipolar or depressive, is about 27 percent.[10]

If one parent has a history of major depression, each child has an elevated risk for developing bipolar disorder and about 20 percent risk for developing either depression or bipolar disorder. The lifetime risk for depression is about 7 percent if neither parent has a mood disorder.

Genetic influences explain about 60–85 percent of the risk for developing bipolar disorder. But identical twins sharing all the same genes do not have a 100 percent likelihood of both developing bipolar disorder. Environmental factors also play some role, but genes are the largest cause for developing bipolar disorder.

The search for specific risk genes has been very difficult. Researchers find that many different genes contribute small amounts of risk for bipolar disorder and any two bipolar individuals who are not closely related will usually have many differences among these risk genes.

Many recent genetic studies take the form of genome-wide association studies or GWAS. Such studies look at hundreds or thousands of people identifying whether they do or do not have a bipolar disorder and map out thousands among the twenty to thirty thousand or so human genes in each of the participants. One such recent study identified about thirty loci: areas on the chromosomes that were different between the bipolar persons and the controls.[11] One such risk gene that has been identified in several separate studies is called CACNA1C. This gene produces a protein that helps control the activity in calcium channels, another type of nerve cell receptor. Calcium channels on the neuron allow calcium ions to diffuse into and out of the neuron when the channel is opened. The concentration of calcium affects the excitability of the neuron, the likelihood it will produce an action potential when stimulated by neurotransmitters.

The CACNA1C gene was found in 36 percent of bipolar patients and 34 percent of controls. Not much difference! The risk gene adds about 6 percent to one's risk of having bipolar disorder. Contrast this with the APOE-e4 gene in Alzheimer's disease. In the white population, having one or two of the e4 genes at the APOE site on the chromosome adds about 150 percent of risk for late-onset Alzheimer's compared to those with no APOE-e4 genes.[12] Although late-onset Alzheimer's also has many genes that affect its risk, the APOE gene can pose a very sizable risk. We have discovered no gene that presents that level of risk for bipolar disorder, but rather there are at least a score of relevant genes, some of which add risk and some that undoubtedly reduce risk.

Some of the genes that play a role in causing bipolar disorder are also present in other psychiatric disorders such as depression, schizophrenia, and attention deficit hyperactivity disorder. This helps us understand why the risk for bipolar disorder is higher in relatives of patients with those other disorders and vice versa.

Other aspects of bipolar disorder that tend to run in families and may have a genetic basis include the polarity of onset (whether manic or depressed), the frequency of episodes, the presence of psychosis, suicidality, rapid cycling, tendency to abuse alcohol or other substances, the presence of panic disorder, and obtaining a therapeutic benefit from lithium.[13]

Is the rate of bipolar disorder increasing? The *cohort effect* is a term that refers to this finding: in patients born since 1970 to a bipolar parent, the children are developing bipolar disorder at a higher rate and at a younger age than in previous generations. The reason for this is unclear. In Huntington's disease, a neurological disorder with a single gene form of inheritance, succeeding generations may develop the disorder at a younger age than their parents did, a phenomenon referred to as genetic anticipation. In this case it appears due to the Huntington's gene making extra copies of itself in the child. These even more mutated genes lead to greater penetrance—an earlier onset of the disorder. However, for bipolar disorder making extra copies of an affected gene does not appear to be what is causing earlier onset, so the reason for this finding is still a mystery.

Research into the molecular genetics of bipolar disorder and other psychiatric disorders is still at an early stage. A dozen or more candidate genes or single nucleotide polymorphisms (SNPs) are of interest. Some, like CACNA1C, have to do with calcium channel receptors on the neuron, some with intracellular messengers inside the nerve cells. It is hoped that further genetic studies will eventually lead to treatments tailored to a particular individual's genome.

What about the environmental causes of bipolar disorder? Research has found that adverse childhood experiences, ACEs, present a risk factor for the development of most psychiatric and substance use disorders and even many medical disorders. Bipolar patients report more childhood traumatic events than controls.[14] These ACEs include physical or sexual abuse or neglect; a parent's death or divorce or separation from a parent; a parent with mental illness, violence, criminality, or a substance use problem; a parent who is jailed; childhood medical illness; and family economic adversity. Adverse childhood events have been associated with more unfavorable outcomes in bipolar disorder such as a greater number and severity of manic and depression episodes, more psychosis, presence of more posttraumatic stress disorder, greater misuse of alcohol and of other substances, an earlier age of onset, more rapid cycling, and higher rates of suicide attempts.[15]

Correlation, of course, does not prove causality. It is not clear that these ACEs truly worsen the course of bipolar disorder. Other possibilities might be that the high genetic loading of parents both with bipolar and other disorders makes ACEs more likely. Many studies in this area have appeared in the last ten to twenty years, so the relationship of these ACEs to bipolar disorder may become clearer soon.

Other social factors have been linked to the emergence and severity of physical and mental disorders in general, and probably play a role in the prognosis for persons with bipolar disorder. These factors are poor access to care; underemployment and insecurity involving jobs, food, and housing; a poorly built environment; discrimination and social exclusion; poor education; and poverty and income inequality.[16] Higher income inequality across a state or a country, even when poverty level itself is controlled, is predictive of worse outcomes for mental and physical illness and greater mortality.

Besides these social and psychological factors, medical factors can increase risk for bipolar symptoms. In chapter 11, Secondary Mania and Late-Onset Bipolar Disorder, we will also touch on medically caused manic syndromes and the fact that late-onset bipolar disorder may have cerebrovascular disease as a major risk factor.

When a person has genetic risk for bipolar disorder, can certain events trigger an episode of mania or depression? We certainly believe they can. Exciting events like a new love relationship, an anticipated job or promotion, or an athletic or artistic achievement may trigger a behavioral activation system that in turn triggers a manic episode.[17] Sleep deprivation appears to be another trigger for mania.

On the other side of the spectrum, losses of a relationship or a job, a financial setback, or ill health may all trigger a behavioral inhibition system and thus a depressive episode. Abuse of alcohol or drugs is a frequent trigger for bipolar episodes, both manic and depressed, and worsens the long-term course of bipolar disorder.[18] Perhaps drug abuse may even bring on bipolar disorder in some individuals who would not otherwise have followed that path. We do not have robust evidence at this time that such is the case, but evidence accumulates that marijuana use can trigger schizophrenia,[19] and that heavy abuse of stimulants can bring on a chronic paranoid state.[20]

In summary, genetic factors play the largest role in causing bipolar disorder. The era of "gene therapy" or directly altering the human genome to treat disease has recently begun with efforts to correct disorders such as the blood disorders sickle cell disease and B-thalassemia that involve only one gene.[21] Treating bipolar disorder by directly manipulating genes may lie in the distant future. Environmental factors both physical and psychological can strongly affect the onset and course of the disorder. Controlling those environmental factors is a strategy available now to help us in preventing episodes and in calming the bipolar storm.

· 4 ·

Setting a Healthy Baseline

$\mathcal{T}$o begin reducing the symptoms of bipolar disorder we can borrow some tips from the wellness movement. Persons with bipolar disorder can gain better control of mood swings by using strategies that promote physical and emotional health in general. Some of these strategies have been well tested in research studies. Others have not been well studied in the bipolar population, but we have evidence from other sources for their usefulness. We shall look at areas of sleep, diet, exercise, substance abuse, and socialization.

Disturbed sleep patterns are often an early sign of a bipolar episode (manic or depressed) developing. After a few nights of poor sleep other manic symptoms of rapid speech, impulsivity, euphoria, and irritability show up. With depression, loss of appetite, low energy, and a loss of the zest for life may soon follow the insomnia. Many patients have a typical pattern of how their episodes unfold. It is important to learn the early warning signs.

Sleep deprivation also can be not only a warning sign, but actually a trigger for a manic episode, and is one of the ways that psychological or physical stress may bring about mania.[1] One of the well-documented psychotherapies for bipolar disorder, interpersonal and social rhythm therapy, focuses on keeping regular patterns in daily activities such as eating and exercise, but especially in sleep.[2]

Sleep specialists have a number of suggestions for improving sleep patterns.[3] Arising at approximately the same time each day is important to help set the body's own circadian clock and to synchronize many neural and hormonal activities with a twenty-four-hour sleep-wake cycle.

An episode of mania or depression can scramble these finely tuned mechanisms and lead to severe insomnia or hypersomnia.

Falling asleep is facilitated by a cool, dark, quiet room. One's body temperature needs to drop a bit to facilitate the onset of sleep. One should avoid caffeine or other stimulating chemicals and activities before bedtime.

Frank was a man in his forties with a rapid cycling bipolar II disorder. He enjoyed working in his yard. But he found if he did this in the evening he got revved up and could not get to sleep. He had to learn to stop these activities several hours before bedtime and transition to some quieter and more relaxing activities, such as reading or watching TV. Can anything make you sleepier than watching a golf tournament on TV?

Sometimes worries about finances, health, jobs, relationships, or other matters prevent sleep. It is hard to simply "not think" about worries. It is more effective to substitute relaxing thoughts or imagery to facilitate sleep. Close your eyes and imagine you are floating in an inner tube on a warm sunny day. Imagine the warm sun on your skin, a light breeze, the calling of shore birds, blue skies and fluffy clouds, the repetitive slapping of the waves, and the bobbing sensation of floating in the tube. These relaxing images may facilitate drifting off to sleep far better than worrying about bills.

Progressive relaxation techniques described by Edmund Jacobson, MD, in his 1929 book of the same name involve tensing and relaxing various groups of muscles to achieve a state of muscular and emotional relaxation. Various YouTube videos illustrate this progressive relaxation technique that can combat insomnia. Going through the steps of the technique make it hard to simultaneously entertain worrisome, sleep-robbing thoughts. By the end of the process relaxed muscles and a calm mind promote sleep.

Sleep is also facilitated by exercise, so long as it is not a few hours before bedtime, when it can sometimes lead to arousal. Numerous studies document benefits of exercise in alleviating symptoms of unipolar depression.[4] Exercise has many other health benefits such as reducing obesity, blood pressure, cholesterol, and blood sugar levels. Exercise gives a boost to the immune system and reduces some aspects of inflammation.

What types of exercise and exactly how much will produce mental health benefits is not clear. General health benefits are seen with even a small increase in exercise, while further increases add more benefit. Aerobic exercises, which can improve cardiovascular function, involve fairly prolonged vigorous use of the muscles in activities like swimming, running, bicycling, dancing, racquet sports, etc. Other exercises like weight lifting or yoga primarily strengthen muscles.

The would-be exerciser should pick activities that are enjoyable for her. The real secret is to incorporate the exercising into one's lifestyle. Having regularly scheduled times for exercise facilitates success. Some people enjoy exercising in a group (e.g., at a gym, in a dance or spinning class, or in a tennis league). For the lone exerciser, watching a video while using the treadmill or stationary bicycle may make it more palatable.

I live in northern Michigan, where often I can cross-country ski for five months of the year. This is an excellent exercise that combines cardiovascular, strength, and balance benefits with the additional emotional benefits from being outdoors in beautiful natural settings. At a moderate pace one can burn about 450 calories per hour—great for weight control. Bicycling, kayaking, golfing, or just walking might work fine for some folks and combine the exercising with an outdoor experience.

Without definite guideposts for the quantity of exercise that confers mental health benefits one can defer to general health recommendations. The World Health Organization recommends at least thirty minutes five times weekly of moderate exercise or twenty-five minutes three times weekly of vigorous activity.[5] Moderate activity would include walking briskly, ballroom dancing, or doubles tennis. Vigorous activity would include jogging, swimming laps, or singles tennis. If one has any significant medical condition or is pregnant or postpartum, one should discuss an exercise plan with one's personal health care provider. If a person has been leading a sedentary lifestyle it is good to begin exercise gently, for example, with just easy walking. But even small amounts of exercise confer health benefits.

The secretary of the U.S. Department of Health and Human Services appointed seventeen experts to prepare Physical Activity Guidelines for Americans, which are summarized below.[6] Children three to five should be active throughout the day. Young people six to seventeen years old should have at least sixty minutes of vigorous activity daily. Adults should have at least 150 to 300 minutes per week of moderate physical activity (such as brisk walking) or seventy-five to 150 minutes per week of vigorous physical activity (such as jogging). In addition, they should have muscle-strengthening activities (such as weight lifting or resistance exercises) at least two days per week. Pregnant and postpartum women should strive for 150 minutes of moderate-intensity aerobic activity. Even adults with disabilities and chronic conditions should aim for this level of activity if possible. Older adults over sixty-five should strive for 150 minutes or more per week of multicomponent physical activity that combines aerobic, muscle-strengthening, and balance activities (such as my cross-country skiing, dancing, or other sports).

In addition to exercise and restful sleep, a health-promoting diet is another building block of a stable baseline. An ideal diet would improve mood stability and reduce the obesity-related problems, such as diabetes and cardiovascular disease, that occur more often in people with bipolar disorder.

The "Western diet" common in North America is rich in processed meats, pizza, chips, hamburgers, white bread, sugar, flavored drinks, and beer. It is high in saturated fats, sugars, and refined carbohydrates, sodium, and nitrites. A Mediterranean diet contains more fish and shellfish and less red meat than the Western diet. It contains more fruits and vegetables, whole grains, fewer processed foods, and healthier unsaturated fats such as olive oil and canola oil. Research studies have shown an association between depression and the Western diet.[7]

Studies of the diets of bipolar patients show they choose the unhealthier high-fat Western diet more than control groups. They tend to have other unhealthy eating patterns, such as eating only one meal per day, eating alone, and having difficulty obtaining food and cooking it. These poor eating patterns may be related to bipolar disorder, or to living in adverse economic circumstances. Medications may stimulate appetite and consumption of fats and sugars. Gorging on carbs could even be an attempt by the body to compensate for stress; high sugar intake lowers stress-induced cortisol levels.[8]

The high-fat Western diet worsens mood through many avenues. High-fat diets may lower levels of neurotransmitters such as dopamine, norepinephrine, and serotonin necessary for mood stability, and promote inflammation, which may play a role in both bipolar disorder and unipolar depression, as well as many medical disorders. High-fat diets lower brain-derived neurotrophic factor, which helps with the growth of neurons. The Mediterranean diet is associated with lower markers of oxidative stress and with more efficient metabolism in our cells and in our mitochondria, the tiny energy factories within our cells.

Sometimes problems result not from excessive eating, but from restriction of food. Christine was a woman whom I treated for a bipolar II mood disorder. She seemed pretty stable for several years on 200 mg/d of lamotrigine. Christine sometimes became enthusiastic about health fads that lacked scientific backing, such as "pyramid power" or copper bracelets. Because she was a few pounds overweight she decided to try a reducing diet she had come across that was strictly vegan, with no protein from meat or eggs, large amounts of grapefruit, and rather limited food choices. I had recommended a more mainstream weight control program, but Christine vetoed that. After three to four weeks on her new diet she slipped gradually into depression. We tried to no avail some medication changes, such as adding lurasidone to her lamotrigine. I urged her to resume her previous dietary patterns, with plenty of protein, even animal protein for the present. Her depression lifted in a few more weeks on her usual, more varied diet.

The neurotransmitters that regulate our mood, such as norepinephrine, serotonin, and dopamine, depend on a sufficient supply of essential amino acids like tyrosine and tryptophan, which come from proteins. "Essential" in this context refers to nutrients that cannot be manufactured by our bodies but must be obtained from dietary sources or supplements. Christine's unusual diet had left her supply depleted. When researchers limited the dietary amount of the amino acid tryptophan, they produced a relapse of depression in their subjects.[9] Clinicians often see depression in patients with anorexia nervosa. Some of this is related to their malnourished state.

Certainly, vegan diets can be part of a healthy lifestyle, but it is important with any vegan diet to include enough protein from nuts, beans, legumes, and grains.

What is the ideal diet to minimize symptoms of bipolar disorder? That is a question we cannot answer at present. We can, however, make some reasonable recommendations regarding healthful diets to minimize mood disorder symptoms. Our brains need many substances to function at an optimal level. Proteins we eat are broken down into amino acids that become neurotransmitters and neurohormones. Fats are needed to supply the fatty tissues in the myelin sheaths that surround nerve fibers and the membranes of nerve cells. Enough calories are needed to maintain blood glucose, which is the fuel for nerve cells. A host of minerals and vitamins are essential to support the chemical reactions that underlie the structure and function of our central nervous system.

A healthy body contributes to a healthy mind. Obesity has been correlated with depression and with systemic inflammation. Many persons with bipolar disorder tend to have less-than-optimal diets. The rates of obesity, diabetes, and high cholesterol among bipolar patients exceed the rates in the general population.[10] Many of the medication treatments for bipolar disorders tend to cause weight gain, diabetes, and high cholesterol. Thus, a diet for bipolar patients should be one that reduces risk for weight gain, diabetes, and high lipids. Current diet recommendations are for lots of fresh fruit and vegetables, lots of whole grains, and healthful fats and oils such as olive oil or canola oil. If one is not vegetarian, getting animal protein from chicken and fish more than from beef and pork sources is recommended, the latter being higher in fats. The "Mediterranean diet," similar to that of people who live near the sea of that name, is a good example of a heart-healthy diet.

Studies of the frequency of depression in various population groups around the world (what is referred to as epidemiology) have found lower rates of depression in Asian groups compared to Western groups and lower rates in some populations that consume a lot of fish.[11] The rates of bipolar I, bipolar II, and other bipolar spectrum disorders were correlated with the average consumption of seafood in about a dozen countries studied.[12] Rates of bipolar disorder in Switzerland and Germany, with low seafood consumption, were several times the rates in Iceland and Taiwan, with very high seafood consumption.

Cold water ocean fish in particular, such as salmon and cod and the shellfish scallops contain high levels of omega-3 fatty acids. Omega fatty acids are necessary components of our brains. The omega-3 fatty acid docosahexaenoic acid (DHA) constitutes 15 percent of the brain's dry weight. Because our body cannot manufacture omega fatty acids, we must obtain them from dietary sources. Besides fish, flax seeds, nuts, and basil are other sources of these essential fatty acids. Thus, I would recommend for bipolar patients a diet high in omega-3 fatty acids found in salmon, cod, scallops, or other cold-water fish, and in flaxseed and nuts. Seafood lovers rejoice!

Throughout most of humankind's history our diet contained an approximate ratio of 1:4 in omega-3 to omega-6 fatty acids. But the modern Western diet reveals a ratio of 1:17 with about a fourfold increase in consumption of omega-6 fatty acids.[13] The omega-6 fatty acids are more pro-inflammatory and the omega-3 fatty acids are anti-inflammatory. A diet rich in omega-3 fatty acids can be helpful in preventing cardiovascular and arthritic diseases, and evidence suggests it improves mood stability.[14] Supplementing a regimen of mood stabilizers with omega-3 fatty acids improved depressive symptoms of bipolar individuals in five studies.[15] Omega-3 doses varied widely from 1 to 10 grams per day. Omega-3s such as DHA and eicosapentaenoic acid (EPA) are suggested as a supplement to mood stabilizers, but certainly not as a replacement.

Glutathione is the principal antioxidant found in our cells. This chemical prevents free radicals from combining with intracellular chemicals that we need to stay healthy. Levels of glutathione are reduced in bipolar persons compared to controls. N-acetyl cysteine (NAC) is a supplement that boosts the synthesis of glutathione. One study found that in doses of 500–1000 mg twice daily during the maintenance phase, NAC reduced depressive symptoms for bipolar patients.[16] One recent study found that NAC plus aspirin added to a medication regimen helped a bit with bipolar depression.[17] Other studies adding NAC to standard treatments for bipolar depression are ongoing. Although other nutraceutical agents such as vitamin D, inositol, and folic acid have been investigated in bipolar disorder, no studies have shown clear benefit from using them. If a patient has a laboratory-documented deficiency of vitamin D or folic acid, that is a different story.

Some diets have been formulated to try to minimize the development and progression of dementias such as Alzheimer's disease. Dr. David Perlmutter (*Grain Brain: The Surprising Truth about Wheat, Carbs and Sugar—Your Brain's Silent Killers*)[18] is a neurologist associated with such a diet that strives to maximize the survival and functioning of individual nerve cells. He recommends extremely low intake of carbohydrates so that the dieter is often in ketosis, a state in which we are breaking down fats to get energy for our moment-to-moment activities, rather than relying only on circulating glucose to supply energy for our cells. There is some evidence that such a diet may help slow the process of older people slipping into dementia, such as Alzheimer's disease.

Such a ketogenic diet has also been shown to help some forms of epilepsy.[19] Case studies of two bipolar women maintaining a low carbohydrate ketogenic diet over at least two years achieved better mood stability than they had with medications alone.[20] This is a trend to watch in the future. We need more extensive controlled studies to confirm the benefits of this strategy. There is also concern that older people on a ketogenic diet may metabolize some of their muscle protein as well as fats when deprived of glucose. Loss of muscle mass in the elderly can bring on other health problems.

The MIND diet has been shown to reduce cognitive deterioration in older adults and reduce the number slipping into Alzheimer's dementia.[21] MIND stands for Mediterranean-DASH Intervention for Neurodegenerative Delay. The MIND diet combines features of the Mediterranean diet mentioned above and the DASH diet (Dietary Approaches to Stop Hypertension), which has been used successfully to reduce high blood pressure. The MIND diet emphasizes these ten foods: leafy green vegetables, other vegetables, berries, nuts, beans, olive oil, fish, poultry, whole grains, and, in moderation, wine. It emphasizes avoiding these five foods: red meat, butter and stick margarine, pastries and sweets, cheese, and fried and fast foods. Although we lack direct evidence for the use of this diet in bipolar disorder, we have considerable evidence that it promotes healthy brain functioning and cardiovascular health and would be the best suggested diet for preventing and managing bipolar disorder at present, given our lack of data specifically on diet in bipolar disorder.

Another fundamental building block of a healthy baseline is avoiding substance abuse. Rates of substance abuse among bipolar patients are much higher than rates in the general population—often twice as high or more in various studies.[22] In chapter 2, on causes of bipolar disorder, we referred to studies showing that a sizable number of genes play a role in the development of bipolar disorder. Many of these same at-risk genes occur in other disorders including substance use disorders. Thus, many patients with bipolar disorder also carry genes that make them more susceptible to substance abuse.

Sometimes the substance abuse occurs before the onset of episodes of depression or mania, and sometimes it starts after a bipolar mood disorder is present. Some studies suggest that substance abuse might play a role in triggering the onset of bipolar disorder, but this is not well established as fact. Heavy abuse of amphetamines can lead to a picture of enduring psychosis with delusions and paranoia that can look like a manic episode.[23] Moreover, studies confirm that bipolar patients have worse outcomes when also abusing substances: more hospitalizations, more rapid cycling patterns, more loss of jobs and relationships, more suicides and suicide attempts, and more frequent mood episodes that do not respond to treatment.[24] We cannot absolutely conclude that the substance abuse causes all these worse outcomes, because the substance abuse could be a marker for more severe bipolar disorder. Nonetheless, there are many reasons to avoid substance abuse to better control bipolar disorder.

Alcohol is the most frequently abused substance among bipolar patients. A study by the Stanley Foundation found 33 percent of bipolar patients have an alcohol use disorder.[25] The rate of alcohol use problems in the general population in that study was 14 percent. More men than women abuse alcohol and other drugs, and that also holds true in the bipolar population.

Rates for abuse of or dependence on other substances among bipolar patients were marijuana 16 percent, stimulants 9 percent, cocaine 9 percent, and opiates 7 percent. One theory regarding the high rates is the so-called self-medication hypothesis.[26] This hypothesis suggests that bipolar patients use alcohol and street drugs to reduce some of their symptoms, for example, using alcohol to try to sleep or cocaine to lift a depressed mood. There appears to be at least a kernel of truth in this concept.

Evidence against this self-medication hypothesis includes the fact that bipolar patients are more prone to stimulant abuse when manic rather than when depressed. Abusing cocaine or stimulants when already on a manic high is certainly not consistent with the self-medication hypothesis. Rather it suggests that in a manic state people tend to lose inhibitions and engage in riskier behaviors or more thrill seeking. Abuse of addictive substances may lead to increased cravings, withdrawal symptoms, and a host of other problems.

Some patients report that marijuana or opiates calm them down, reducing anger and agitation. At this point all the research, however, indicates that use of marijuana is associated with worse outcomes, showing an increase in manic episodes.[27] One study found better outcomes for bipolar patients who stopped cannabis use compared to those who continued to use marijuana.[28] If teenagers want to lower their IQ a few points, heavy marijuana use is a reliable way to do it![29] Although medical marijuana was approved by the state of Michigan for use with posttraumatic stress disorder (PTSD), research by the Veterans Administration at this point shows marijuana use making the course of PTSD worse rather than better.[30]

Marijuana contains myriad substances. It is possible that some chemicals derived from marijuana, such as cannabidiol, may have antipsychotic effects. But smoking the ground-up marijuana plant delivers far more of the harmful chemicals.

One way in which substance use may worsen the course of bipolar illness is through noncompliance. Persons who use alcohol and street drugs extensively often do not take prescribed medications reliably. That can certainly lead to a rockier road for the bipolar patient.

Many of the medications used for bipolar disorder have a contraindication to their use along with alcohol. Thus, to maximize one's healthy baseline, avoid use of alcohol and street drugs, or if taking an occasional drink, keep them few and far between. Most communities have access to twelve-step groups such as Alcoholics Anonymous or Narcotics Anonymous or, for family members of those afflicted, Al-Anon. Frequently clinics and therapists who specialize in substance abuse treatment are available, sometimes at the same site where bipolar disorder is treated. One of the community mental health agencies I worked at had a "co-occurring group" for persons with both mental health and substance abuse problems.

One further step in promoting a stable base of emotional health is to cultivate a social support system. Wanting and enjoying relationships is part of our human nature. A social support system can ease the misery that accompanies episodes of depression. Often a family member or close friend may see clear signs of an impending manic episode before the patient is clearly aware of it. This can lead to earlier, more successful intervention—another way that a support system helps.

People may experience emotional support from their family, workplace, place of worship, educational institution, neighborhood, a community mental health clubhouse program, or from various community and volunteer organizations. A severe bipolar disorder may lead to a loss of employment. Sometimes friends and family may become alienated by behaviors of a bipolar person and pull away. Such loss of job and friends can be devastating. However, friends and family and even employers with a solid understanding of bipolar disorder are more likely to stick by a bipolar person and remain supportive, more able to see some of their negative behaviors as a product of bipolar disorder and not of the patient's usual personality.

At other times patients might find that some relationships are "toxic" for them. That is, the relationship always leads to negative consequences of emotional pain or low self-esteem. Perhaps a friend always pushes one into substance abuse or a lover is physically or emotionally abusive. The patient may be better off distancing herself from such toxic situations. Relationships that bombard the bipolar patient with vehement negative criticism or that smother them, like a "helicopter" parent, by taking away their independence can also be toxic.

Having relationships that make one feel better supports one's emotional health. Sometimes helping others gives one an emotional boost. It is good to seek out and maintain such relationships in one's life. The value of emotional support is verified in research studies. For example, emotional support is one of the biggest factors in successfully dealing with the loss of a spouse.[31] For family and friends of the bipolar patient, learning about the disorder can certainly help them to provide more beneficial emotional support.

Sometimes, despite living a healthy lifestyle, bipolar patients can relapse. In the next chapter we discuss treatment for acute manic and mixed episodes.

Treatment of Mania and Mixed States

TREATMENT CONSIDERATIONS

$\mathcal{T}$he first step in getting treatment for bipolar disorder is selecting treatment providers. Psychiatrists are well trained to provide much of the needed treatment for bipolar disorder. A psychiatrist is a medical doctor (MD or DO) who then spends another three or more years of training in the specialty of psychiatry: diagnosing and treating persons who have a significant mental or emotional disorder. Not only do psychiatrists receive up-to-date training in medications used in bipolar disorder, and in some of the psychotherapeutic techniques that can be used to help bipolar persons, but they are trained to detect medical problems that might masquerade as emotional disorders or complicate the treatment of psychiatric disorders. When problems such as substance abuse, anxiety disorders, or eating disorders complicate the treatment of a bipolar patient, psychiatrists are well trained to deal with those problems as well. In the United States, after passing a national examination they become board certified. Psychiatrists may be found in private practice, associated with a private clinic or community health center, or through the Veterans Administration or community mental health centers (CMHCs).

Primary care physicians, such as family practice doctors; medical specialists, such as neurologists; internal medicine doctors; or pediatricians may sometimes treat bipolar disorder. Some psychiatry is included in the curriculum for all doctors in medical school and sometimes as part of their residency training, for example, in family practice. Many primary care doctors, however, may not feel sufficiently well informed to treat a patient's bipolar disorder, or may be willing to do so only with close collaboration with a psychiatrist.

In recent years, more nurse practitioners (NPs) and physician assistants (PAs) with psychiatric training are practicing and can prescribe a wide variety of medications. In some states, such as Michigan, where I practice, psychiatric nurse practitioners must collaborate with a psychiatrist so that they have ready consultation for cases that are challengingly complex. In some states they are able to practice independently. NPs and PAs may also be found in private practices, private clinics, or through the VA and CMHCs. NPs have training beyond their nursing degree that usually includes a year of classroom instruction in psychiatric issues and a year of internship under the mentorship of a psychiatrist. Nurse practitioners must pass a certifying examination in their area of specialty practice.

Registered nurses and sometimes medical assistants may play a significant role in the treatment of the bipolar patient. Besides tasks such as checking vital signs and drawing blood, they may gather information, fill out rating scales, do exams for abnormal movements, and inject intramuscular drugs. Often, they may be the point of contact in person or on the telephone when problems occur.

Training in psychotherapy (talking therapy) varies among psychiatric training programs. Some offer quite a bit, some very little. Programs expose trainees to at least some of the major forms of psychotherapy used in bipolar disorder: cognitive-behavioral therapy, interpersonal therapy, supportive therapy, and psychodynamic therapy. Forms of family therapy and psychoeducation are often included. However, it would be unusual for a psychiatrist to emerge from residency training with expertise in all these forms of therapy.

Other therapists may play a role in the treatment of bipolar patients. Psychologists, social workers, substance abuse specialists, and other counselors may offer psychotherapy, such as those types mentioned above, or other types of psychotherapy, for the bipolar patient. Today in many settings mental health treatment is split treatment: a psychiatrist or nurse practitioner or primary care doctor oversees the medication treatment and a therapist focuses on issues that can benefit from intensive talking therapy. A case manager may also assist in solving many day-to-day practical issues and in offering emotional support.

Most therapists tend to be well versed in just one or a few forms of psychotherapy in which they have trained under an experienced mentor. Psychologists may have a master's degree after a few years of training beyond their bachelor's degree, or a PhD in psychology or a doctor of psychology (PsyD) degree after at least four years in graduate school training. Social workers may have a bachelor's degree or an MSW, (master of social work) gained after a few years of graduate training. Other therapists might have degrees in counseling or in substance abuse therapy. These various therapists must have the training and credentials to be licensed by the states, provinces, or regions in which they practice.

Treatment works best when the patient likes and trusts her treatment providers. Simply having a positive, trusting relationship with another human being can be healing. Some research studies have found this positive rapport with the provider to exert more benefit than the specific type of psychotherapy.[1] Even in studies of medication effects, the patient's improvement may correlate more with the patient's positive relationship with the prescriber than with the effects of specific medications.[2] Thus, finding a provider or treatment team that one can trust and work with is very important. This does not mean that the patient may always like what she is hearing from her treatment providers. Sometimes treatment involves confronting a patient with problem behaviors (e.g., substance abuse or lack of exercise), that may be unpleasant to face. When a patient trusts her clinical provider, she can better hear and make constructive use of such confrontations.

Medication treatment in bipolar disorder can be conveniently broken down into treatment for mania or mixed states, treatment for bipolar depression, and maintenance treatment. In many ways treatment of the manic phase is the most straightforward, and many effective treatment options exist. Recommended treatment in a manic or hypomanic phase usually involves prescribed medications, such as a mood stabilizer and/or an antipsychotic drug. Treatment also involves stopping behaviors such as alcohol or drug abuse that may perpetuate mania and treating insomnia, which drives mania.

Shannon, who had no previous psychiatric history, began feeling more upbeat and energetic and sleeping only a few hours at night. She had always liked Mick Jagger from the Rolling Stones, but now became obsessed with him. Watching a televised concert, she was convinced Mick was communicating specifically with her, and that he wanted to have a relationship with her. She began hearing his voice speaking to her. Her family was concerned with her behavior and her progressive disorganization. When her husband heard her out on the front lawn in her pajamas singing and dancing, he brought her to the hospital's emergency department. She agreed to a voluntary admission and was diagnosed, as her mother had been, with a bipolar I disorder, manic phase. After starting on olanzapine, a second-generation antipsychotic, she improved within days, sleeping better and no longer hearing voices. She gained insight that the voice of Mick Jagger originated in her and was not real. Years later she would sometimes joke about it. Within a few weeks she had fully resumed her functions as a mother, wife, and homemaker while continuing on 10 mg per day of olanzapine.

MOOD STABILIZERS

Today we take for granted that medications exist that target various psychiatric syndromes such as bipolar mania or depression, obsessive-compulsive disorder, or social phobia. But even the concept that medications could effectively treat such disorders was foreign to clinicians in the first half of the twentieth century. The discovery by Dr. John Cade in 1949 that lithium could effectively treat mania marked the beginning of the era of modern psychopharmacology.[3] Looking back, it is surprising that Dr. Cade discovered lithium's effective antimanic activity.

That discovery of lithium's efficacy was preceded by many attempts in the first half of the twentieth century to use physical methods to treat severe mental illnesses such as mania, schizophrenia, and severe depression. Cold packs calmed agitation. Prolonged "sleep cures" extending for about five days often brought some improvement to patients, but many relapsed and a few died from pneumonia contracted during the long stretch of sedation. Sedating drugs, such as barbiturates or bromides, could make patients sleepy, but did not help the core hallucinations of schizophrenia or the grandiose delusions of mania. Controlled high doses of insulin were used to lower blood sugar to the point of "insulin coma," another treatment of that era. The observation that some patients with both epilepsy and psychosis functioned better mentally after a seizure triggered the use of seizures as therapy, first using the drug pentylenetetrazol (Metrazol) and later in the 1930s with electroconvulsive therapy, for which Ugo Cerletti received the Nobel Prize in Medicine.[4]

Prior to Cade's work, lithium already had a presence in the world of medicine. The disorder gout causes painful swollen joints when uric acid crystallizes in joints. Uric acid can also form kidney stones. The British physician Sir Alfred Garrod proposed that gout was caused by an excess of uric acid in the body. What followed was the "uric acid diathesis" as a theory of disease. Claims were made that headaches, asthma, diabetes, skin disorders, digestive problems, obesity, and rheumatism were also caused by excess uric acid. Even many types of psychiatric disorders were hypothesized to be a result of excess uric acid.[5]

In the chemistry lab lithium citrate was shown to dissolve uric acid crystals and even kidney stones, forming the more soluble lithium urate. Doctors hypothesized that lithium citrate taken by mouth might relieve symptoms of gout and dissolve kidney stones. Unfortunately, that technique did not work.

In Denmark, physician Carl Lange (most famous for the James-Lange theory of emotion) noted in 1886 that many of his patients with mild recurrent depression had a sediment in their urine. He thought this was uric acid and treated them with lithium, achieving some success in reducing their bouts of depression. Since Lange's publications were not translated into English until 2001, Cade had no knowledge of this. Carl's younger brother Fritz, also a physician working in an asylum, tried lithium on hundreds of acutely depressed patients in 1894. Some of them improved within days to weeks.[6]

In the United States, psychiatrist Dr. William Hammond, working at Bellevue, noted in his textbook published in 1871 that lithium bromide, also used as an antiseizure drug by the famous neurologist Dr. Silas Weir Mitchell, rapidly calmed agitated manic patients. Strangely, there was no mention of lithium in his subsequent textbooks.[7]

Perhaps because of lithium's hypothesized benefits for the "uric acid diathesis," lithium spas and lithium water became popular. Even the now-popular soft drink, Seven-Up, first formulated in 1929, included among its original seven ingredients lithium citrate. The modern version contains no lithium.[8]

As the twentieth century progressed it became clear that the uric acid diathesis of disease was a mistaken concept, except for uric acid's well-established role in gout and kidney stones. The popularity of lithium water and spas declined. But recent research[9] suggests some correlation of high uric acid levels in the blood with bipolar disorder, and some success in treating acute mania with allopurinol, a drug used to lower uric acid levels. Perhaps there is a link between uric acid and bipolar disorder yet to be fully revealed.

John Cade grew up in Australia, living as a child on the grounds of mental asylums where his father worked as a psychiatric director. Cade himself later served as a director of some Australian asylums. In that era many patients with bipolar disorder, schizophrenia, or severe depression were hospitalized for months, even years, with no effective medication treatments available.[10]

During his military service in World War II, Cade, along with thousands of other Allied troops, was captured by the Japanese and held for several years in the Changi prison camp in Malaya. There he functioned as both a general medical officer and a psychiatrist in the small makeshift hospital. Food rations were slim and the imprisoned troops suffered from malnourishment and beriberi, caused by a deficiency of thiamine (vitamin B1). To combat beriberi Cade had the imprisoned soldiers supplement their meager diet with a liquid derived from mashing the juice from local grasses, which contained some thiamine. His wartime experiences solidified his belief that many severe mental illnesses had a physical cause.[11]

After the war ended, and Cade renourished his emaciated body at home in Australia, he resumed duties at a mental asylum. There he set up a crude lab, storing patient urine samples in the family refrigerator. Precisely why he settled on lithium for a therapeutic trial in mania is not clear. He noted a calming effect on guinea pigs, and even tried it on himself for several weeks to confirm its safety.[12]

All ten manic-depressive patients reported in his 1949 paper had a good or an excellent response to lithium. His first patient, who had been chronically manic and hospitalized for five years, was able to go home.[13]

Even as Cade was conducting his landmark treatments, lithium was making news in the United States. Lithium carbonate was introduced in 1948 as a salt substitute; it was not long before reports of toxic symptoms such as tremor, confusion, loss of balance, seizures, and even a few deaths occurred. In 1948 the U.S. Food and Drug Administration banned lithium from beer and soda and in 1949 banned the lithium salt substitutes. Most significantly, this era of lithium toxicity made the

American medical community reluctant to use lithium even after its therapeutic potential became clear.[14]

After Cade's 1949 paper was published in the *Medical Journal of Australia*, and other Aussie psychiatrists began treating acute mania with lithium, incidents of toxicity and a few deaths occurred, including the very first patient Cade had treated with lithium. At that time there was no established means of measuring lithium blood levels, a practice that today helps us avoid toxicity. Thus within a few years of his publication Cade had abandoned his use of lithium and was recommending against the use of lithium because of its dangerous side effects.[15]

However, a German refugee physician, Dr. Edward Trautner, developed a means to measure lithium levels and published in 1951 a paper describing successful treatment without any serious toxicity of thirty manic patients employing use of blood lithium levels. Measuring blood levels was key to both delivering a therapeutic dose and avoiding toxic side effects.[16]

Researchers in Europe, most notably Dr. Mogens Schou in Denmark, learned of Cade's success with lithium and confirmed its benefits in therapeutic trials in his country. Medical research had not yet become as highly structured and "evidence based" as it is today. Many of his earlier studies were criticized for lacking the scientific rigor of "randomized, double-blind controlled" studies, which rapidly became the standard for testing new drugs. Randomized means the experimental group, (e.g., those getting lithium), and the control group, those getting a chemically inactive placebo that is disguised to look like the experimental drug, are randomly selected. Double-blind means that both the patients and the clinicians who rate their levels of improvement do not know which patients are getting the active drug and which the placebo. Measurement of mania or depression uses a well-standardized, valid, and reliable rating scale.[17]

Psychiatrists in Great Britain were slow to accept lithium, perhaps because of the lax scientific standards in early reports, while in the United States bad memories of the salt substitute era probably delayed approval of lithium by the FDA until 1970. Dr. Schou also showed lithium to be effective in preventing relapses both of bipolar disorder and of highly recurrent unipolar depression. Schou's younger brother, who suffered from debilitating depressions for decades, resumed a productive fulfilling life when on lithium.[18]

Lithium remains a frequently used mood stabilizer today. A mood stabilizer is a medication that provides effective treatment during some phase of bipolar disorder and does not worsen bipolar symptoms in any of the phases. The antipsychotic drugs, both first- and second-generation, are not considered "mood stabilizers," although many would otherwise fit the definition. Other mood stabilizers used in the manic phase are valproate, carbamazepine, and oxcarbazepine, and, for depression prevention, lamotrigine. The four antimanic mood stabilizers come in various forms of quick or slow release, liquid or solid, and various brands. Their therapeutic action is to reverse the manic state and bring the patient back to a neutral mood state. They all have established therapeutic blood levels, meaning the medication has to reach a certain level to give optimal treatment results. Typically, it takes about four or five days to get the medication to a full therapeutic level, and that long again to show significant impact on manic symptoms. More rapid dosing strategies have been developed for some drugs, such as valproate.[19]

Lithium is a naturally occurring element. We all have trace amounts in our bloodstream, but the therapeutic blood level is 0.6 to 1.2 mEq/L (milliequivalents per liter). In acute treatment a level above 0.8 is more effective. Lithium is eliminated through the kidneys and can cause an increase in urination, followed by an increase in thirst to help compensate for the increased urine output. All the mood stabilizing medications can have effects on other bodily organ systems, so frequently a number of tests are carried out when starting them. Typically, when starting lithium, we check blood electrolytes (sodium, potassium, chloride, and carbonate), and serum creatinine and blood urea nitrogen, which reflect kidney function, and do a standard urinalysis. Often an EKG (electrocardiogram) is ordered; lithium can affect the electrical conduction system in the heart or rarely lead to arrhythmias.[20]

Lithium has side effects on the central nervous system, such as causing a resting tremor, and sometimes troublesome memory difficulties. Sleepiness or fatigue can occur. At high doses incoordination and sedation may occur. Lithium can occasionally lead to hypothyroidism and rarely to hyperparathyroidism. When starting lithium, thyroid levels are checked, as is serum calcium, which reflects parathyroid function. Periodically during lithium treatment TSH (thyroid stimulating hormone) and serum creatinine are measured along with serum lithium levels. Diarrhea or upset stomach can sometimes occur. Hair loss and worsening of acne or psoriasis are other possible troubling side effects.[21]

Valproate in the form of Depakote (sodium valproate) was FDA approved to treat mania in the 1990s.[22] Valproate had been previously used in medicine as an anticonvulsant and for prevention of migraine headaches. Therapeutic blood levels range from around 50 to 125 μg/mL (micrograms per milliliter), but in acute treatment, levels above 80 μg/mL are more effective. These can be achieved in four or five days or rapid loading techniques can be used, with larger doses given on the first day of treatment. When used alone, the mood stabilizers take around three weeks to have a good antimanic effect and several weeks more to bring the patient back to his usual neutral mood state.

Valproate can cause a decrease in blood platelets and other abnormalities in the blood,[23] so a complete blood count is usually ordered before treatment, along with liver enzymes. Both hepatotoxicity and benign reversible increases in liver function tests can occur. Pancreatitis and a high serum ammonia state are rare but serious potential side effects. Like lithium, valproate can also cause tremor, diarrhea, heartburn, weight gain, and hair loss. But overall it usually causes fewer side effects than lithium and has become the most frequently used antimanic mood stabilizer.

Carbamazepine (CBZ) is another well-established anticonvulsant that was later used as a mood stabilizer. It has established blood levels between 4 and 12 μg/mL. It can rarely cause abnormal changes in blood cells such as low white count or anemia (low red cell count), so a blood count is taken prior to starting treatment. Elevations of liver enzymes and liver toxicity can occur, as can low sodium levels, especially in the elderly.

Rare but very severe allergic skin rashes (Stevens-Johnson syndrome and toxic epidermal necrolysis) can sometimes occur. When psychiatrists were just beginning to use CBZ in bipolar patients who were nonresponders to lithium, I described what was probably the first reported case of Stevens-Johnson syndrome in a patient treated with CBZ for bipolar disorder.[24] His rash was so severe that he had to be transferred to a university burn unit. Fortunately, he ultimately had a full recovery. This severe allergic skin reaction can also occur with oxcarbazepine, lamotrigine, and rarely with valproate. Today we have some tests than can help predict which patients are most at risk by doing genomic testing. This test uses saliva or a swab from inside the cheek to gather the patient's DNA. Persons with Asian ancestry are at higher risk for these severe skin reactions.

CBZ can also cause dizziness, drowsiness, fatigue, unsteadiness, double vision, nausea, and vomiting. With the anticonvulsants the higher the dose used, the more likely that side effects with the central nervous system will occur—from drowsiness to clumsiness to double vision. Cardiac toxicity, thyroid abnormalities, and gastrointestinal side effects can occur.[25]

CBZ also has many interactions with other drugs, leading to increases or decreases in the blood levels of the other drugs. For example, CBZ might lower the level of a birth control pill below its therapeutic level, leaving a female patient vulnerable to becoming pregnant. CBZ even changes the parameters of its own metabolism by inducing liver enzymes that shorten its half-life from around twenty-four hours when starting to around eight hours after two to four weeks of treatment.[26] Half-life is the duration of time it takes for the blood level of a drug to be reduced by 50 percent. Thus, a dose of carbamazepine that effectively stabilizes mood might become subtherapeutic and ineffective after several weeks and need readjusting. Because of its extensive side effect profile and its drug interactions, CBZ is not usually the first choice among mood stabilizers. Rather it tends to be used if other mood stabilizers have failed.

Oxcarbazepine (Trileptal) is an anticonvulsant that is chemically related to CBZ, but has fewer side effects and drug interactions. It has never been FDA approved in the United States for use in bipolar disorder, but is approved in some European countries. Only a handful of research studies support its efficacy as a mood stabilizer, but it has been used quite often "off-label" in the United States, where it is FDA approved as an anticonvulsant. It can manifest the central nervous system side effects of fatigue, sedation, clumsiness, abnormal eye movements, and double vision that CBZ can show, as well as low serum sodium levels and rarely the severe allergic skin rashes associated with CBZ.[27]

If the patient presents in a mixed bipolar state (symptoms both of mania and depression), valproate is usually the first choice among mood stabilizers. Similarly, if the patient has a rapid cycling pattern (four or more episodes per year) valproate may work better than lithium.[28] Antidepressant drugs are usually avoided in mixed states, which are treated like manic states with mood stabilizers and/or antipsychotics, which will be discussed next.

ANTIPSYCHOTICS

Patients presenting with hypomania or milder manic symptoms are often treated initially with one agent, a mood stabilizer or an antipsychotic. The antipsychotic agents act much more rapidly than mood stabilizers. A calming effect may occur within hours of an injection or oral dose of antipsychotics. If a bipolar patient is severely agitated or combative, the antipsychotic can bring rapid relief to the patient and to those around him. The antipsychotic effects of reducing hallucinations and delusional thinking occur more slowly over days. Patients with more severe manic symptoms have been shown to respond more quickly to a combination of a mood stabilizer plus an antipsychotic. Certainly, the patient's own personal history of response to medications is of paramount importance. Usually if a particular drug or combination of drugs has worked well in the past for a patient's manic or depressive episodes, that same set of drugs is likely to work well again. If the patient tolerated those drugs without any problematic side effects, that is another reason to consider using what worked well in the past.

Antipsychotic drugs have been around since the use of chlorpromazine (Thorazine) in the 1950s and were used to treat both schizophrenia and bipolar mania. Chlorpromazine (Thorazine, Largactil), trifluoperazine (Stelazine), thioridazine (Mellaril), perphenazine (Trilafon), and haloperidol (Haldol) are examples of FGAs, first-generation antipsychotics. The development of clozapine (Clozaril) in the 1970s and then risperidone (Risperdal) in the 1980s marked the first "atypical antipsychotics" or second-generation antipsychotics (SGAs). They were dubbed "atypical" because they caused significantly fewer of the neuromuscular side effects common to the FGAs.

I shall describe side effects of the antipsychotics extensively in this chapter, because so often minimizing the side effects makes a therapeutic drug more palatable for patients. Many drugs are available that effectively target manic symptoms, but often a drug's side effect profile determines whether patients will stay with it.

The antipsychotic effect of both the old and newer drugs hinges on the drug's ability to block the dopamine 2 receptors in the limbic system of the brain. The limbic system, which includes the hippocampus, the amygdala, and the cingulate gyrus, among other brain structures, functions in the organization and expression of emotions. The dopamine-dependent receptors in the limbic system mediate psychotic symptoms such as hearing voices or having delusions of persecution. Blocking those dopamine receptors reduces hallucinations and delusions. This blockade of dopamine by antipsychotic drugs also occurs in other parts of the brain, such as the basal ganglia, which are involved in muscular control. A host of possible side effects can ensue from this blockade.[29] Pathology in the basal ganglia, structures lying beneath the cerebral cortex, plays a role in the movement disorders seen in Parkinson's disease and Huntington's disease.

One of these neuromuscular side effects caused by antipsychotics is acute dystonia, which refers to a sudden onset of abnormal muscle contractions. For example, a patient's eyes might look upward uncontrollably (oculogyric crisis) or the patient might experience a painful and often frightening turning of the neck. These problems are usually readily reversed by an injection of diphenhydramine (Benadryl), lorazepam (Ativan) or benztropine (Cogentin).

Pseudoparkinsonism, another side effect from dopamine blockade, usually occurs at least a few days after starting an antipsychotic, but may not occur for months. This side effect mimics Parkinson's disease. The patient has a resting tremor, a shuffling gait, poor balance, stiffness of the muscles, an emotionally flat face with reduced blink rate, and overall difficulty with movements. This syndrome too can be alleviated with antiparkinsonian medications, such as benztropine (Cogentin), trihexyphenidyl (Artane), diphenhydramine (Benadryl), or amantadine (Symmetrel). Reducing the dose of the offending drug can also alleviate pseudoparkinsonism, but may take days to weeks to do so.

Akathisia refers to an overall restlessness and urge to move and is a third type of side effect brought on acutely by dopamine-blocking antipsychotics. Frequently it is experienced as a restless urge to pace. It can be extremely uncomfortable for some patients. Propranolol (Inderal) or lorazepam (Ativan) or similar antianxiety medications can alleviate this side effect.

Tardive dyskinesia (TD) refers to a syndrome of abnormal involuntary movements (dyskinesia) that occur at least several months (tardively or late in onset) after taking an antipsychotic or other dopamine-blocking drug. Abnormal movements can occur in the mouth, tongue, or face, such as puckering, blinking, chewing, grimacing, or tongue protrusion. Abnormal movements can occur in the limbs, such as wiggly movements in the fingers or squirming movements of the feet, or even in the neck or torso. The movements of TD are irregular in frequency, in contrast to the regular movements of a parkinsonian tremor. When discovered early, the movements of TD might go away if the offending agent is stopped. Unfortunately, many cases show continued abnormal movements indefinitely, although they may become milder in intensity and frequency over time.

The atypical or second-generation antipsychotics (SGAs) showed significantly fewer of these dopamine blockade side effects. The SGAs also block a serotonin receptor that blunts the dopamine blockade of the system controlling muscle movements. Although dystonias, pseudoparkinsonism, akathisia, and tardive dyskinesia occur as side effects of the SGAs, they occur much less often than with the older antipsychotics or FGAs such as haloperidol or chlorpromazine. Thus, the newer SGAs are used much more frequently now than the older FGAs. The SGAs have become first-line agents in treating bipolar disorder in all three phases: mania, depression, and maintenance.

With the FGAs patients developed TD at a rate of about 5–8 percent per year of treatment. Many studies confirm that the incidence of TD is consistently lower with the SGAs, in the range of 0.8 percent to 2.9 percent per year of continuous treatment.[30] Risk factors for developing TD include the cumulative dose of antipsychotic, female sex, presence of cognitive disturbance, African American ethnicity, presence of diabetes, a substance abuse disorder or a mood disorder rather than schizophrenia, and the use of lithium or an antiparkinsonian medication along with the antipsychotic. Those patients showing a movement disorder problem early in treatment, such as acute dystonias or pseudoparkinsonism, are at more risk for TD. Older age, beyond fifty-five, is a very significant risk factor, with several times higher rates of incidence of TD.

In 2017 the FDA approved valbenazine, a prescription drug treatment for TD. At a dose of 80 mg once daily it reduced symptoms of TD significantly more than placebo.[31] About 10 percent of patients reported one of these side effects: headache, urinary tract infections, or sleepiness.[32] Through the years I had a number of patients on tetrabenazine, a drug closely related to valbenazine, for TD. This drug was never FDA approved, but was available in the United Kingdom and later Canada, and could be used in the United States in unusual circumstances or in research studies, usually through a movement disorder clinic within a university neurology department.

Tardive dystonias show a slower, more prolonged abnormal movements than the usual tardive dyskinesias in which the movements are described as athetoid (wormlike) or choreiform (dancelike). Tardive akathisia also occurs rarely, when the restless urge to move is a persisting effect long after the offending drug has been discontinued.[33] One patient of mine with a schizoaffective disorder developed tardive dystonia with a tendency for her neck muscles to contract so that she was looking downward. This rendered her unable to drive an automobile. She had been on FGAs such as thiothixene and perphenazine before the advent of the SGA risperidone. Eventually she obtained significant relief from botulinum toxin (Botox) injections into her neck muscles. These would suppress the abnormal movements for close to three months. She was able to take olanzapine, an SGA, to control hallucinations and delusions, without any worsening of her tardive dystonia.

Some small studies indicate that high doses of vitamin B6 may bring some reduction of the severity of TD.[34]

Data on vitamin E do not support a role for vitamin E in improving TD, but perhaps it may lessen the worsening of the movement disorder in patients staying on antipsychotics.[35]

Another rare neuromuscular side effect of FGAs and SGAs is neuroleptic malignant syndrome (NMS). Neuroleptic is another term for antipsychotic medication. NMS may occur in up to 1 percent of psychiatric admissions started on antipsychotic medication.[36] It is usually seen within the first month of treatment. It is characterized by elevated temperature, autonomic instabilities such as elevated blood pressure and rapid heart rate, muscle rigidity, and often other dystonias. The patient often has clouded consciousness and/or agitation. Abnormal laboratory signs such as very elevated creatine phosphokinase, white blood cell count, and urinary myoglobin occur, the latter reflecting a breakdown of muscle tissue. NMS is a medical emergency usually treated in the intensive care unit, where antipsychotics are stopped, the patient is kept hydrated and sometimes the muscle relaxers bromocriptine or dantrolene are used to decrease symptoms. In up to 25 percent of cases NMS can be fatal.[37] After recovery, patients can sometimes be successfully treated with antipsychotics other than the offending agent or lower doses of that agent, obviously with great caution.

When used in treating mania the SGAs can be used alone or with a mood stabilizer. The combination can lead to more rapid and complete resolution of the mania, but the risk of side effects becomes greater.[38] Antipsychotics exert their antimanic effects rapidly, often producing a decrease in agitation within hours. Some are available as intramuscular injection (aripiprazole, ziprasidone, olanzapine) for rapid response. Some have a wafer form that rapidly dissolves in the mouth (risperidone, olanzapine, asenapine) or a liquid form to be swallowed. The rapid improvement in manic symptoms can prevent dangerous situations where a manic patient may be close to physical aggression. Sometimes these medications may head off the need for hospitalization by helping a manic patient calm down enough to realize he needs help and to become willing to participate in outpatient treatment.

The list of SGAs continues to grow and some have gained new uses in depression treatment, which we shall discuss more thoroughly in the next chapter. The current list of SGAs includes clozapine (Clozaril), risperidone (Risperdal), olanzapine (Zyprexa), quetiapine (Seroquel), ziprasidone (Geodon), aripiprazole (Abilify), paliperidone (Invega), iloperidone (Fanapt), asenapine (Saphris), lurasidone (Latuda), brexpiprazole (Rexulti), and cariprazine (Vraylar). Some are available now in generic form, which can make a huge difference in cost if one is paying out of pocket. Many private insurers include the lower cost generics as first-line choices. To get authorization to cover newer non-generic agents, the doctor often must show evidence that several generic agents were tried and failed. In the state of Michigan, Medicaid covers all psychotropic agents, giving clinicians a wider choice of medications. This class of drugs has many side effects in common, so I shall discuss these side effects as a group, highlighting when particular drugs differ or stand out.

I have discussed above the group of neuromuscular side effects. Some SGAs show fewer of these side effects, especially clozapine and quetiapine. Often if a patient has problems with those neuromuscular side effects, providers may switch to one of those agents. In patients developing TD we often switch to quetiapine or the older SGA clozapine because of the lesser tendency for those drugs to worsen TD. Clozapine, olanzapine, risperidone, and quetiapine have lower rates of the restlessness side effect called akathisia than ziprasidone, aripiprazole, asenapine, and lurasidone.[39]

The *metabolic syndrome* is a name given to a cluster of side effects than can occur from SGAs. It includes obesity; high blood pressure; elevated levels of lipids, such as triglycerides, cholesterol, or LDL; and diabetes mellitus. Patients on SGAs often experience an increase in hunger and gain a significant amount of weight within two weeks. This is a fairly reliable sign that further weight gain will ensue if the drug is continued. Weight gain by itself can lead to hypertension (high blood pressure), elevated lipids, and type II diabetes mellitus. But some patients who do not gain significant weight can also develop diabetes. There is evidence that the SGAs can directly affect the body's mechanisms of glucose metabolism, but exactly how they do so is not yet understood.

The SGAs differ in their tendency to cause weight gain. Olanzapine is the worst offender—about on a level with clozapine. Quetiapine and risperidone are intermediate, while ziprasidone and aripiprazole have the least risk for weight gain. Lurasidone, asenapine, iloperidone, cariprazine, and brexpiprazole can all cause the metabolic syndrome, but less so than olanzapine. When a bipolar patient is prescribed one of these drugs, it is important for patients to partner with their prescriber in keeping track of weight gain, blood sugars, and lipid levels. Patients need to focus as well on getting exercise and watching calorie intake. It is a truism that weight gain occurs when a person takes in more calories than she expends. So even on these medications, patients can maintain a heathy weight. Patients do not all manifest the tendency to gain weight equally. Some seem to easily maintain a stable weight, while others notice progressive weight gains within a few weeks of starting these drugs. I have had many patients who took olanzapine or clozapine for many years without developing obesity or diabetes problems. We currently have some genomic tests than can help predict who will be at risk for weight gain on olanzapine and who will not.

When the first (typical) antipsychotic, chlorpromazine, was developed it had a brand name of Largactil in Canada. The name was chosen to reflect the large number of different actions of this compound. Besides the antipsychotic effects, it had antihistamine effects, blood pressure lowering effects via alpha-adrenergic receptors, anticholinergic effects such as dry mouth and constipation, and effects to block hiccups and nausea. The newer SGAs continue the tradition of affecting many types of receptors, not only in the brain, but throughout the body.

Two of the SGAs, risperidone and iloperidone, have the greatest tendency to elevate prolactin, which is a type of hormone. This hormone is normally quite elevated in a woman after childbirth and promotes breast enlargement and lactation. I have had patients, both male and female, experience leakage of milk from the nipples and breast enlargement. Sometimes it is just the feeling of an uncomfortable swelling beneath the nipple. Elevated prolactin can cause a decrease of sexual desire or impotence. These sexual side effects and lactation go away when the offending medication is stopped. Prolactin levels can be readily measured in the blood and are elevated when lactation occurs. Many of the older FGAs also caused this side effect. It is possible for any of the SGAs to cause this, but among SGAs I have encountered it primarily with risperidone and iloperidone. If elevated for years, prolactin has the potential to cause osteoporosis or thinning of the bones.

Antipsychotics (both first- and second-generation) can reduce blood pressure or cause orthostatic hypotension—a drop in blood pressure from sitting to standing causing the patient to feel dizzy or lightheaded. They can cause fatigue or sleepiness. Quetiapine especially can cause sleepiness. Usually this occurs at doses of 50 to 200 mg per day and does not get worse as the dose is raised. As with many side effects, it often improves over days to a few weeks. Sometimes, however, the sedation continues and prompts the need for trying a different drug. Aripiprazole and ziprasidone are among the least sedating of SGAs.

Many antipsychotics produce what is referred to as anticholinergic side effects, caused by blocking the receptors for the neurotransmitter acetylcholine. These side effects include dry mouth, constipation, difficulty passing urine, blurry vision, increased heart rate, and sometimes, especially in the elderly, confusion.

Other side effects listed for SGAs as a group include increased risks of mortality if used in dementia-related psychosis, seizures, impaired swallowing, impairment of the body's temperature regulation mechanisms, impairment of thinking and coordination that might impact ability to use machinery, and increased suicidality.[40]

Although we occasionally can see a decrease in white blood cells, especially neutrophils, with various SGAs, it occurs much more often in clozapine. Clozapine is actually the oldest SGA or atypical antipsychotic. It has found a special treatment niche because it is the single most effective antipsychotic in treating schizophrenia. Patients who did not adequately respond to trials with other antipsychotics improved the best with clozapine. This has been borne out in many research studies. It is sometimes used in bipolar or schizoaffective disorder if patients continue to have severe psychotic manic episodes or poorly controlled mood swings despite other treatments with mood stabilizers and SGAs. Such treatment-refractory patients have been known to improve with clozapine.

So frequent were problems with reduced white blood cell counts that in the United States we have developed a clozapine registry. After its initial introduction in the United States, clozapine was withdrawn from the market after a few years (in 1974) because it had caused some deaths from dangerously low blood counts. When reintroduced for treatment of schizophrenia in 1989, special mandatory blood monitoring was required. Patients must have their blood drawn to document their absolute neutrophil counts every week when starting clozapine. Neutrophils are the white blood cells that are very important in attacking invading bacteria. If no serious reductions in the neutrophils occur, the blood draws are extended to every two weeks and eventually to every four weeks. Registered pharmacies will not dispense the medication without verification of the neutrophil count. Without this close monitoring some patients would die from bacterial infections that they simply could not fight off when their neutrophil levels dropped too low.

Clozapine has other unique but rare side effects including cardiomyopathy (a disorder of the heart muscle) and pericarditis (inflammation of the membranous sac surrounding the heart). Like many other antipsychotics it can lower the seizure threshold, making the patient more likely to have a seizure. A troublesome side effect is excessive salivation, especially at night. This can be relieved by other medications if needed. Despite some of these unusual and severe side effects, clozapine can still be useful, giving patients back improved control of their mood when other drugs have failed. Clozapine is FDA approved only for use in treatment-resistant schizophrenia and for suicide prevention in schizophrenia. Although not FDA approved for use in bipolar disorder, it is occasionally used in treatment-refractory cases.[41] See table 5.1.

Table 5.1. FDA-Approved Treatments for Mania

	Drug alone	Drug plus lithium or valproate
Mood Stabilizers		
lithium	+	
valproate, valproate ER	+	
(Depakote, Depakote ER)		
carbamazepine ER (Tegretol ER)	+	
First-Generation Antipsychotics		
chlorpromazine (Thorazine)	+	
Second-Generation Antipsychotics		
olanzapine (Zyprexa)	+	+
risperidone (Risperdal)	+	+
quetiapine, quetiapine XR	+	+
(Seroquel, Seroquel XR)		
ziprasidone (Geodon)	+	+
aripiprazole (Abilify)	+	+
asenapine (Saphris)	+	+
cariprazine (Vraylar)	+	

OTHER TREATMENTS FOR MANIA

Electroconvulsive therapy (ECT) is occasionally used for acute mania if medication trials have failed or may be inadvisable for medical reasons (e.g., a pregnant woman with acute mania).[42] ECT involves the application of electrodes to the scalp of an anesthetized patient. The alternating electrical current causes a neurologic seizure that seems crucial to its effectiveness. ECT and its side effects are discussed in chapter 6, Treatment of Bipolar Depression. ECT remains the most effective treatment for severe unipolar depression.

Insomnia and agitation frequently accompany episodes of mania or of mania or depression with mixed features. Drugs usually used as antianxiety agents or sleep aids can be added to a patient's primary antimanic drugs. These include the benzodiazepines and the "Z drugs."

The benzodiazepines as a group have been around since the 1950s and include familiar names such as diazepam (Valium), alprazolam (Xanax), and temazepam (Restoril). They can aid sleep and also cause sleepiness and lethargy. They also have some muscle relaxant and antiseizure effects. They differ in how rapidly they are absorbed, metabolized, and eliminated. When used at moderate dosages for extended periods (many weeks or months) patients can develop a tolerance for them or a dependence on them, and can experience a withdrawal syndrome when abruptly stopping them. Patients with a history of addiction to other substances, such as alcohol and pain medications, are more prone to develop abuse or dependence on the "benzos." In treating bipolar mania, they can usually be used briefly over days or a few weeks until mood stabilizers or antipsychotics quell the manic symptoms including insomnia.

The Z drugs zolpidem (Ambien), zaleplon (Sonata), and eszopiclone (Lunesta) were developed more recently, specifically as sleep aids. They tend to target just one of the synaptic receptors that the benzos target but lack the muscle relaxant and anticonvulsant properties of the benzos. They also are best used briefly or intermittently in treating insomnia associated with bipolar disorder. Sometimes adding a Z drug or benzo to a mood stabilizer such as lithium or valproate may be enough to get some patients through a hypomanic spell without risking some of the side effects of an SGA.

While acute manic and hypomanic symptoms respond well to medications within days to weeks, bipolar depression has been more difficult to control, as we discuss in the next chapter.

· 6 ·

Treatment of Bipolar Depression

*K*evin had been struggling with mood problems since his early teens. When he came to me for treatment in his senior year of high school he was experiencing intense spells of depression that typically lasted several weeks. He felt sad, discouraged, and had unexplained crying spells that could come on during a class. He felt fatigued with no energy and complained about poor concentration. Usually an excellent student, he would struggle to complete assignments. Sometimes he would have suicidal thoughts and contemplate overdosing. His depression appeared to improve with bupropion and quetiapine, but as we increased the dose of quetiapine toward a full therapeutic level the side effects of drowsiness became a problem. Some previous treaters had diagnosed him with bipolar disorder and others with recurrent major depression. Any uncertainty about his bipolar diagnosis vanished when he experienced a high spell for several weeks. He was energetic with bubbly enthusiasm, convinced an essay he wrote for a class would become a well-recognized boon to all humankind. His speech was noticeably rapid, and he was up half the night writing assignments without apparent sleepiness the next day. We were not able to achieve a satisfactory level of mood stability before he went to college in a distant town and sought another provider there.

Bipolar patients tend to have many more days of depression than of mania or hypomania. Bipolar I disorder patients spend about three times more days in depression than they do in mania. Bipolar II disorder patients spend on average thirty-nine times more days in a state of depression than in hypomania.[1] Clearly, having effective and tolerable treatments for bipolar depression is a major need.

Often the depressed state follows an episode of mania. This pattern of mania-depression-euthymia (neutral mood state) is more frequent than the pattern of depression-mania-euthymia.[2] At other times patients may slip from euthymia into depression, which may or may not be followed by mania. In fact, many patients show such a pattern for years before ever exhibiting a manic episode.

Not only is depression more frequent and more persistent than mania in bipolar disorder; it is also harder to treat effectively.

Understanding why a patient's mood shifts to depression is important. Perhaps the change coincided with starting a new blood pressure pill, which perhaps could be changed. Perhaps the patient began drinking excessively and this is an issue to address. Perhaps a family death or job loss triggered the depression, in which case psychotherapy might be very helpful. If the depression is a recurrence of yearly wintertime depressions, perhaps bright light treatment (used for seasonal affective disorder) could be considered. Sometimes no triggering factors are apparent.

The goal in treating bipolar depression is not just improvement (response), but eliminating the depression, getting the patient back to baseline (remission). Because most medications take weeks to show their full benefit, one has to approach treatment systematically, neither abandoning ship too soon if a medication strategy is not working, nor continuing too long with an ineffectual combination of meds. Often, we see partial improvement, in which case it makes sense to augment the helpful treatment with other medications or nutritional supplements that may boost the response, or with psychotherapy, meditation, or an exercise regimen, all of which can foster an antidepressant response. Once in remission one should not be in a hurry to stop what has helped. After a period of time—say about six months in remission—it is reasonable to think of tapering off certain medications, unless they seem vital to a preventive, maintenance regimen.

Let's look at drug treatment strategies for the patient in the midst of a bipolar depression. If the patient is already on a mood stabilizer, optimizing the blood levels of that drug makes sense (e.g., pushing lithium levels to 0.8 mEq/L or above and valproate levels to 80 µg/mL or above). If the patient takes lamotrigine with no problematic side effects, dosages of lamotrigine might be increased. Sometimes just that adjustment of the mood stabilizer might bring improvement. As with manic episodes, using treatments that worked well for a particular patient in the past without troubling side effects makes sense. It is important to individualize the treatment, looking at both the patterns of the bipolar disorder (e.g., psychotic features or rapid cycling), and any comorbid disorders (e.g., panic disorder or an alcohol use disorder). One needs to look at other medical conditions and medications a patient is taking. For example, a patient who also has frequent bouts of migraine might benefit from valproate, which helps prevent migraines as well as mood swings.

For many years, physicians used antidepressant medications to treat bipolar depression. Many research studies of antidepressant efficacy used both unipolar and bipolar patients. Careful analysis of past data specifically with bipolar patients led to a conclusion that treating bipolar depression with antidepressants had not been very effective. Therefore, researchers sought more effective treatments for bipolar depression. Four new medication options have become available in the past eighteen years.

Studies of the combination of fluoxetine and olanzapine (Symbyax) won FDA approval for the treatment of bipolar depression in 2003.[3] In the studies, each drug by itself showed some efficacy, but the combination did best. It comes in five sizes (mg of olanzapine, followed by mg of fluoxetine): 3/25, 6/25, 6/50, 12/25, and 12/50, with recommended starting dose 6/25. The brand combination drug, Symbyax, can be closely duplicated by using less expensive generic fluoxetine (Prozac) and olanzapine (Zyprexa). The olanzapine/fluoxetine combination or OFC was successful in bringing depressed bipolar patients into remission. The OFC understandably may manifest side effects from both drugs, including weight gain, elevated blood sugars and blood lipids, sleepiness, fatigue, dry mouth, and sexual dysfunction. The original studies were done on the OFC by itself, but in practice many times a mood stabilizer is also prescribed. OFC has also been approved for treatment of refractory unipolar depression (i.e., depressions that have not responded to at least two adequate trials of an antidepressant).

Quetiapine has also been FDA approved since 2006 for treatment of acute bipolar depression, both by itself and along with the mood stabilizers lithium or valproate.[4] It was approved for both bipolar I and II depression. The original studies used two dosage groups: 300 mg/d and 600 mg/d. Both groups improved to a similar extent. Some patients improved at even lower doses of quetiapine. Sleepiness is the most common side effect with quetiapine, occurring in about 50 percent of patients at therapeutic doses. Sometimes somnolence (sleepiness) improves over days to weeks, but sometimes doctor and patient decide to try a less sedating regimen. Quetiapine has also been approved for maintenance treatment of bipolar disorder, so that it is one of two second-generation antipsychotics, along with olanzapine, approved in all three treatment phases: mania, depression, and maintenance.

Quetiapine also has FDA approval for treatment of unipolar depression when added to an antidepressant. Occasionally clinicians see patients for whom the diagnosis (unipolar versus bipolar depression) is simply not clear. There may be a possibility of previous episodes of hypomania, but they were not recognized as such at the time. Quetiapine can be considered here since it can help both unipolar and bipolar depression. In a similar fashion, OFC can be used in these ambiguous situations, because it also has indications for both unipolar and bipolar depression.

In 2013 the FDA approved lurasidone, both as single therapy and combined with a mood stabilizer for treatment for bipolar depression.[5] It showed a good antidepressant effect at doses between 40 and 120 mg/day. It has a lighter side effect burden than quetiapine and OFC. Compared with those two treatments, sleepiness with lurasidone is much less common, as are weight gain and the associated metabolic side effects. In one study about 7 percent of patients had sleepiness at doses between 20 to 60 mg/day and about 14 percent felt too sleepy at 80 to 120 mg/day. This compares with about 56 percent of patients taking a therapeutic dose in the quetiapine studies. A weight gain of 7 percent over baseline is considered worrisome in a six-to-eight-week study. This occurred in 19.3 percent in the OFC studies and 8 percent with quetiapine, but only 2 percent with lurasidone. Occasional nausea and vomiting occurred with lurasidone, as did akathisia (drug-induced restlessness) in about 11 percent and pseudoparkinsonism (showing side effects that mimic Parkinson's disease) in 13 percent. These neuromuscular side effects occur a bit more often with lurasidone than they do with quetiapine or OFC. The neuromuscular side effects of antipsychotics, including akathisia and pseudoparkinsonism, are discussed in chapter 5, Treatment of Mania and Mixed States.

Lurasidone treatment is usually started at 20 mg/d and slowly increased over a period of weeks, giving the drug a chance to work at a given dose before increasing it. Lurasidone needs to be taken with food, at least 350 calories. I usually recommend it be taken with the evening meal. Taking it on an empty stomach results in blood levels about two-thirds lower. Although not FDA approved as a maintenance treatment, if lurasidone is successful in improving depression it is often continued.

All three of these bipolar depression treatments show a response rate (significant improvement) of better than 50 percent and remission rates (depression symptoms gone) of 40 to 50 percent. Although these rates are not stellar, they are better than most other drug treatment rates for bipolar depression. The antidepressant response to these medications is much slower than the antimanic response to SGAs, with depression gradually improving over several weeks. A full antidepressant response may take four to six weeks.

Some response to bipolar depression has been shown with the mood stabilizers lithium, lamotrigine, and valproate, although not greater than the 50 percent response rates we have seen with lurasidone, quetiapine, and the olanzapine/fluoxetine combination.[6] See table 6.1.

Table 6.1.   FDA-Approved Treatment for Bipolar Depression

olanzapine + fluoxetine (Symbyax)
quetiapine, quetiapine XR (Seroquel, Seroquel XR)
lurasidone (Latuda)
cariprazine (Vraylar)

Lurasidone was tried in an older (fifty-five years and beyond) population of depressed bipolar patients, both as monotherapy and along with lithium or valproate. Significant reduction in depressive symptoms was seen after six weeks with doses from 20 to 120 mg/day compared with placebo. However, in those elderly patients where lurasidone was added to lithium or valproate, any improvements did not reach statistical significance beyond the benefits of the mood stabilizer alone.[7]

A fourth second-generation antipsychotic, cariprazine (Vraylar), has shown efficacy and safety in treating bipolar I depression in an eight-week study.[8] Patients treated with 1.5 mg/day of cariprazine showed significant improvement compared with placebo, as did many patients receiving 3.0 mg/d. Slightly less than 50 percent of patients showed a therapeutic response after six weeks on the 1.5 mg dose and 30–35 percent achieved remission in that time frame. Cariprazine is a potent blocker of D3 dopamine receptors as well as the D2 dopamine receptors that all antipsychotics block. Whether this D3 blockade is crucial to its antidepressant effect is not yet clear, although suggested by animal research. Any untoward physical or laboratory effects were very minimal in this short study, with no significant weight gain. The 3.0 mg dose caused some akathisia (restlessness) in 17 percent and the 1.5 mg dose in 8.3 percent of patients taking it. This drug gained FDA approval for treatment of bipolar I depression in June 2019.

For many years bipolar depression has been treated with antidepressant medications, alone or with mood stabilizers. Overall, they were not very effective. Some patients might have a brief response, only to lapse back into depression. Or worse, some patients on the antidepressant alone might soar into a manic or hypomanic phase. In light of those findings, it is strongly recommended that if bipolar patients use an antidepressant that they should already be on a mood stabilizer or antipsychotic to prevent launching them into mania. There is additional concern that antidepressants could trigger a rapid cycling pattern in bipolar patients. Rapid cycling means more than four distinct mood episodes in a year's time. Rapid cycling patterns tend to be more difficult to stabilize than the usual slower cycling bipolar disease. The older antidepressants (tricyclics and monoamine oxidase inhibitors) and the newer serotonin-norepinephrine reuptake inhibitors (SNRIs) tend to be more likely to cause mania or rapid cycling than the serotonin reuptake inhibitors (SSRIs) or bupropion (Wellbutrin).[9]

One meta-analysis (analysis of results from multiple studies) of bipolar depression treatment found that adding an antidepressant did not significantly increase the benefit provided by a mood stabilizer alone.[10] Side effects tended to be fairly minimal and switching to a manic or hypomanic state was minimal, around 0.5 percent, when a mood stabilizer was on board. But experts sometimes disagree. A different review of ten studies with over one thousand total patients in bipolar depression found a significant response rate of 44.8 percent with antidepressants versus 33.4 percent with placebo.[11] This response rate was not clearly less than the response rate of antidepressants in unipolar depression, which often is lukewarm at best. Many antidepressant response rates are only 10 or 15 percent better than placebo rates in many published studies on unipolar depression. In severe unipolar depression, antidepressants clearly outperform placebo, but in mild and moderate unipolar depression the placebo rate is high enough that antidepressants struggle to outperform it.

A consensus statement about use of antidepressants from the International Society for Bipolar Disorders made twelve recommendations.[12] Among these were to avoid use of antidepressants in depression with mixed features (two or more manic symptoms), and in patients with a history of rapid cycling. Antidepressant use was permissible in those with a history of positive response to them or a history of lapsing into depression when the antidepressant was stopped. They also recommended avoiding antidepressants in bipolar I disorder.

SSRIs came into use in the United States in the 1980s with the advent of fluoxetine (Prozac). Other SSRIs available in the United States include paroxetine (Paxil), sertraline (Zoloft), citalopram (Celexa), escitalopram (Lexapro), and fluvoxamine (Luvox). These drugs inhibit reuptake of serotonin into the presynaptic nerve terminals from which it has been released, leaving more serotonin within the synaptic cleft between nerve cells where the serotonin can have more effect on the postsynaptic serotonin receptors. SSRIs have had success in treating not only unipolar depression, but obsessive-compulsive disorder and anxiety disorders such as panic disorder, generalized anxiety disorder, and social anxiety disorder. The SSRIs have had some usefulness in treating bulimia (an eating disorder) and posttraumatic stress disorder. They are safer than the older tricyclics and monoamine oxidase inhibitors (MAOIs) in the case of an overdose and less likely to cause certain side effects, like a blood pressure drop when standing, or severe dry mouth, constipation, or urinary retention. However, the SSRIs can show gastrointestinal side effects such as nausea, vomiting, or diarrhea. They can cause sexual dysfunction ranging from a loss of sexual desire to delayed orgasm or no orgasm at all. Especially in older patients they might cause low sodium levels in the blood. In youth and young adults, they might increase the frequency of suicidal thoughts. But overall their side effects are more troublesome than life threatening.[13]

SNRIs are serotonin-norepinephrine reuptake inhibitors. These include venlafaxine (Effexor), desvenlafaxine (Pristiq), duloxetine (Cymbalta), and levomilnacipran (Fetzima). They have a side effect profile that includes most of the SSRI side effects. Because of the effect on norepinephrine they can sometimes cause a slight increase in blood pressure (usually no more than 5 mm) or effects on the heart such as rapid heart rate or extra beats. They have also shown benefit in treating some pain syndromes such as peripheral neuropathy pain, fibromyalgia, and even pain from osteoarthritis. Duloxetine and levomilnacipran might have fewer sexual side effects than most SSRIs.

A number of newer antidepressants inhibit serotonin reuptake like the older SSRIs plus exhibit an effect on one or more other presynaptic or postsynaptic receptors. None have been judged any more effective than the SSRIs. These include vilazodone (Viibryd), and vortioxetine (Trintellix). These newcomers appear to have less tendency for weight gain and sexual side effects than the older SSRIs but can have the same gastrointestinal side effects. Older antidepressants trazodone (Desyrel) and nefazodone (Serzone) are serotonin 2 receptor antagonists and along with mirtazapine (Remeron) tend to be rather sedating. They are often used if insomnia is a prominent feature of depression. High doses of trazodone are often hard for patients to tolerate because of dizziness side effects. Nefazodone is rarely used now because of rare cases of liver toxicity. Mirtazapine often causes significant weight gain.

Among older antidepressants imipramine was the first tricyclic antidepressant, having been formulated in the 1950s. This group of antidepressants was dubbed "tricyclics" because their chemical structure has three rings. Amitriptyline, nortriptyline, desipramine, protriptyline, clomipramine, and trimipramine are other tricyclics available in the United States. Like the SSRIs and SNRIs, they are not FDA approved for treating bipolar depression, but only unipolar depression, or in the case of clomipramine, obsessive-compulsive disorder. They have found additional uses, not approved by the FDA, in the treatment of anxiety disorders and pain syndromes. They can cause a drop in blood pressure from sitting to standing, dizziness, rapid heart rate, cardiac arrhythmias, dry mouth, constipation, urinary retention, and sexual side effects. They can be deadly if taken in large amounts in an overdose. They may be more prone than SSRIs to cause mania and rapid mood cycling.

MAOIs were the first antidepressants—discovered accidentally. When the MAOI iproniazid was used to treat patients' tuberculosis, many of them showed remarkable improvement in their depression. Today in the United States, phenelzine, tranylcypromine, and iso-carboxazid are the only oral MAOIs available.[14] There is also a trans-dermal patch form of selegiline. Oral MAOIs can show the "cheese reaction" with foods containing the amino acid tyramine. Such foods include aged cheese and meats, fava beans, and also pharmaceuticals such as pseudoephedrine, some asthma medications, and meperidine (Demerol). The cheese reaction can lead to severe high blood pressure, necessitating emergency treatment to protect patients from outcomes such as a stroke. In addition, MAOIs have many of the side effects listed for tricyclics. The selegiline patch does not have a risk for the cheese reaction at its lower dose. MAOIs are seldom used these days because of the potential side effects. Through the years, however, I have had a number of patients with bipolar depression who improved with them, when other treatments had failed.

Jack was a middle-aged man with bipolar II disorder. He came to me experiencing a prolonged depression that had lasted many months. He had low energy and interest and his speech and movements seemed visibly slowed down. His wife was taking care of him because he lacked the energy to make his meals and otherwise take care of himself. He did not have suicidal ideation, however. His depression had not responded to additions of a tricyclic (imipramine) or an SSRI (fluoxetine) to his lithium. When we added phenelzine (Nardil) he soon returned to a normal mood. This occurred many years before the FDA had approved OFC, quetiapine, lurasidone, or cariprazine for bipolar depression. He continued for many years on lithium and phenelzine, experiencing some hypomanic ups, but never again severe depressions.

Many early research studies on antidepressants included both unipolar and bipolar patients. Studies through the years indicated very modest effect on average, in bipolar depression, not nearly as robust as that of lurasidone, quetiapine, or OFC. However, patients differ in their responses to medications, so some bipolar patients may show an antidepressant response to certain antidepressants. The patterns of drug responsiveness in an individual patient are more important than the results of controlled studies. People are variable in their physiology and we each have our own patterns of response to drugs. These response patterns tend to hold true over time, so a drug or drug combination that worked well in the past to alleviate depression may work well again in the future.

Other pharmaceutical agents sometimes used in bipolar depression, usually in combination with other drugs, have included stimulants such as methylphenidate (Ritalin) or amphetamines (Adderall), agents to promote wakefulness such as modafinil (Provigil) or armodafinil

(Nuvigil), or agents such as pramipexole (Mirapex) that increase do-pamine levels in disorders such as Parkinson's disease and restless legs syndrome. They lack consistent robust evidence for their effectiveness in bipolar depression and are not FDA approved.[15] The calcium channel blocker nimodipine, used for high blood pressure, has shown benefit used along with lithium for stopping rapid cycling episodes.[16]

Herbal and nutritional agents used for unipolar depression such as St. John's wort, SAMe, and 5-hydroxytryptophan, are occasionally used. We lack research studies on these agents for bipolar disorder. However, omega-3 fatty acids showed a positive benefit in bipolar depression when added to mood stabilizers in a meta-analysis of five studies.[17] Citicoline used in a study with patients having both a mood disorder, either unipolar or bipolar, and methamphetamine use disor-der showed an antidepressant response.[18] Citicoline is an intermediate chemical in the synthesis of phosphatidyl choline and may contribute to an increase in several neurotransmitters.

N-acetyl cysteine or NAC is another nutritional supplement with moderate evidence for augmenting a bipolar antidepressant regi-men. This substance has also shown benefits in obsessive-compulsive disorder (OCD), many substance abuse problems, trichotillomania (hair-pulling) and even gambling. It may reduce irritability in autistic persons. It is usually started at 500 mg twice daily for a week, then the dose is doubled.[19]

Thyroid hormone in the form of T3 or T4 has been a commonly used augmenter to drugs in unipolar depression. There is modest evidence that T3 may help bipolar II depression. Very high dose T4, such as 300ug/d in women, has had good evidence as an augmenter in bipolar depression.[20]

A sizable number of bipolar patients have low or borderline low levels of vitamin D3. When that is the case, supplementing medications with vitamin D3 makes sense. Some evidence suggests it may help bi-polar depressives with normal vitamin D3 levels as well.[21]

Ketamine is a pharmaceutical agent used for about fifty years as an anesthetic that has been used in a flurry of studies to treat depression, both bipolar and unipolar. It is not FDA approved, but still investiga-tional. However, several studies have shown a very rapid and significant reduction in depressive symptoms.[22] Ketamine treatment has the poten-tial to lead to a paradigm shift in the treatment of both unipolar and bipolar depression, because the treatment is fast acting and benefits many patients who have not responded to traditional medication regimens.

Ketamine is administered as an intravenous infusion over about forty minutes at dosages much less than those used in anesthesia. Some antidepressant effects may occur as early as forty minutes and peak in about a day. The benefits last about three to twelve days.[23] In other studies the benefits are more short-lived,[24] but some research centers are using repeat maintenance infusions every two to four days. A recent study in bipolar depressives showed rapid reduction in suicidal think-ing.[25] A reported side effect with ketamine is brief (up to four hours) dissociative symptoms after the injection, wherein patients may experi-ence a dreamlike or out-of-body experience. Elevations of pulse and blood pressure can occur.

A drug called esketamine, which like its chemical cousin ketamine acts on N-methyl-d-aspartate (NMDA) receptors, improved depres-sion and relieved suicidal thinking within two hours of being sprayed into the nostrils of depressed patients.[26] It was FDA approved in March 2019 for clinical use in unipolar depression. It is first being released only in selected treatment centers to be used along with a standard antidepressant in unipolar depression. We will likely see trials soon in bipolar depression.

Other modalities to treat depression include sleep deprivation. I have had quite a few patients, both unipolar and bipolar, who re-sponded with marked improvement of depression with one night of sleep deprivation. Usually awakening by 3:00 a.m. is recommend in these trials. Some bipolar patients manifest hypomanic mood after the sleep deprivation. Sometimes the mood settles back to neutral. Other times, after the patient gets a solid night of sleep, the depression returns. But just knowing the depression is not unrelenting can give patients a surge of hope. In one study, bipolar depressed patients were kept awake for three thirty-six-hour stretches followed by recovery sleep and bright light treatment.[27] In the second week they received bright light each morning. Patients also received lithium. They showed a substantial response rate over 70 percent. There was no placebo control group, but the substantial response rate suggests that more such studies are in order.

Patients with seasonal mood disorder become depressed in the shortening daylight of fall or winter and show improvement when the days become longer. Some of them respond well to bright light treatment: 10,000 lux of brightness delivered from about eighteen inches away for thirty minutes, preferably in the morning each day. Such treatment may help some bipolar and unipolar depression sufferers even if they do not have a seasonal pattern. Exercise was discussed in chapter 4, Setting a Healthy Baseline, and can certainly be added to a regimen to alleviate depression.

A recent study found bright white light of 7,000 lux from twelve inches away delivered around midday for about forty-five minutes daily to have very significant success in alleviating bipolar depression.[28] Those treated with bright light showed a 68.2 percent remission rate at three to six weeks of treatment compared to 22.2 percent in the placebo/control group, which received dull red light, not likely to trigger an improvement. The effects of treatment did not clearly show until four weeks. Patients started with only fifteen minutes of light the first week, thirty minutes the second, forty-five minutes the third, and sixty minutes in the fourth week if they had not responded. No switches to mania or hypomania occurred. Most of the patients were on mood stabilizers and many also on antidepressants. These were not patients with seasonal affective disorder, who get depressed each winter, but bipolar depressives without seasonal fluctuations.

A combination of sleep deprivation and bright light treatment can sometimes yield rapid improvement in bipolar depression.[29] I treated a woman with a rapid cycling bipolar I disorder who often cycled into depressions with prominent suicidal thinking despite being maintained on valproate. Often a night of sleep deprivation after being awakened at 3:00 a.m. by hospital staff would rapidly catapult her out of her depression. Sometimes she would slip back into depression after a full night of sleep, but other times the improvement would continue, leading to a very shortened hospital stay.

Repetitive transcranial magnetic stimulation (rTCMS) was approved by the FDA in 2008 for treatment of unipolar depression that has not responded to at least one trial of an antidepressant drug.[30] It might hold promise for bipolar depression. An electromagnetic coil placed on the scalp generates a magnetic field that alternates rapidly. This creates electrical stimulation to the underlying cerebral cortex at a depth of 2–3 cm. Typically patients are treated five days per week for up to six weeks in an outpatient setting. Patients remain awake during the half-hour-long sessions and may occasionally experience headache, but overall the treatments are easily tolerated. In a review of nineteen randomized controlled trials of rTCMS with 181 depressed bipolar patients, 44.3 percent showed a positive response at the end of active treatment, while only 25.3 percent of sham-treated controls did so.[31] In those studies targeting one side of the brain, either the left or the right dorsolateral prefrontal cortex was effective. Bilateral magnetic stimulation did not prove effective. Side effects such as headache are minimal.

Among neuromodulation techniques, transcranial direct current stimulation (tDCS) is a relative newcomer. A direct current passes between two electrodes placed on the scalp, stimulating the underlying cerebral cortex. It has advantages of being relatively inexpensive and an easily mobile form of treatment. In contrast, repetitive transcranial magnetic stimulation requires expensive and more substantial hard-to-move equipment. A recent review extracted records of only forty-six bipolar patients treated in several studies of tDCS for major depression. Those original studies included unipolar depressives as well. The tDCS treatment was found to be significantly beneficial for bipolar depression.[32] In a randomized, double-blind study of tDCS added to ongoing treatment, 67.6 percent of bipolar depressives had a positive response. A sham control group that received electric current only very briefly (essentially a placebo group) showed a 30.4 percent response rate.[33] Some pain at the site of stimulation on the scalp was the primary side effect.

Electroconvulsive treatment is the single most effective treatment we have for severe unipolar depression. Larger numbers of patients respond and go into remission than with any single drug regimen available.[34] Likewise, in bipolar depression ECT can be highly effective for inpatients who have not responded to other treatments, or who are psychotic or in desperate straits, either highly suicidal or not taking adequate nourishment. ECT works more rapidly than antidepressant drugs, with one-third showing a response in a week and 75 percent showing a response by three weeks.[35]

ECT can also be used for the depressed bipolar pregnant patient, avoiding lengthy exposure of the fetus to drugs. A randomized, controlled trial of ECT for treatment-resistant bipolar depression conducted with seventy-three patients in Norway found 73.9 percent of the ECT-treated group responding versus 35.0 percent of the control group treated with medications.[36] However, the remission rates did not differ significantly (34.8 percent versus 30.0 percent). In other words, the patients improved, but their depression did not go away completely. This is a problem we see with both unipolar and bipolar depression: many of our treatments help substantially, but a sizable number of patients still have residual symptoms of depression and are not back to a normal mood.

ECT is often administered to inpatients, but can be an outpatient treatment, often in the outpatient surgery section of a hospital with an anesthesiologist or nurse anesthetist present. During ECT the brain receives an alternating electric current of sufficient strength and duration to cause an electrical seizure. Patients are given anesthesia and muscle relaxants so that they do not have actual convulsions of their muscles. Their vital signs are monitored closely, as well as blood oxygen levels and EEG readings. The treatment is delivered about three times a week. Between six and twelve treatments are usually enough to bring a patient out of her depression. Patients' memories for the days surrounding their treatment and just before tend to be lost or severely dimmed (retrograde amnesia). Learning new information may also be mildly impaired for several weeks after ECT (anterograde amnesia). Studies have shown that patients' overall memory function, executive function, general intelligence, and creativity a number of weeks after the procedure is no worse than that of a control group of patients with histories of severe depression but no ECT treatment.[37]

Right unilateral ECT with an electrode on the forehead and another on the right temple is effective with somewhat fewer cognitive side effects than bilateral ECT with electrodes applied to both temples. Post-ECT confusion for minutes to hours is common, as are nausea, headaches, and muscle aches.

Vagal nerve stimulation (VNS) was FDA approved for treatment of epilepsy in 1997. When patients were noted to have improvement of their mood, trials of VNS for treatment of depression were carried out. In 2003 VNS was approved for treatment of treatment-resistant depression, that is, patients with four or more failed trials of antidepressant regimens. Bipolar and unipolar patients were included in the trials so the FDA approval extends to bipolar depression.[38] Outpatient surgery must be performed to implant a pacemaker-like stimulator beneath the skin attached by electrodes to the vagus nerve in the neck. The vagus nerve delivers nerve impulses from the parasympathetic branch of the autonomic nervous system up to the brain stem's tractus solitarius. Usually messages from the heart, gastrointestinal tract, and other internal organs follow this pathway. Nerves from the tractus solitarius connect to the brain's emotional centers in the limbic system (hypothalamus and amygdala) and then on to the ventromedial prefrontal cortex. This latter cortical area appears underactive in depression; stimulation via the VNS may be what gradually reduces depression.

One study of VNS treatment of refractory depressed patients showed a 27 percent response after one year compared to 13 percent response in the treatment-as-usual group. Besides the usual risks of surgery, side effects such as alteration of the voice in 55–60 percent and shortness of breath in 13 percent tended to persist. Other side effects such as cough in 24 percent, neck pain in 15 percent, and laryngismus (spasm of the voice box) in 10 percent diminished over time.[39]

In summary, we have many drugs that can help bipolar depression including four relative newcomers that are fairly effective. Various neurostimulation techniques that act directly on neural tissues are in early stages of development. Nutritional supplements can boost the antidepressant response to medications. Manipulation of the body's biorhythms through bright light treatment and sleep deprivation show promise. Psychotherapy in bipolar disorder, which can be not just useful, but lifesaving in bipolar depression, is discussed in chapter 8,[40] right after our next chapter on maintenance treatment, that is, treatments designed to minimize relapses.

· 7 ·

Maintenance Treatment
for Bipolar Disorder

𝑊hat happens once an episode of mania or depression has been treated and the patient is feeling better? Can medications be stopped or changed?

Some authorities on bipolar disorder refer to a continuation phase of treatment that lasts about two to six months after the acute mania or depression.[1] In the era before effective treatments, many observations were documented about the course of manic-depressive illness, and how it waxed and waned over time. Episodes of bipolar depression or mania lasted on average two to six months, with depression tending to last longer than mania. We can think of the continuation phase as treating the underlying depression or mania that has been suppressed by the medications, but still lingers beneath the surface with mood symptoms ready to manifest themselves in a relapse if treatment is interrupted.

If the medications are reduced or stopped too quickly, the patient moves from remission into a relapse, with full-blown mood disorder symptoms returning. When the mania or depression has run its natural course (roughly two to six months) and the patient is close to euthymic (neutral mood), he is considered to be in recovery. This is a more stable state than just remission. But it is the nature of bipolar disorder to be recurrent. The patient in recovery is still at risk of a recurrence, triggered by factors that are sometimes identifiable and sometimes not. If a person has one manic episode his likelihood of another manic episode or of a major depression in the next five years is 81 to 91 percent.[2]

Kraepelin observed that as his manic-depressive patients aged, they would have more severe episodes that occurred more frequently. This was a pattern in most, but certainly not all patients, because "the multiplicity of the courses taken by manic-depressive insanity . . . is absolutely inexhaustible."[3]

Robert Post, MD, a well-known researcher at the National Institutes of Mental Health, strongly advocates ongoing preventive treatment when a patient has had one manic episode.[4] This helps to prevent the pattern of more frequent and severe episodes, which Post dubs "the malignant transformation of bipolar disorder." Years earlier, he had applied the concept of "kindling" to bipolar disorder.[5] This concept was borrowed from the field of epileptology and referred to a phenomenon in which the occurrence of seizures caused a worsening of the seizure disorder, causing more frequent and severe seizures. We now have in the field of epigenetics a solid basis for understanding molecular mechanisms involved when environmental occurrences (such as seizures or mania) alter the output from our genes.[6]

Besides the risk of recurrence into major depression, mania, or hypomania, many patients have subsyndromal patterns of symptoms, that is, a cluster of symptoms that does not meet full criteria for a major mood episode, but that are still bothersome. Most often these are depressive symptoms that keep them from reaching a fully functional level. In a long-term follow-up for a mean of 12.5 years, researchers described patients as symptomatic 47 percent of the time, mostly with mild depressive symptoms.[7] But individual patients differ widely in how fully and how rapidly they recover from mood episodes. Roughly one-third of bipolar patients have a good functional recovery, one-third have a remission of symptoms but do not have a good functional recovery, and one-third remain significantly symptomatic.[8] Thus, the treatment goals of the maintenance phase include not only preventing relapse or recurrence, but maximizing mood stability and enhancing optimal levels of functional recovery, such as returning to work and pursuing fulfilling life goals in the interpersonal and cultural realms of existence.

How can medication maintenance strategies best prevent relapses and recurrences? Most research studies do not really acknowledge the distinction between continuation phase and long-term maintenance phase, or distinguish between relapse and recurrence. Usually they compare one group of patients in remission taking drug A for prevention versus a group that appears equally well and then stops drug A and substitutes a placebo. When the second group shows more relapses over time this provides evidence of the preventative effects of drug A. Sometimes several drugs are compared (e.g., drug A is compared to lithium or another well-established preventative agent).

Mood-stabilizing drugs that have been FDA approved for long-term preventive treatment in bipolar disorder include lithium and lamotrigine. Valproate, carbamazepine, and oxcarbazepine are often used for long-term maintenance, although they are not specifically FDA approved for that. Lamotrigine is currently the most prescribed mood stabilizer overall in the United States. Research studies also support valproate and carbamazepine as providing protection from relapse.[9]

One large study that compared lithium and lamotrigine found that while both had preventive effects, lithium did a better job preventing manic episodes, but lamotrigine did better at preventing depression.[10] Those studies paved the way for FDA approval in 2003 for lamotrigine as a preventive treatment for bipolar depression. Lithium had been approved in 1974 and had been the sole FDA-approved treatment for prevention of bipolar mood relapses for nearly thirty years.[11]

Certain features can help predict which patients are likely to be good lithium responders, meaning lithium will help prevent relapses for these patients. These features include having mania with a euphoric mood, having classical bipolar I mania with no mood-incongruent delusions and no comorbidities (associated disorders) such as substance abuse or anxiety disorders. A mood-incongruent delusion during a manic phase is one that does not have a grandiose or expansive aspect. The delusion does not fit with the mood. A patient I treated had the belief, during a manic phase, that he had invented a perpetual motion machine. This is a mood-congruent delusion that fits his grandiose state of mind. Another patient had a delusion that others believed she had committed certain criminal acts. That delusion has more paranoid, not grandiose qualities, and would be a mood-incongruent delusion during a manic phase.

Other features that predict a good preventive response to lithium include showing the temporal sequence of mania-depression-euthymia, having relatively few previous episodes, having a history of a good response to lithium or a family history of either a good lithium response or of bipolar disorder, not showing a rapid cycling pattern (four or more episodes per year), and showing a good quality of recovery between mood episodes.

In contrast, a poor lithium response is predicted by a rapid cycling pattern, a mixed or dysphoric mania, the temporal pattern depression-mania-euthymia, three or more prior episodes, a nonclassical mania such as bipolar II or bipolar spectrum, or mania with mood-incongruent delusions. A poor response to lithium is also predicted by a bipolar disorder accompanied by comorbidities such as substance abuse and other psychiatric disorders, severe mania, secondary mania, adolescent mania, or a personal history of nonresponse to lithium.[12] The predictive value of these features is modest: some patients with these features will respond well to lithium.

The propensity to have a good therapeutic response to lithium runs in families and researchers are tracking down the genes involved in this beneficial propensity. Much as with the genetic basis for bipolar disorder itself, many genes seem to be involved, making the research more challenging. However, one study found the presence of a particular genetic variant in a Chinese population could predict a positive lithium response correctly 93 percent of the time.[13]

Lithium is available in immediate release and extended release pills or capsules of lithium carbonate, and as a liquid, lithium citrate. Common side effects include increased thirst and urination, tremor, gastrointestinal irritation and diarrhea, weight gain, and sleepiness.[14] Some people complain of trouble with short-term memory or cognitive slowing, but I have had many patients with mentally challenging jobs as doctors, nurses, teachers, and attorneys who continued working while taking lithium. A small percentage of people will develop hypothyroidism, usually detected first by an elevation of the lab test TSH (thyroid stimulating hormone). If lithium is stopped, the thyroid may revert to normal. However, if lithium is having a significant preventive effect it is possible to continue lithium and take a thyroid supplement. Usually such hypothyroidism is very easy to treat with one tablet daily of thyroid supplement.

When beginning lithium, the patient usually has a battery of blood tests and often an EKG, because lithium could worsen some cardiac arrhythmias. The lithium dose is adjusted based on the patient's response, side effects, and blood levels. Lithium levels are drawn more frequently at first, such as every week, then gradually reduced to once every three to six months. Preventive maintenance levels between about 0.6 and 0.8 mEq/L (milliequivalents per liter) are sought, but some patients have too many side effects at those levels and must further reduce the dose. One study found lithium levels between 0.4 and 0.6 mEq/L better tolerated but not as effective for prevention as levels from 0.8 to 1.0.[15]

TSH and serum creatinine levels are checked every six to twelve months, the latter to assess kidney filtration rates. Many patients will develop a pattern of excessive fluid drinking and excessive urination, sometimes urinating three or four times at night. Some may have to give up lithium because of this polyuria/polydipsia pattern. I have had a few long-term lithium patients who showed a gradually rising serum creatinine that reflected eventual kidney failure. Several had to go on dialysis. Besides decades taking lithium, these patients all had additional risk factors for kidney failure: problems like diabetes mellitus and hypertension.

Aging and dehydration can lead to increased lithium levels. Some types of medication can increase lithium levels: certain medications for blood pressure control such as thiazide diuretics, angiotensin converting enzyme inhibitors (ACE inhibitors), and angiotensin II receptor type I antagonists; and medications that help arthritis such as NSAIDS and COX-2 inhibitors. Caffeine and the bronchodilators theophylline and aminophylline can reduce serum lithium levels, as can diuretics mannitol and acetazolamide.[16] When starting any such medications, communication between the medical provider and the prescriber of lithium is essential.

Lithium has another attribute that is rare to find documented for psychotropic medications: it prevents suicide. A number of studies from different medical centers were meta-analyzed showing a robust eightfold reduction in completed suicide rates attributable to lithium.[17] A meta-analysis involves combining the results of a group of individual research studies all of which deal with a similar research question. Patients taking lithium had an overall reduction in their mortality rates from any cause. However, in this study lithium did not reduce nonsuicidal self-harm behaviors such as the superficial cutting that is often seen in borderline personality disorders. Chapter 10, Suicide and Bipolar Disorder, contains more information about lithium's antisuicidal effects.

If it becomes necessary to stop an established regimen of lithium treatment (e.g., because of side effects), it is best to taper off gradually over at least four weeks. Rapid discontinuation leads to higher risk of relapse.[18]

Lamotrigine has become the most prescribed mood stabilizer because it has few side effect problems while providing substantial prevention of depressive relapses. Incidence of somnolence and weight gain is fairly similar to that for lithium. Common side effects are headache, diarrhea, itching, benign rash in around 10 percent, and abnormal dreams.[19] The incidence of severe rash in mood disorder adult patients is .08 percent when used alone and .13 percent when used adjunctively (e.g., with other mood stabilizers).

Severe skin rash such as the Stevens-Johnson syndrome are life threatening. Besides a symmetrical red, raised rash that spreads over the patient's body in a matter of days, in this syndrome mucous membranes (like the throat) and other organs are affected, accompanied by systemic symptoms of fever and debilitation. Thus, the recommendation is to stop lamotrigine when the patient develops a rash, until it can be established that the rash is not drug related. The dermatologists in my region of practice were very good about seeing my lamotrigine patients with rash to render a timely diagnosis. Persons of Asian ancestry are more prone to these severe rashes and we now have genomic tests that can further pinpoint who is at highest risk.

Lamotrigine is available in various sized tablets. Patients usually start at a low dose of 25 mg/d (milligrams per day) for two weeks, 50 mg/d for the next two weeks, then 100 mg/d. A reasonable dose for many bipolar patients is 100–200 mg/d. Lamotrigine is FDA approved only up to 200 mg/d for bipolar disorder, but as high as 500 mg/d for some seizure disorders. Thus, there is plenty of evidence for its safety and tolerability at these higher doses, if circumstances are such that pushing the dose beyond 200 mg/d is indicated.

Joe was a bipolar patient whose episodes of depression had declined significantly in frequency and severity on 200 mg/d of lamotrigine, but they were still occurring every few months. He had shown very poor tolerance of lithium and valproate. When his lamotrigine was increased further to 300 mg per day, he was free of mood swings for the next two years.

FDA approval has also been given to a number of second-generation antipsychotics (SGAs) for long-term maintenance treatment, some as single drug therapy: olanzapine, risperidone long-acting injectable, and aripiprazole. Some have FDA approval to be used along with lithium or valproate for maintenance. These include olanzapine, risperidone long-acting injectable, quetiapine and quetiapine extended release, aripiprazole, and ziprasidone.[20]

Olanzapine showed good prevention of mood episodes, preventing mania better than depression, but around 51 percent of patients gained more than 7 percent of body weight. The weight gain/metabolic syndrome has put a damper on olanzapine's popularity because some other SGAs have less tendency to cause obesity. Lithium and lamotrigine are also less prone to cause weight gain. However, some patients appear not to gain significant weight on olanzapine. Usually rechecking a patient's weight after about four or eight weeks on olanzapine will reveal the course. If the patient has gained more than a few pounds, she is highly likely to keep gaining if left on olanzapine. A genomic test that may detect those destined for weight gain on olanzapine has come out, but it is not clear whether it captures all those at risk.

With use of any of the SGAs it has become routine to check a baseline height, weight, body mass index, blood pressure, fasting blood sugar, cholesterol, and triglyceride levels and to recheck those measurements in three months and twelve months, omitting the lipid panel if that has been stable. Checking a weight in the first four, eight, and twelve weeks after starting the SGA gives an early warning as to whether the metabolic syndrome is developing. If the patient gains more than 5 percent of her baseline weight at any point, one needs to consider a switch of medications.[21] The metabolic syndrome was discussed in chapter 5, Treatment of Mania and Mixed States, in the Antipsychotics section.

Aripiprazole (Abilify) has gained FDA approval for bipolar maintenance as monotherapy and as an adjunct to lithium or valproate. It helped prevent mania better than depression. It also gained approval for such use in those ten to seventeen years of age. It failed to show added benefit to lamotrigine in prevention of bipolar depression, however.[22] Aripiprazole has a fairly minimal propensity for causing weight gain and does not clearly add risk for diabetes or lipid disorder.[23] Sometimes akathisia and tremor can be a problem, but overall it is tolerated better than olanzapine, risperdal, and quetiapine. Aripiprazole is available in tablet and oral dissolving forms and as both a short-acting injectable and a long-acting injectable called Abilify Maintena, although this long-acting injectable has not been FDA approved for bipolar prevention.

Risperdal long-acting injectable (LAI) is FDA approved for bipolar maintenance as both monotherapy and as an augmenter of lithium or valproate. It prevents mania better than depression, with some studies actually showing more depression episodes with Risperdal LAI than with placebo, but not at a statistically significant level. Weight gain is less of a problem than with olanzapine and propensity for diabetes and hyperlipidemia is unclear. Neuromuscular side effects may occur.[24]

Quetiapine is FDA approved for bipolar maintenance as an adjunctive medication along with lithium or valproate. Quetiapine in both its immediate-release form and extended-release form is approved for that purpose. Quetiapine had good results preventing both depression and mania. About 30 percent of patients experience excessive sleepiness that sometimes relents as the patient gets used to it. Sometimes sleepiness persists and is significant enough that patients discontinue quetiapine or use caffeine or other wakefulness-inducing agents to combat the sleepiness. Weight gain can be a problem. Risperdal and quetiapine have less weight gain than olanzapine, but more than aripiprazole and ziprasidone. Quetiapine as monotherapy also showed good preventive effects, but it has not been FDA approved for bipolar maintenance as monotherapy.[25] See table 7.1.

Table 7.1.   **FDA-Approved Single Medications for Bipolar Maintenance**

Drug	Target Dosage
Lithium	900–1200 mg/d
Lamotrigine	100–200 mg/d
Olanzapine	5–20 mg/d
Risperdal LAI	25–50 mg IM q 2 weeks
Aripiprazole	15–30 mg/d

Ziprasidone is FDA approved as an adjunct to lithium and valproate for bipolar maintenance use. It does better in preventing mania than depression. As mentioned above, weight gain is minimal. Akathisia (a restless urge to move) may occur in around 8 percent. Taking it with food aids ziprasidone's absorption. See table 7.2.

Table 7.2. FDA-Approved Medications to Add to Lithium or Valproate for Bipolar Maintenance

Drug	Target Dosage
Risperdal LAI	25–50 mg IM q 2 weeks
Aripiprazole	15–30 mg/d
Quetiapine	200–400 mg/bid, 400–800mg qpm extended release
Ziprasidone	40–80 mg/bid with food

Neuromuscular side effects such as tardive dyskinesia that can occur with long-term use of SGAs are discussed in chapter 5, Treatment of Mania and Mixed States.

Divalproex or valproate, although not FDA approved as maintenance monotherapy, is commonly used that way in practice. Numerous studies support its ability to prevent bipolar mood episodes. Valproate prevents depression slightly better than it prevents mania.[26] In addition, the FDA has approved four medications to be used adjunctively with valproate or lithium for prevention of bipolar episodes. In a study that looked at preventive effects of lithium, valproate, and the combination of lithium and valproate, lithium did best with just 53.6 percent recurrence rate compared to 69.1 percent for valproate. The combination of lithium and valproate did not do better than lithium alone.[27]

Valproate may have a special role for patients who cannot tolerate lithium well, for rapid cycling forms of bipolar disorder, for those with comorbid substance abuse, for those with more than three previous episodes, and for those with dysphoric or mixed mania.[28] Common side effects with valproate include tremor, nausea, vomiting, diarrhea, stomach irritation, weight gain, mild sleepiness, and hair loss. A multivitamin with selenium and zinc, such as Centrum Silver, may prevent or reverse the hair loss. Tremor from valproate, like that from lithium, may be controllable with small doses of propranolol. Very uncommon but serious side effects include pancreatitis, liver toxicity, and a state of high serum ammonia.[29] Some increase in the polycystic ovarian syndrome has been associated with valproate. That syndrome and the teratogenic (producing birth defects) effects of valproate are discussed in chapter 9, Pregnancy and Bipolar Disorder.

Serum valproate levels between 50–100 mg/L (milligrams per liter) are considered in the maintenance range, with levels above 80 targeted if relapse is occurring at more conservative doses. Lab tests such as complete blood count, including platelets and liver functions, are often checked in practice every six to twelve months.

Carbamazepine, while somewhat effective, has been less effective than lithium in monotherapy maintenance trials. It may have a role for treatment of nonclassical bipolar patients, bipolar II, bipolar spectrum disorders, bipolar with mood-incongruent delusions, bipolar patients with comorbid substance abuse or anxiety disorders, and patients who do not tolerate lithium or valproate. Common side effects with carbamazepine include dizziness, nausea, fatigue, sedation, diplopia (double vision), and incoordination.

As reviewed in chapter 5, Treatment of Mania and Mixed States, carbamazepine has many drug interactions and potential side effects on blood cell production and on the liver. About 7 percent of adults may show a decrease of white blood cells, but more sinister effects on blood cells such as aplastic anemia, agranulocytosis (reduced numbers of bacteria-fighting white blood cells called neutrophils) and thrombocytopenia (low platelet count) occur less than once in 10,000 cases. Many authorities think periodic blood counts offer no value because the blood dyscrasia can develop so rapidly. Instead, patients need to be alert to report to their providers symptoms such as fever, bleeding, petechia (tiny reddish or purple skin spots), excessive bruising, and sore throat. The severe rashes of Stevens-Johnson syndrome and toxic epidermal necrolysis can occur in one to six patients in 10,000 among the white population.[30] The incidence is about ten times greater in the Asian population and is associated with the HLA-B*1502 gene, one now detectible with many genomic test kits. Carbamazepine serum levels of 4–12 µg/L (micrograms per liter) are established for epilepsy treatment and similar levels are used for bipolar maintenance.

A young man had recently been discharged from hospital on carbamazepine (CBZ), after discontinuing lithium, which had not prevented another manic episode. Within a few days of his discharge a reddened symmetrical rash spread over his body. When he arrived in our emergency department, he was very ill with fever and such an extensive rash that he required a lifesaving transfer to a burn unit at a major university hospital. He had CBZ-induced Stevens-Johnson syndrome, a potentially fatal side effect.[31] Fortunately he made a full recovery over several weeks.

Oxcarbazepine has been used in the maintenance phase as a safer and less complex cousin of carbamazepine, but good studies documenting its benefits as a maintenance drug are lacking.

Antidepressant use in acute bipolar depression generates some controversy. This controversy becomes even more heated when we look at the use of antidepressants as maintenance medications. A meta-analysis of seven studies found the combination of antidepressants plus mood stabilizers able to prevent relapse somewhat better than placebo plus mood stabilizers: 35.5 percent versus 25.3 percent.[32] But the antidepressant group had more manic switches: 29.8 percent versus 16.3 percent for placebo. One study found that patients who stayed well for six months on an antidepressant regimen had fewer relapses the next six months by staying on that antidepressant rather than by stopping it.[33] The International Committee on Bipolar Disorders and Antidepressants supported the preventive use of antidepressants in bipolar disorder in exactly those circumstances—namely, when there is a history of relapses when stopping them.[34]

The FDA requires that drugs be compared with a placebo to document their efficacy and safety. Thus, many drugs FDA approved for acute treatment of mania or bipolar depression have not undergone that placebo comparison in the maintenance phase. These include monotherapy with lurasidone, olanzapine/fluoxetine, ziprasidone, asenapine, and quetiapine. Often these medications showed a good response compared to a known effective maintenance medication. Thus, the question may arise in the course of treatment whether to continue an effective drug from the acute treatment phase into the maintenance phase or to switch, for example, to a mood stabilizer. This decision must be individualized for each patient. My tendency as a treater has been to continue an agent such as lurasidone or quetiapine as a maintenance treatment if the patient is doing well and having no side effects. The old rule of thumb, "If it ain't broke, don't fix it" applies. However, if a patient in stable mood on quetiapine is progressively gaining weight, it might be a time to consider tapering off quetiapine and trying lamotrigine or aripiprazole, which are less prone to cause weight gain.

It usually makes sense to carry out such medication changes gradually over a period of weeks. Then, if mood symptoms occur with a drop in dose, one can return to the previously successful regimen without having the patient slip into a major mood episode. Cessation of lithium has been well studied, with the notable result that stopping lithium abruptly (say in a taper of less than two weeks) leads to more mood relapses in the subsequent year than if one tapers over four weeks or more.[35]

In the real world, very few bipolar patients continue their maintenance phase long-term on just one drug. One study found that only 6.9 percent did so.[36] Often small relapses or mild-to-moderate mood symptoms arise and other medications are added. Besides the FDA-approved augmenting drugs mentioned in this chapter, many doctors may combine two mood stabilizers or add an SGA or an antidepressant to a mood stabilizer. Clinicians are practicing the "art of medicine" when they must make their best judgment about complex medication regimens where there are no randomized, double-blind controlled trials to guide their choices. But this constitutes the majority of practice.

It is relatively uncommon to combine two SGAs other than in a cross-tapering scenario. This is because SGAs have a fairly similar mode of action: blocking dopamine D2 receptors and serotonin 5HT2 receptors. Mood stabilizers lithium, lamotrigine, valproate, and carbamazepine all have distinct modes of action, so that theoretically one might gain greater preventive power by combining some of them. Lamotrigine may have particularly good effects preventing depression relapse, while the others may have a stronger mania-preventing effect. Drug interactions between lamotrigine and valproate and carbamazepine require careful dosage adjustments when any of these are combined.

As patients improve from the symptoms of mania or depression and return to their usual activities, they may feel hampered by side effects from the drugs that aided in their improvement. Sleepiness or tremor that was tolerable when in the hospital may be a major problem when returning to work or family responsibilities. When depression has lifted, a drug-induced sexual problem may hamper a patient's enjoyment of life. Often dosages of medications can be reduced to alleviate these side effects. Sometimes we can use another strategy or use another medication to counteract side effects if stopping the drug is too risky. The maintenance phase involves balancing the risks for relapse against the side effect burden of the medications. Many of the mood stabilizers and antipsychotics have a more robust preventative effect at higher doses, but their side effects may also be worse.

Often experience will shed light on what dosages or what blood levels of agents like lithium or valproate will keep patients in remission. If dropping below a certain level repeatedly leads to more symptoms, it may be important to draw that line in the sand and not cross it.

Claudia first was hospitalized with a psychotic manic episode in her twenties. Despite maintenance treatment with lithium she continued to have relapses, usually in the late fall of each year, requiring hospitalization. She recovered from the episodes well and continued her roles as wife, mother, and part-time worker. After decades of taking lithium and experiencing hypertension, her serum creatinine kept rising, indicating renal insufficiency. Her kidneys were doing a poor job of filtering and eliminating wastes from her blood. She was transitioned off lithium and on to carbamazepine, which unfortunately provided imperfect preventive effects. Meanwhile, she began renal dialysis and ultimately had a renal transplant. The addition of 25 mg/d of aripiprazole to her carbamazepine improved her preventive drug regimen. She has remained free of psychiatric hospitalizations for many years on a combination of a mood stabilizer and SGA for prevention.

Rare patients who have had poor preventive effects from medications and good acute responses to electroconvulsive therapy may use electroconvulsive treatment in a maintenance mode, receiving ECT about once per month.[37] Vagal nerve stimulators, discussed in chapter 6, Treatment of Bipolar Depression, are intended as long-term preventive treatment of depression episodes. Some of the patients implanted have been bipolar. Very possibly in the future we shall see more neuromodulation techniques such as transcranial magnetic stimulation and transcranial direct current stimulation tested for bipolar disorder maintenance and approved for clinical practice.

Freedom from relapses is enhanced by following the health-promoting practices discussed in chapter 4, Setting a Healthy Baseline, namely getting adequate sleep and exercise, following a healthful diet, avoiding substance abuse, and seeking gratifying social support systems. The considerable benefits of psychotherapy for prevention of bipolar relapse are discussed in chapter 8, Psychotherapy for Bipolar Disorder.

· 8 ·

Psychotherapy for Bipolar Disorder

$\mathcal{I}$ used to think that because bipolar disorder had such a strong biological component, psychotherapy had relatively little effect on its course. However, my experience, as well as research, has shown that psychotherapy plays a very important role for bipolar patients.

In the early 1900s as psychoanalysis was a growing force in psychiatry, some practitioners hoped that psychoanalysis might cure manic-depressive illness if only the right childhood fixations could be dealt with. This has certainly not been the case.[1] However, modern forms of psychotherapy have been developed and adapted for treating bipolar disorder. Today we regard psychotherapy as a way to learn skills to lessen the severity of the depressive episodes, to prolong and enhance the periods of euthymia or neutral mood, and to better manage mood swings and the many anxieties, losses, and conflicts that are part of life.

Some studies have indicated that bipolar patients are more sensitive to stressors than the average person.[2] Losses can precipitate depression; sleep deprivation or emotionally exciting factors can precipitate mania. Adverse childhood events may make bipolar patients more susceptible to stressors or to dysfunctional behaviors such as suicide attempts and substance abuse. Psychotherapy can help patients gain coping skills to deal with depressive and manic episodes when they arise and to handle the stressors of life more effectively so they do not trigger full-blown episodes of mood disorder.

Psychotherapies developed specifically for bipolar disorder are most often introduced during the maintenance phase, when the patient is not severely manic or depressed and is more able to fully participate in psychotherapy. Many patients may respond to these therapies during depressive episodes as well. During mania any therapy is primarily focused on helping the patients acknowledge their situation, comply with medications or hospitalization, and avoid substance abuse or other self-destructive behaviors. During the manic phase patients are often not in a frame of mind to fully participate and benefit from these specific psychotherapies.

Some forms of psychotherapy have been rigorously examined in bipolar patients and compared with treatment as usual. Psycho-education is a form of talking therapy in which the clinician provides information to patients or family. The clinician helps to educate them about aspects of bipolar disorder (e.g., how to recognize symptoms of impending mania or the important role of medications in controlling mood swings). Psychoeducation can be done individually or in a group. Three psychotherapies specifically developed for bipolar disorder all contain a component of psychoeducation.

One such form of treatment is interpersonal and social rhythm therapy (IPSRT), an offshoot of interpersonal psychotherapy. Interpersonal therapy was developed as a treatment for depressive disorders.[3] Therapy focuses on role transitions like divorce, coping with losses, handling interpersonal conflicts, and shoring up interpersonal deficits (e.g., self-defeating or avoidant patterns). Social rhythm therapy emphasizes the benefits of following a regular pattern for one's bodily functions such as sleeping and waking times, mealtimes, exercise, and social interactions. Establishing a regular pattern of these functions has been found to reduce mood swings during the maintenance phase of treatment for bipolar mood disorder.[4]

Family-focused psychotherapy directed toward bipolar teens or young adults also reduces episodes of hospitalization and speeds recovery from an episode.[5] A therapist meets with the designated patient and parents, spouse, or other significant persons in the patient's life. Educating both family members and the patient about bipolar disorder has been a useful intervention. Emphasizing the importance of following a medication regimen, keeping regular contact with health professionals, and contacting them at times of crisis all help prevent relapses. Along with those psychoeducational functions, the therapist helps develop active listening skills and facilitates better communication and problem-solving patterns within the family. Sometimes family-focused therapy is conducted in groups of patients and parents, and sometimes with one family only.

Cognitive therapy was an outgrowth of the work of psychiatrist Dr. Aaron Beck. Originally trained as a psychoanalyst, Dr. Beck found that in treating unipolar depressed patients, automatic thoughts and core dysfunctional beliefs produced pessimism, low self-esteem, and helplessness in their assessments of situations. A depressed patient starting a new job might think "This is too hard, and I am going to fail at it." This thought may stem from a dysfunctional belief that he is an incapable person, destined for failure. Such thoughts and beliefs can become self-fulfilling prophecies, coloring one's attitude and perceptions and facilitating failure. Beck found that he could restructure the automatic negative thoughts and core dysfunctional beliefs, thus alleviating and preventing depression.[6]

On a strictly behavioral plane, therapists found that helping depressed patients to document what activities made them feel better or made them gain a sense of proficiency was helpful. Doing more of these positive behaviors often improved mood.[7]

Cognitive-behavioral therapy (CBT) combined these two therapeutic techniques and has been adapted to many specific disorders including bipolar disorder. In various studies bipolar patients underwent from twelve to twenty sessions of CBT with outcomes compared to briefer psychoeducation, supportive therapy, or treatment as usual. In some studies the CBT group had fewer relapses, but in others they did not.[8]

All four of these specific forms of psychotherapy—psychoeducation, social rhythm and interpersonal therapy, family-focused therapy, and cognitive-behavioral therapies—have shown documented benefits in bipolar disorder. These treatments reduce the frequency of relapses or hospitalizations and lead to fewer days spent in depression. Most patients with bipolar disorder can benefit from psychotherapy at some point in their treatment.

Besides the benefits of psychotherapy during the maintenance phase of bipolar disorder, psychotherapy is often useful and sometimes lifesaving during acute bipolar depression. Some research studies have looked at the outcomes of psychotherapy for bipolar depression.

In the multicenter STEP-BD study, 163 patients received intensive psychotherapy such as thirty fifty-minute sessions over nine months. The psychotherapies took the form of cognitive-behavioral therapy (CBT), family-focused therapy (FFT), or interpersonal and social rhythm therapy (IPSRT). A control group received only three sessions of fifty-minute psychoeducation. The psychotherapy group outshined the control group with 64.4 percent recovery versus 51.5 percent.[9] Interestingly, the benefit held for patients who had one lifetime anxiety disorder such as panic disorder, generalized anxiety disorder, or social anxiety disorder. But those with no anxiety disorder or two or more such disorders did not show the benefit from psychotherapy. In addition, patients with frequent episodes—more than twelve lifetime mood episodes—did not show benefit either.

In a study with ninety-five depressed bipolar II patients, 74.5 percent of those treated with IPSRT and quetiapine showed a greater than 50 percent reduction of symptoms in twenty weeks. Sixty percent of those treated with IPSRT and placebo showed a similar improvement, but the difference did not reach statistical significance. The quetiapine group showed a little more weight gain. The authors concluded that IPSRT might be a reasonable monotherapy (without medication) for some bipolar II patients experiencing acute depression.[10] Interestingly, they found that patients randomized to receive the treatment they preferred (psychotherapy alone or psychotherapy plus medication) did far better than those who did not receive their preferred treatment. Sometimes patients have an inner wisdom regarding what treatments will work for them.

The practice of psychotherapy is rather different from the practice of managing the medications for bipolar disorder. Whereas most psychiatrists or advanced practice nurses are familiar with the full gamut of approved bipolar medications, most psychotherapists are skilled at only one or a few types of psychotherapy. Many training programs for mental health providers focus on just a few forms of treatment, such as psychodynamic therapy, cognitive or cognitive-behavioral therapy, interpersonal therapy, rational-emotive therapy, or family therapy. There are scores of types of psychotherapy. Only a few have had rigorous research as to their benefits for bipolar disorder.

Most mental health practitioners tend to be eclectic and pragmatic. Eclectic means they take what seems useful from a wide variety of approaches to apply to the situation at hand. Most mental health practitioners have continuing education after their degrees are conferred and learn more techniques at conferences and workshops, or from a more experienced mentor.

Many mental health practitioners use "supportive therapy" with bipolar patients. Supportive therapy is centered on the present, rather than dwelling on the past, and takes a problem-solving approach. For example, if a bipolar woman is being physically abused by her partner, the focus of psychotherapy shifts to helping her get safely out of that situation before focusing on other issues. If a patient is suicidal, the focus is on maintaining safety first. With safety secured, one can explore why suicide seems like a solution, and look at healthier alternatives for the patient to pursue.

During depressive phases simply instilling and reinforcing realistic hope is a beneficial intervention, reminding the patient what it was like to feel reasonably good a few weeks or months previously and reassuring him that such a mood state can be achieved again.

Much psychotherapy can be characterized as falling on an expressive/supportive continuum. In the situation discussed above, finding a safety plan for a patient with suicidal urges would be a very supportive intervention. Understanding what is making suicide seem like an inviting option falls more on the expressive end of the continuum. The therapist shapes his intervention to the patient's particular circumstances, symptoms, and mental framework.

I first treated Nancy in her twenties when she was having periods of depression. She had several hospitalizations for episodes of strong suicidal ideation. Despite being a lover of animals, at one point in her desperation she concocted a plan to terminate her pets' lives and then her own. But she reached out for help and was hospitalized.

Over time a pattern emerged of cycling mood swings about every three weeks. She had brief highs with less need for sleep, more energy, and the ability to accomplish tasks around the house more easily. These high periods alternated with depressive lows with low energy, where every small chore seemed monumental and she might just stay in bed all day. Medication treatment appeared to make these mood swings milder, but they still were quite apparent.

Nancy had many stressors in her family life. Her parents argued a lot; she sometimes felt caught in the middle. Her father could be very cold, stingy, and unloving, focusing more on hunting and fishing than the family. Her sister had become alienated from the family—not communicating for long periods of time. Once her sister was silent and unresponsive to any calls for more than a year. We discussed these interpersonal stressors and her responses to them in our sessions. As her parents aged, she often felt compelled to spend time with them in a nearby city to help with household chores or to drive them to doctors' appointments. She had to limit her stays, however, or she would drop into a deeper than usual depression. For Nancy, supportive psychotherapy focused on dealing with these personal relationships, rather than following the format of one of the specific therapies for bipolar mentioned above. But it helped.

Although not the subject of as many studies as CBT or IPSRT, supportive therapy has documented benefits in bipolar disorder. One study looked at outcomes over nearly three years after twenty sessions of CBT or of supportive psychotherapy, finding that both prevented relapses about equally.[11] Another study extending over three years compared results of supportive psychotherapy with IPSRT, finding both equally beneficial in reducing relapses.[12]

In chapter 12, Disorders Associated with Bipolar Disorder, I present the fact that many bipolar patients have other associated psychiatric disorders such as alcohol or substance use disorders, anxiety disorders, posttraumatic stress disorder, and others. Sometimes marital or family conflicts arise that are not necessarily a direct result of the bipolar disorder. Bipolar patients with such disorders can benefit from the psychotherapies developed to treat those specific problems. If the treating psychiatrist or nurse practitioner cannot provide the psychotherapy (because of lack of training, lack of time, or restriction by the insurance carrier), they can make a referral to another mental health clinician skilled in the type of psychotherapy needed.

Paul was a man in his thirties whom I treated for bipolar I disorder. His manic episodes, characterized by paranoia and agitation, had led to several hospitalizations over the years. However, his mood was fairly stable on a regimen of valproate and risperidone without troubling side effects. He became understandably distressed when he discovered his wife was having an affair. I referred them as a couple to a psychologist with whom I often shared patients. Despite his competent marital treatment, they divorced. Before long Paul found a new partner and was once more enjoying life. His marital treatment focused on serious marital issues and not his bipolar disorder. However, the extra therapy may have prevented him from slipping into a major mood episode.

In our age of burgeoning apps and artificial intelligence there are even online computerized forms of some therapies (e.g., CBT). These are helpful, although I would still favor regular interactions with a human therapist. In chapter 5, Treatment of Mania and Mixed States, I discussed the powerful benefit that comes from having good rapport with a doctor or a therapist. That human component is absent or certainly modified with computer-based treatment. In the future we are likely to see more mental health services delivered via video technology and more computer-assisted forms of psychotherapy. For the present we have quite a few forms of psychotherapy proven to be helpful in reducing bipolar relapses and residual symptoms and improving the quality of patients' lives, especially when used during depressive episodes and during the maintenance phase.

· 9 ·

Pregnancy and Bipolar Disorder

$\mathcal{A}$s if the treatment of bipolar disorder were not challenging enough, pregnancy adds an additional layer of complexity with the need to understand the risks and benefits of treatment for both mother and fetus. At one time it was thought that the state of pregnancy offered a certain level of protection against episodes of mood disorders such as depression or bipolar mood episodes. However, in recent years extensive research has indicated that pregnancy does not offer such protection.[1]

During the postpartum period, in the days and months after giving birth, women are more prone to episodes of both unipolar depression and of bipolar depression and mania. Many women with bipolar disorder experienced their first mood episode in a postpartum period. If a woman with a bipolar diagnosis or a close family member has experienced a previous postpartum psychosis, her risk of having a postpartum psychosis is 50–75 percent if she is untreated during pregnancy.[2]

During pregnancy and even when planning to become pregnant, it is especially important for a young woman with bipolar disorder to maintain close consultation with her psychiatrist and with the providers of her obstetrical care. The health care providers too need to communicate. When I worked at a community mental health agency, I had more telephone calls with obstetrical providers than with any other specialty.

Many of the medications we use for bipolar maintenance and for the treatment of acute episodes are potentially toxic for the developing fetus. This tends to change the risk/benefit ratio of medication treatments during pregnancy. Approximately half of pregnancies are unplanned. Those women with bipolar disorder who are in a situation where pregnancy is a possibility need to consider that prospect carefully.

Using effective birth control measures until one is ready to embark on pregnancy makes a great deal of sense.

The developing fetus is most vulnerable to birth defects and to other long-term negative consequences from medications in the earliest parts of pregnancy. Thus, many women who desire to get pregnant should have a careful discussion with their prescribing clinician about their medications and pregnancy. Often some or occasionally all medications might be discontinued for a time, in order to have a pregnancy free of chemicals that could be toxic to the fetus. In other situations, a woman's bipolar disorder may be sufficiently severe that stopping preventative medicines is asking for a devastating relapse. One study found that women who stopped their bipolar medications during pregnancy faced a relapse rate of 80 percent or more during the remainder of pregnancy and the postpartum period.[3]

Certainly, having a pregnant mother in a state of mania or severe depression is not necessarily good for a fetus either. In a hypomanic or manic state women are more prone to taking risks, including using alcohol or street drugs, which may have far more negative consequences for the fetus than prescribed mood stabilizers. In a state of severe depression women may not maintain their nutrition, prenatal vitamins, or other necessary medications and may be at higher risk for suicide. Pregnancy is, however, often a deterrent to suicide.

Ideally if one were evaluating negative effects of a medication used for bipolar disorder, one would compare the medicated group to an unmedicated group of women with bipolar disorder with similar age and health history. This is not always possible, so sometimes birth defect rates from the general population are used. This is not as accurate for comparison, because the children of mothers with major mental illnesses such as bipolar disorder, major depression, or schizophrenia have higher rates of birth defects and other perinatal disorders than the general population.

Research has found that bipolar mood disorder increases the risks for certain problems in the mothers and offspring beyond that for a comparison group without a mood disorder. These risks include a higher rate of Caesarean section and induced labor, infants that are smaller for gestational age, or that have microcephaly (head circumference lower than normal), premature birth, gestational hypertension, and neonatal hypoglycemia (low blood sugar). Bipolar mothers have higher rates of smoking, overweight, and of alcohol and substance misuse than mothers with no mental illness. Although these factors can increase negative birth outcomes, the studies still showed higher rates of the complications listed even when adjusting for those maternal risk factors. Bipolar mothers treated with lithium, carbamazepine, valproate, or antipsychotics during pregnancy did not show higher rates of those complications listed above than the untreated bipolar mothers. However, rates of certain congenital malformations (such disorders as cleft palate and heart defects) are slightly increased by lamotrigine, lithium, valproate, and carbamazepine.[4] More on this issue later in this chapter.

When trying to assess the effects of a particular medication on the developing fetus, it is rare to have data from randomized controlled double-blind prospective studies, which are considered the most reliable studies for "evidence based" medicine. Women become pregnant but are not randomly designated to become so in a research study. Rather, studies may be retrospective, that is, looking backward in time, at a group of bipolar women (and their offspring) who took a particular drug during pregnancy compared to another group of pregnant women who did not take the drug and their children.

Another way that medications are tested for toxic effects in pregnancy is through experiments with animals. Often rodents are given various dosage levels of medications during pregnancy to determine what level of the drugs starts to cause death or other harmful effects in the offspring of the rodents.

In 1979 the FDA established Pregnancy Risk Categories: A, B, C, D, and X, with the earlier letters indicating a safer medication (https://www.drugs.com/pregnancy-categories.html). The categories were based on how well the effects of the drug on pregnancy were documented and on the risk versus benefit ratio of the drug in question. Assessments were made of the drug's toxicity by looking at the rate at which various negative drug effects (e.g., learning disabilities or birth defects) occur in the offspring of mothers who have been on a drug during pregnancy and comparing that to a group not exposed to that drug. Controlled studies were also carried out on other mammalian species.

Category A means that adequate and well-controlled trials have failed to demonstrate a risk to the fetus in the first trimester and there is no evidence of a risk in the later trimesters. The thyroid hormone levothyroxine and the B vitamin folic acid are in this category.

Category B means that animal reproduction studies have failed to demonstrate a risk to the fetus and there are no adequate and well-controlled studies in pregnant women. Examples include metformin, amoxicillin, pantoprazole, and lurasidone or Latuda (a second-generation antipsychotic used in bipolar disorder).

In category C animal reproduction studies have shown an adverse effect on the fetus and there are no adequate and well-controlled studies in humans, but potential benefits may warrant use of the drug in pregnant women despite reported risks. Examples include lamotrigine, gabapentin, trazodone, and most other antidepressants and antipsychotic agents.

Category D indicates there is positive evidence of human fetal risk based on adverse reactions in data from investigational or marketing experience or from studies in humans, but potential benefits may warrant use of the drug in pregnant women despite potential risks. Examples would include alprazolam, clonazepam, lorazepam, lithium, valproate, and carbamazepine.

In category X, studies in animals or humans have demonstrated fetal abnormalities and there is positive evidence of human fetal risk based on adverse reaction data from investigational or marketing experience, and the risks involved in use of the drugs in pregnant women clearly outweigh potential benefit. Examples include atorvastatin, warfarin, and methotrexate.

In June 2015 a new system of characterizing the risk of drugs and pregnancy went into effect with the FDA. This will be applied to newly approved drugs and gradually phased in on existing drugs. This new information will include data from pregnancy exposure and registries, risk summaries, and clinical considerations of the effects in lactation as well as in pregnancy.

Many of the mood stabilizing medications used in bipolar mood disorder such as lithium, valproate, carbamazepine, and oxcarbazepine are in FDA class D, clearly manifesting some risks to the human fetus. Lamotrigine is ranked C, as are most of the second-generation antipsychotics, which include risperidone, olanzapine, ziprasidone, quetiapine, and aripiprazole. However, lurasidone and clozapine received a B ranking.[5]

Lamotrigine had a classification of C under the FDA guidelines. Thus, despite some harmful effects in animal testing, its use may be warranted during pregnancy. Much of this data came from the epileptic population using lamotrigine as an anticonvulsant. During pregnancy we often substitute lamotrigine for more toxic agents such as valproate or lithium. After delivery, if the mother plans to nurse, we often have to change lamotrigine again to another agent such as valproate, because lamotrigine is delivered in larger quantities through breast milk to the newborn, whereas valproate is present in very small amounts in breast milk. Quantities of these drugs in breast milk are smaller than the amounts the unborn fetus is exposed to from the mother's bloodstream. For this reason, some authorities say it is unnecessary to change drugs after birth and when starting breastfeeding. The baby has already been exposed to the drug and at a higher level. While there are advantages in minimizing the number of different drugs that a fetus and infant is exposed to, sometimes the properties of a particular drug override this consideration. Lamotrigine passes freely through breast milk so that nursing infants may have blood levels from 6 percent to 50 percent of the mother's blood level. Valproate is expressed minimally in breast milk—infants show only 1–2 percent of the blood levels of their nursing mother.[6] The question of switching a drug used during pregnancy to a different one during lactation is one of those areas where expert opinions differ.

Another category B drug used in bipolar mood disorder is lurasidone, brand name Latuda. This may be an appropriate choice for a pregnant bipolar patient who is depressed, or one who needs some prophylactic protection from major mood swings. Latuda is presumably more benign than most of the mood stabilizers.

Veronica had experienced several hospitalizations with psychotic manic episodes as well as with one severe postpartum depression. She had been stable for several years on valproate and quetiapine. On one of her appointments she told me she had just discovered she was pregnant (about six weeks along), despite her use of birth control pills. After I called her obstetrician, I transitioned her to lamotrigine, stopping the valproate and quetiapine. She had a few minor depressive symptoms during her pregnancy. After delivery her lamotrigine was stopped and she began valproate and quetiapine again because this combination had worked so well for her in the past. She opted for bottle feeding her healthy newborn. She was a happy mother with no postpartum mood episodes.

We can also look at three potential hazards of maternal drugs during pregnancy: actual malformations, medical complications in the postpartum period, and neurobehavioral problems in the developing child months or years later.[7] Congenital malformations are an observable (by eye or imaging technique) abnormality in the anatomy of the newborn (e.g., a cleft lip or a hole in the wall of the heart).

Lithium has been known to cause the Ebstein anomaly (a heart disorder with blockage of the right ventricle's outflow) when taken by the mother in the first three months of pregnancy. Even so, the risks for Ebstein anomaly are very small, only 0.1 percent.[8] The rate of Ebstein anomaly in pregnancies without lithium is one-twentieth of that. When a mother continues on lithium during pregnancy, an ultrasound and an echocardiogram are recommended between sixteen and eighteen weeks gestation.[9] The overall rate of malformations was 2.8 percent in a prospective study of lithium, near the baseline rate of malformations, which is 2–3 percent. However, a retrospective study (which is usually more prone to error than a prospective one) found a malformation rate of 11 percent with lithium.[10] Perinatal complications in the newborn whose mother has been on lithium during pregnancy include increased birth weight, cyanosis (poor oxygenation), hypotonicity (floppy baby), neonatal hypothyroidism, and nephrogenic diabetes insipidus, which is a failure of the kidney to concentrate urine.[11] Risks for learning problems or other neurobehavioral difficulties in the developing child appear low.[12] One recent study found no decreases in verbal, performance, or full-scale IQ in children exposed to lithium in utero, compared to controls.[13] Lithium is often reduced or discontinued in the mother when labor begins or a day or two before a planned delivery to minimize her risk of lithium toxicity, because there is a massive fluid loss and diuresis at the time of delivery, which might cause her lithium concentration to rise to a toxic level.[14]

Infants nursing from mothers on lithium show blood levels about 20 percent of their mother's, generally low enough to avoid side effects. Using supplemental formula feedings will further reduce the infant's blood levels.[15]

Carbamazepine has substantial rates of untoward pregnancy outcomes such as craniofacial defects in 11 percent, spina bifida in 3 percent, developmental delays in 20 percent, and fingernail hypoplasia in 26 percent.[16] Cleft palate has been associated with low levels of serum folate in pregnant women, and anticonvulsants can lower folate levels in women. Thus, if a woman remains on one of the anticonvulsant/mood stabilizers (carbamazepine, oxcarbazepine, lamotrigine, and valproate) during pregnancy, she needs to take supplemental doses of folic acid, such as 4–5 mg/day. Pregnant women in general, who are not on one of these anticonvulsants or mood stabilizers, are given smaller doses of folic acid, such as 0.4 mg/d to help prevent midline birth defects such as cleft palate and spina bifida.[17] Perinatal complications with carbamazepine include vitamin K deficiency. Long-term problems with cognitive deficits can occur, but less so than with valproate.[18]

Valproate has been associated with neural tube defects, such as spina bifida, cranial defects, and other major malformations in 6.2–13.3 percent of fetuses exposed during pregnancy. Risks are higher with doses greater than 800 mg/d. Perinatal complications include poor growth, abnormal muscle tone, heart decelerations, and vitamin K deficiency. Long-term behavioral problems such as lowered intelligence, autistic spectrum disorders, and ADHD have been associated with valproate, their occurrence more likely with doses greater than 800 mg/d.[19] Valproate appears to cause more birth defects than other anticonvulsants, and several countries have enacted special rules to limit valproate usage during pregnancy and for fertile women.[20]

Valproate is often not a first choice for women of childbearing age for an additional reason. It has been associated with polycystic ovary syndrome. This is an endocrine disorder characterized by obesity, abnormal hair growth and loss of normal hair, menstrual irregularity, seborrhea, acne, and infertility.[21] Sometimes these symptoms will subside when valproate is stopped.

Lamotrigine has a low rate of malformations (1.9–4.6 percent) such as cleft lip or palate. Folate supplements during pregnancy might prevent these. We lack sufficient data regarding cognitive or behavioral problems in offspring, but the risks seem to be much less than for valproate.[22] Lamotrigine is considered a safer alternative during pregnancy than lithium or valproate.[23]

The first-generation antipsychotics, such as haloperidol, perphenazine, and chlorpromazine, have not shown an increase of major malformations, but might give the neonate neuromuscular side effects that would generally subside in days to weeks. We have less data on SGAs (second-generation antipsychotics) and other mood stabilizers, except lamotrigine, referred to above. Studies of the use of antipsychotics, including SGAs, during pregnancy for mothers with bipolar disorder, did not find an increase in malformations,[24] and concluded that "the most reasonable and less harmful choice for treating future mothers with bipolar disorder or schizophrenia appears to be maintaining them at the safest minimum dosage" of the SGA.[25] One study found slightly increased risk of malformations with risperidone,[26] and another found a slight increase of gestational diabetes in mothers on quetiapine or olanzapine.[27]

In the later stages of pregnancy after the basic structure of the heart is formed, it is much safer to use lithium in a mother without high risk for cardiac abnormalities in the fetus. Many of the SGAs seem to have a lower risk for birth defects than the mood stabilizers. SGAs might be another alternative when medications are needed during pregnancy, instead of using the more toxic valproate, carbamazepine, or oxcarbazepine.

Postpartum depression or mania is something to watch for carefully after the mother gives birth. In the last days of pregnancy entering the birth process mothers are often severely sleep deprived. They undergo a radical change in hormone levels with high progesterone levels dropping dramatically after giving birth and oxytocin levels rising. All these factors may play into the relatively high risk for mothers in the postpartum period. A previous episode of postpartum depression or mania is also a high-risk factor for occurrence of such a disorder after a subsequent birth. Having a relative who has had postpartum mood episodes increases the risk twofold for a postpartum mood episode.[28]

Whereas we try to keep both the number of medications and their dosages to a minimum during pregnancy, it is often wise to reinstate a more robust mood stabilizing regimen after the mother gives birth to prevent a postpartum mood episode. Here again we must remain watchful for the effects on the newborn if the mother is nursing. There exists a fair amount of research on drug levels in breast milk. The Lact-Med® database (https://www.ncbi.nlm.nih.gov/books/NBK501922) has up-to-date information. This can help to guide our choice of medications in the postpartum period. As discussed above, the serum levels of lithium in breastfeeding infants can rise to up to 50 percent of the mother's serum levels, which could be high enough to cause side effects. With valproate the nursing infant's levels are 1–10 percent and with

SGAs less than 5 percent, both reassuringly low.[29] Mothers may also try to structure the timing of medication dosing and of breastfeeding to minimize the exposure of the newborn to possibly toxic medications. Formula supplements for baby can further lower drug levels.

In 2019 brexanolone (Zulresso) was approved by the FDA for treatment of postpartum depression. This drug is chemically identical to allopregnanolone, which is a metabolite of the hormone progesterone. Progesterone and allopregnanolone peak at high levels during the third trimester of pregnancy, then drop abruptly after birth. Brexanolone must be administered in the hospital intravenously. It is very expensive and is "modestly more effective than placebo," according to the *Medical Letter*.[30] Studies on brexanolone excluded bipolar patients, so whether it could be helpful for them we simply do not know at present.

If a mother does exhibit a postpartum psychosis, which is usually a manic or mixed episode with hallucinations and/or delusions present, she should be monitored very carefully. Sometimes admission to a psychiatric inpatient unit is necessary. Sometimes the infant can be allowed lots of time with the mother there to facilitate bonding. Sometimes having another family member home with mother and baby to continuously monitor them is a safe plan. Very rarely tragic cases occur such as one well publicized case in Texas where a psychotic mother killed her newborn, provoked by hallucinations she thought were from God. Initially convicted of murder, she was later judged not guilty by reason of insanity.

Florence had several hospitalizations with manic or mixed episodes but wished to become pregnant. After meeting with her and her husband, we agreed on a plan for her to go off medications during attempts to conceive and during pregnancy, with her husband empowered to call me if she showed any signs of recurrence. Her pregnancy went well, but after delivery she showed the same wide-eyed, confused, suspicious demeanor she had shown in her previous episodes. Despite her psychosis she seemed able to bottle feed the baby and had no thoughts whatsoever of harming the child. Some of her treatment team advocated an involuntary hospitalization for her. However, her husband, whom she totally trusted, agreed to stay home with her and the baby as we restarted a regimen of valproate and olanzapine. In addition, we had monitoring from child protective services at home. Florence rapidly went into remission and we eventually stopped the olanzapine, while maintaining her valproate, which had a strong preventive effect for her. She also proceeded with a tubal ligation.

If a mother happens to be on one of the SSRI or SNRI antidepressants in later stages of pregnancy, we often make efforts to taper down or even discontinue the drug just before delivery. This is done to try to avoid or minimize the poor neonatal adaptation syndrome.[31] In the womb, the blood that flows through the fetus is detoxified in the mother's liver. After delivery, only the infant's immature liver is available to detoxify medications coursing through the bloodstream of the newborn. Sometimes newborns whose mothers were taking SSRIs like sertraline (Zoloft) or citalopram (Celexa), or SNRIs like venlafaxine (Effexor) or duloxetine (Cymbalta), during later stages of pregnancy were jittery, not eating or sleeping well, and sometimes had to stay in the hospital a day or two longer. This syndrome is self-limiting and goes away in a matter of a few weeks. But if we can avoid it completely, so much the better.

A few studies suggested that the use during pregnancy of SSRI and SNRI antidepressants might cause autism and/or persistent pulmonary hypertension in offspring. The FDA has judged the evidence to be insufficient. Studies find when a control group is carefully matched to the group on these drugs that there are no statistically significant differences in these undesired outcomes. One SSRI, paroxetine, has been linked to an approximately 1 percent increase in cardiac birth defects and should be avoided.[32] Paroxetine has been labeled category D for this reason, while other SSRI antidepressants are ranked category C.

Benzodiazepines, which include alprazolam (Xanax), diazepam (Valium), lorazepam (Ativan) and clonazepam (Klonopin) can cause a malformation such as cleft palate in .01 percent (one in ten thousand) births. Although rare, it is 80 percent over the rate in the general population. Benzodiazepines combined with SSRI antidepressants may increase the risk of congenital heart disease. Perinatal problems associated with the benzos and also the "Z drugs," which are the sleep aids zolpidem (Ambien), zaleplon (Sonata), and eszopiclone (Lunesta), include preterm birth, low birth weight, and a 24 percent increase in congenital malformations.[33]

I have treated many mothers through the years who were on several psychotropic medications when they discovered they were pregnant. Often, we rapidly discontinued some or all of them. For others, because of the severity of their disorder, we agreed to have them continue mood stabilizers, antipsychotics, or antidepressants during their pregnancy. In most cases they had healthy children who did not manifest any signs of toxicity from these medications. Surely pregnancy is a time for prospective bipolar mothers to maintain close contacts with both their obstetrical and mental health providers in order to optimize not only their own health, but that of the next generation.

New mothers can often benefit from social support. Husbands, mothers, mothers-in-law, sisters, and friends, among others, can often smooth the rocky road that follows childbirth. Practical help such as supplying meals or feeding and bathing baby or being there emotionally can assist any mother, including those with bipolar mood disorder. If the new mother has a significant mood episode, others may need to do a great deal more of the childcare for a while.

When reinstating a birth control plan, it is vital that psychiatric and obstetrical prescribers communicate. Some birth control pills containing combinations of estrogens and progestogens can severely lower blood levels of lamotrigine, while mood stabilizers such as carbamazepine can lower blood levels of birth control pills enough to render them ineffective. In these situations, options such as intrauterine devices or long-acting injections of progestogens can be considered.[34]

Careful teamwork between the pregnant bipolar mother and her health providers can make pregnancy a time of excited anticipation and the postpartum period a time to celebrate a joyous family event.

• 10 •

Suicide and Bipolar Disorder

$\mathcal{G}$reg had coped with a bipolar II mood disorder since his late twenties. His episodes of depression were much more frequent than his highs, and lithium had proved very effective in preventing both. However, after twenty years taking lithium, and undoubtedly affected also by his diabetes and hypertension, Greg's kidneys started to fail. His serum creatinine and his creatinine clearance began to rise, reflecting impairment in his kidneys' filtration rate. I had to take him off lithium to prevent further renal insufficiency. Despite stopping lithium, his kidney function deteriorated further and he began hemodialysis.

Even worse, his depressive moods now plunged out of control. Despite trials with lamotrigine, quetiapine, olanzapine/fluoxetine, and antidepressants he had severe depressive episodes. When his wife was gone, he injected himself with an overdose of insulin, lying in a coma until his wife returned unexpectedly early. Rushed to the hospital, he survived, but his brain and other organs suffered damage from the prolonged low blood sugars caused by the insulin overdose.

Bipolar disorder has one of the highest suicide rates among psychiatric disorders. The likelihood of a bipolar person dying by his own hand ranges among various investigators from around 6 percent[1] to 19 percent.[2] This compares with lifetime suicide rates in the general population of 0.4–0.7 percent, that is, 4–7 per thousand. Another study found 164 suicides per 100,000 person-years among bipolar patients compared to 10.6 per 100,000 among controls.[3] Bipolar persons are ten to thirty times more likely to die by suicide than nonbipolar persons.[4] Between a quarter and a half of bipolar persons will make a suicide attempt during their lifetime. This compares to about 3 percent of the general population. Given this high risk for suicide, preventing this tragic out-come is certainly a priority in the treatment of bipolar disorder.

Throughout my psychiatric career I have seen hundreds of patients who survived suicide attempts, some of them by highly lethal methods like a gunshot to the head or to the chest, by hanging, or by jumping from a tall building. Almost universally after the suicide attempt the survivors are once again glad to be alive. Sometimes it takes weeks of treatment to reach that point. Suicide is, with rare exception, a perma-nent solution to a temporary problem.

In the midst of a depression people are often overcome by pes-simism, seeing the future darkly and yielding to hopeless, helpless feelings. Giving the depressed person a sense of hope is crucial and also realistic. I often tried to help patients look back to a recent time when they were not depressed and to the likelihood that they could feel that way again. Bipolar patients, especially those with a mixed episode or mixed features, may also experience high impulsivity or delusional thinking that contributes to suicide attempts.

Many factors affect suicidal thinking and suicidal behavior beyond having a bipolar disorder. It appears that there are some genes that affect suicidality, which differ from the set of genes that contribute to depression or to bipolar disorder. We can see such patterns of suicide in some families. This is certainly not to say suicide in such people is inevi-table. Far from it. That is why one needs to mobilize helpful mitigating factors and to reduce factors that contribute toward suicide.

Alcoholism and other substance abuse contribute to suicide risk. The disinhibiting effect of alcohol is well known, and applies to suicidal behaviors as well as to other risky behaviors. The intoxicated person is more likely to be argumentative or belligerent, and more likely to break the law or to be promiscuous. Intoxication also raises suicide risk sub-stantially, impairing the neural circuits that course through our frontal lobes, where rational thoughts about effects on our loved ones and moral and religious concerns counteract emotionally fueled wishes to die.

Benzodiazepines, such as alprazolam (Xanax) or diazepam (Va-lium), can have a disinhibiting effect similar to alcohol in some people. If this is the case in a particular person, he should strive to minimize or avoid such medication. The FDA posts class warnings for antide-pressants, anticonvulsant-type mood stabilizers, and SGAs (second-generation antipsychotics) as posing possible risk for increased suicidality. These effects in antidepressants are seen in teenagers and young adults, but seem to disappear in adults, as a group, after the mid-twenties. Suicidality in the studies constituted suicidal thoughts and urges as well as suicide attempts. However, data from other studies support the contention that antidepressants do not increase suicide risk or that they sometimes decrease it.[5]

In antiepileptic drugs as a group (which includes some mood stabilizers), the risk of suicidality (thinking and behaviors) was about four persons in one thousand on mood stabilizers and about two persons per thousand on placebo.[6] So the risk of these agents causing suicidality is very small. Data regarding valproate and carbamazepine (drugs that are both antiepileptic and mood stabilizing) indicate they do not increase suicidal risk and may even lower it.[7] Those two mood stabilizers differ in that fashion from the other nine antiepileptic drugs studied by the FDA. But the FDA gave all these drugs as a class the warning regarding suicidality.

Suicide attempts differ significantly from completed suicides. Suicidal behaviors can be seen on a continuum from those with high intent for completed suicide to those seeking consciously or unconsciously some interpersonal impact. This often involves eliciting some caring response from a significant other or family member. Sometimes suicidal behavior may be an expression of anger intended to cause guilt or distress in others. Some suicide attempts manifest a hopeless giving up and seeking an end of emotional distress. Many suicide attempts include components of several of these motives.

The despondent veteran who chooses a time when no one is likely to visit him to shoot himself in the head is showing high intent for completing suicide, and choosing a very lethal means. A young woman who has just had a spat with her boyfriend over his seeing another woman, and then consumes a half dozen Xanax from her bottle of one hundred, and calls her best girlfriend to tell her what she has done before she gets too sleepy, is on the other end of the continuum. She has chosen a very nonlethal method and has called out for help. She may be hoping her actions will magnify her boyfriend's guilt and elicit a more caring response from him. At the same time, she has felt hurt and humiliated by his behavior and a part of her wishes she could just exit the situation.

I have chosen these man and woman roles advisedly. Women, in fact, have more suicide attempts than men, but men have more completed suicides. Men tend to choose more lethal means such as fire-arms and hanging. More men than women are familiar with firearms. Bipolar men are about twice as likely as bipolar women to die by suicide. In the general population that ratio is 4:1.[8]

Suicides often represent a "perfect storm" of long-term factors pushing a patient toward discouragement or hopelessness and acute loss or disappointment adding the "last straw." Most studies of suicide are retrospective assessments of possible contributing factors. However, in such retrospective studies the knowledge that a person has died from suicide may color recall and reporting of symptoms and problems preceding the suicide.

A prospective study of suicide avoids those issues of biased reporting. Dr. Jan Fawcett (no close relation, but perhaps we share a distant Huguenot ancestor) and colleagues followed nearly one thousand patients in a mood disorder clinic with either bipolar or recurrent unipolar depressive disorders. After four years, twenty-five had committed suicide. They found among risk factors were hopelessness, anhedonia (inability to experience pleasure), global insomnia, and panic attacks or anxiety. They recommend addressing these risk factors. Benzodiazepines or antianxiety drugs, sleep aids or sedating antidepressants, or SGAs may be literally lifesaving in such situations. With benzodiazepines one must weigh potential benefits against risks of addiction or disinhibition.[9]

The long-term risk factor with the strongest association with attempted or completed suicide is a family history of suicide in a first-degree relative. History of a previous attempt is a strong risk factor. Other long-term risk factors include an early age of onset of bipolar disorder and the severity of bipolar illness, with more time in a depressed state correlating with suicide. Risk increases when the first mood episode for a bipolar patient is depression. A rapid cycling pattern (four or more mood episodes within a twelve-month period) adds to suicidal risk. A history of physical or sexual abuse, a pattern of impulsivity or aggression, and medical disorders that affect the central nervous system are all risk factors.[10]

Among bipolar persons, suicide tends to occur during depressed or mixed states, only rarely during mania. While the ratio of suicide attempts to completed suicide is about 30:1 in the general population, it is only 3:1 among bipolar patients. Their attempts tend to have higher intentionality and lethality.[11]

Protective factors lessen the risk for suicide.[12] These include restricted access to highly lethal methods such as firearms, feelings of responsibility to children or other family, pregnancy, strong religious beliefs, a general satisfaction with life, positive coping and problem-solving skills, positive social support and the ability to make use of it, access and adherence to care, and a positive therapeutic relationship. Resources such as intelligence, good health, job skills, and money can also provide some protection against suicide.

Sometimes suicides are planned and carried out over a short period of desperation. That is why it is important to restrict access to firearms and ammunition when a depressed patient is having strong suicidal urges. More than half of all suicides occur with firearms. Only in the age group ten to fourteen is suffocation (e.g., by hanging) a more frequent cause. Women choose poisoning by overdose most often as a means.

It is not true that the depressed person will simply choose another method if the gun is not there. Sometimes that happens. But often the depressed person, usually ambivalent about suicide, will have a change of heart or a glimmer of hope and decide to abort his suicidal quest. The British found that changing the gas in stoves from a lethal gas to a benign one reduced suicide rates in Great Britain. People who were putting their heads in the oven to die from lethal gas (a fairly quiet, effortless method) were not reverting to some other means to kill themselves.[13]

When a person, especially an adolescent, has episodes of depression with suicidal thoughts, removing the firearms from their access can be lifesaving. The gun that sits in the hall closet to ward off dangerous intruders is far more likely to be fired in an act of self-destruction than in one of self-protection.[14]

Large numbers of patients make direct or indirect threats about suicide before committing the act. Some may give away prized possessions or behave with friends in a fashion that could be interpreted as "saying goodbye." This provides an opportunity to channel persons at risk into treatment or to increase the intensity of their treatment. However, a substantial number of suicides do not give a discernible warning. Some, even when closely assessed by clinicians, may deny any suicidal intent days or hours before ending their life.[15]

The effect that suicide might have on family members and other loved ones is often a deterrent to suicide. Helping the suicidal patient recognize that negative effect may help them put their suicidal urges on the back burner. Letting the suicidal patient know that they are loved and needed can thus be very helpful. I have talked with patients who put away a gun simply because a friend called them as they were planning a final exit. Patients with young children or another adult dependent on them are less likely to commit suicide. Sometimes even concern for a pet acts as a strong deterrent to keep from acting on suicidal thoughts.

When suicidal thoughts or planning enter the patient's mind, this becomes an especially important time to be working closely with the mental health professionals involved in the patient's care. They are skilled in evaluating suicidal risk and implementing a treatment plan proportionate to that risk. Sometimes extra monitoring by the family and extra therapy sessions may get a patient through a period of higher risk. Other times a patient may need psychiatric hospitalization to provide a safe environment and to alleviate depression more rapidly. Hospitals can provide close monitoring and removal of dangerous objects ranging from sharp objects to belts and shoelaces. With daily monitoring, medication regimens can be more rapidly optimized. Skilled psychological support is readily available. Electroconvulsive therapy can be a rapid lifesaving intervention in the hospital for severely depressed or delusional patients, or those who have failed several medication regimes.

It is wise to have a plan in place for a bipolar patient should they experience severe suicidal depression. Know which providers should be called and how to move forward with psychiatric hospitalization should that be needed.

At times a patient's usual mental health clinicians might be unavailable. Many people access help through hospital emergency rooms. Many places have access to telephone crisis hotlines than can help people in crisis or refer them for further help if needed. Most community mental health systems have emergency services available.

If the bipolar patient appears at risk to harm himself or others, police can be helpful in providing safe transport to an emergency room setting. Sometimes one or a few trusted friends or family may be sufficient to convince the patient that he needs immediate help and professional evaluation. If the patient appears at risk, but not immediately so, and refuses voluntary help, a process of involuntary hospitalization is available with applicable laws differing by state. In Michigan a petition is filed with the probate court and with the judge's approval, law enforcement officers are empowered to bring the patient to an emergency room for evaluation.

Periods after hospitalization are a high-risk time for suicide attempts.[16] The length of stay in psychiatric hospitals has shortened considerably over the decades. Typically, patients now leave the hospital better than when they arrived, not experiencing active suicidal urges, but far from well. The hope is that these patients will continue on their path to wellness with the help of an improved medication regime and some active psychotherapy. But sometimes the patient stumbles on that path to wellness and begins to sink back into a depressed and suicidal state. Sometimes patients omit prescribed medications, or use alcohol or other substances, which weaken the benefits of their bipolar meds. Sometimes events in the patient's personal life, such as loss of a relationship or a job, will trip up their progress. The post-hospital period is a time for vigilance. In recovery from depression, energy levels and sleep typically improve before mood and thinking patterns normalize. Thus, an improving depressed person might find himself with the energy to carry out a suicide plan that demanded too much effort to perform at the depth of his depression.

When a patient does make a suicide attempt, successful or not, it often engenders feelings of anger, abandonment, or guilt in those close to them. The concept that the patient is willing to abandon the other person via death can be hard to accept. In the midst of suicidal depression patients are usually not thinking clearly, not weighing all the effects of their acts in a rational manner. Certainly, it is not good to heap mountains of guilt on a suicide survivor, which might drive them deeper into depression. But loved ones can express the hurt they felt if they accompany that by an expression of how much they need the patient and how glad they are that she survived.

Feelings of guilt in those close to a suicide are common. Family, friends, and clinicians alike usually play the "Monday morning quarterback" game: reviewing what they might have done differently. Sometimes this yields some productive ideas. Sometimes guilt may be an appropriate response to having treated the suicide attempter poorly. But often the guilt is irrational, a part of our mind's attempt to undo a tragic occurrence.

These feelings of guilt and anger, as well as the knowledge that the suicide was a conscious choice, makes grief after suicide a complex matter. Grief counseling individually or in a group may facilitate processing the grief and healing. In larger population centers specific groups for those grieving suicide may exist.

Hundreds of studies confirm that a wide variety of antidepressants improve the overall symptoms of depression, but I have found it disappointing and a bit surprising that research has not shown antidepressants to consistently reduce suicide rates in depressed persons. Effective drugs used to treat cancer or heart disease clearly show reductions in death rates. Yet we have been unable to consistently show a reduction in suicide rates from antidepressant medications.

Lithium, however, is a horse of a different color. Researchers reviewed thirty-four studies of patients on lithium versus twenty-five studies of patients not on lithium assessing risks for suicide. Overall, lithium reduced suicide rates five or six times better than other treatments and reduced suicide attempts fifteen times better.[17] Lithium treatment benefited not only bipolar I and bipolar II patients, but those with recurrent depression as well.

A lengthy study of more than three hundred bipolar persons treated in a clinic in Sardinia kept careful account of suicidal behaviors as well as medication regimens. Here once more a robust anti-suicide effect was documented for lithium. It seemed to kick in particularly well after patients had been on lithium for a year or two, reducing suicide rates about eightfold.[18] However, if patients abruptly stopped lithium, their rate of suicide jumped above the baseline rate. Other studies confirm that rapid discontinuation of lithium (say in two weeks or less) often leads to a bipolar episode.[19] If that episode is one of depression or a mixed episode, the suicide risk jumps. Tapering lithium over at least one month is recommended when it needs to be stopped, unless there are some immediate medical concerns (e.g., pregnancy or toxicity).

Compared with lithium, suicide was 2.7 times more likely with valproate.[20] Another meta-analysis of thirty-two studies comparing lithium against other mood stabilizers, antidepressants, or placebo found that lithium reduced self-harm (including suicide) by 70 percent.[21]

Thus far other mood stabilizers and most SGAs have not shown this robust anti-suicide effect in bipolar disorder manifested by lithium.

This is one reason to consider lithium as a long-term maintenance medication.

However, one SGA, namely clozapine, has shown an anti-suicide effect in schizophrenia.[22] In another study clozapine reduced suicidal thoughts in patients with schizoaffective disorder and bipolar disorder.[23]

The single best strategy to prevent suicide in bipolar disorder is to follow an effective treatment program including maintenance medications that prevent relapse. Lithium, with its strongly documented anti-suicide effect, may be part of that regimen.

• 11 •

Secondary Mania and
Late-Onset Bipolar Disorder

$\mathscr{I}$n 1990 I reported the following case:[1] A local internist had referred a sixty-one-year-old businessman for psychiatric evaluation after several days with a persisting headache in his left forehead and changes in his behavior. He had no personal or family history of psychiatric disorder. He was agitated, sleeping poorly, and ruminating about taxes and the federal government, which he thought had a plot against him. Mr. Carson was a large man whose voice boomed as he spoke rapidly, jumping from one topic to another with no apparent connection. He was demanding and suspicious, and his mood shifted suddenly from euphoria to irritability to occasional tearfulness. He knew the correct date and was able to perform simple memory and calculation tasks correctly. When asked to interpret a common proverb his response wandered off task.

Mr. Carson took several medications for atrial fibrillation (the rapid chaotic contractions of the heart's upper chambers), for hypertension, and a blood thinner because of previous thrombophlebitis (blood clots). His physical exam was unremarkable. Routine laboratory studies revealed an elevated serum creatinine of 1.9, reflecting renal insufficiency or abnormally slow filtration of the blood by his kidneys. His thyroid studies including TSH were normal. A CT scan of the brain with contrast revealed a recent ischemic infarct (a non-bleeding stroke) of the right frontal lobe. His electroencephalogram was abnormal with generalized background slowing of his brain waves. Psychological testing revealed a normal score of 29 out of 30 on the Cognitive Capacity Screening Test and some minor errors on the Bender Gestalt test, indicating scores below age expectation for visual motor coordination and spatial visualization skills. The Wexler Adult Intelligence Scale-revised

127

gave a verbal IQ of 96 and a performance IQ of 81, with the disparity between performance and verbal skills suggesting a significant right cerebral hemisphere deficit. His full-scale IQ of 89 appeared lower than would be expected from this businessman. Overall the psychological testing suggested diffuse cerebral impairment with predominant effects in the nondominant right hemisphere. Mr. Carson had suffered a stroke in the right frontal lobe of his brain that had triggered a manic syndrome.

Treatment with the FGA haloperidol brought improvement within days. Lithium carbonate was started, but stopped quickly because of his subnormal renal status. He was discharged from an inpatient unit in fifteen days on 4 mg per day of haloperidol, which was tapered and discontinued over the next seven weeks. He recovered and continued to do well three years after discharge.

Mr. Carson's case exemplified a syndrome of secondary mania, with manic symptoms that mimic those of bipolar disorder, but are directly caused by a drug or a medical disorder, in his case a stroke in his right frontal lobe. Secondary mania was described in a classic 1978 paper by psychiatrists Krauthammer and Klerman.[2] You may be familiar with Charles Krauthammer as a Pulitzer prize–winning newspaper columnist recently deceased. He pursued a career in journalism after his psychiatric training.

In secondary mania, as they defined it, a patient had to display for at least one week an elated or irritable mood. He had to manifest at least two of the following symptoms as well: hyperactivity, decreased sleep, grandiosity, push of speech, flight of ideas, distractibility, or lack of judgment. If a patient had a previous history of mood disorder (bipolar disorder or depression) or was currently experiencing a confusional state (as we might see, for example, in delirium tremens from alcohol withdrawal), he was excluded from fitting the definition of secondary mania. Although other investigators had used the term "secondary mania," Krauthammer and Klerman were the first to thoroughly review and define the syndrome.

Through the years the psychiatric classification schemes made various alterations to this definition. In the current *DSM-5* the criteria for "bipolar and related disorders due to another medical condition" are similar.[3] However, besides a persistent state of abnormal mood (irritated, expansive, or elevated) the patient should also manifest an increase in energy or activity. The required length of time is not precisely defined. The manic picture must be the result of some medical disorder, and it must cause impairment in social, occupational, or other areas of life or necessitate hospitalization. And, much as in Krauthammer and Klerman's definition, this manic picture is not just part of a delirium, nor is it caused by another mental disorder.

Delirium is an organic mental disorder characterized by significant mental confusion, such as disorientation in time, place, or person, impaired short-term memory, and impaired attention.

Krauthammer and Klerman cited previously reported cases of secondary mania that could be classified into various medical causes. Metabolic derangements such as postoperative state or hemodialysis were included. Infectious etiologies such as influenza and Q fever (caused by rickettsial bacteria) triggered a number of reported cases of secondary mania. Central nervous system tumors and epilepsy were two other classes of disorders leading to secondary mania. They also reported drug-induced cases of secondary mania. Our current *DSM-5* separates into its own category substance/medication-induced bipolar and related disorders. Krauthammer and Klerman cited cases related to amphetamines, levodopa, isoniazid, and various other medications.

Through the years, various case reports added further drugs to the list of those inducing mania, further infectious etiologies such as St. Louis encephalitis, and further examples of central nervous system tumors that cause secondary mania. In addition, further categories of disorders have been added such as cerebrovascular related, head injuries, other central nervous system diseases, and degenerative and immunological disorders.[4] See table 11.1.

A variety of drugs have been reported to precipitate mania.[5] Stimulants such as methylphenidate, cocaine, and sympathomimetic amines (such as those used to treat asthma), steroids, steroid withdrawal, and androgens are well-known causes. Corticosteroid drugs are widely used to treat autoimmune disorders, such as systemic lupus, and inflammatory disorders, such as asthma or severe allergic skin rashes. But other reported medications include anti-tuberculous drugs (isoniazid and iproniazid), procarbazine, procainamide, metrizamide, procyclidine, levodopa, methyldopa withdrawal, hallucinogens (e.g., LSD and PCP), alcohol, bromides, bromocriptine, metoclopramide, cimetidine, cyclobenzaprine, yohimbine, amantadine, tolmetin, benzodiazepines (triazolam, alprazolam, lorazepam), buspirone, zidovudine, guanfacine, and lisinopril. Even hyperbaric oxygen has been reported to cause secondary mania.

Table 11.1. Causes of Secondary Mania

Brain Disorders

Brain tumors	Parkinson's disease
Cerebrovascular disease (e.g., stroke)	Huntington's disease
Traumatic brain injury and brain lesions	Wilson's disease
Alzheimer's dementia	Idiopathic calcification of the basal ganglia
Frontotemporal dementias	Epilepsy

Infectious Diseases

Q Fever	HIV/AIDS
Cryptococcal meningitis	Herpes Simplex
Influenza	Tuberculosis
Viral encephalitis	Epstein-Barr virus
Syphilis	Hepatitis

Metabolic Diseases

Uremia/renal failure	Folate deficiency
Hypercalcemia	Anemia
Hepatic failure	Gout
Amyloidosis	Anoxia
B12 deficiency	

Endocrine and Genetic

Hyperthyroidism	Acromegaly
Cushing's syndrome	Hypothyroidism with starvation diet
Hypothyroidism	Hyperaldosteronism
Diabetes mellitus	Klinefelter's syndrome
Addison's disease	Kleine-Levin syndrome
Hyperparathyroidism	

Immunologic

Systemic lupus	Giant cell arteritis
Multiple sclerosis	Regional enteritis (Crohn's disease)
Rheumatoid arthritis	Ulcerative colitis
Periarteritis nodosa	Migraine
Sarcoidosis	

Malignancy Related

Carcinoma of the pancreas	Carcinomatosis
Lung cancer	Lymphoma
Other paraneoplastic syndromes	Carcinoid syndrome

Samantha worked as a health care professional. In her thirties she developed chronic fatigue syndrome. Her energy was extremely low. She was depleted after working a few hours. She tended to sleep more and her appetite was poor. She had no energy and lost interest in her hobbies. She had to leave her job and go on disability. She also had diffuse muscle aches and pains and was diagnosed with fibromyalgia and chronic fatigue syndrome. Understandably she was depressed and sought me out for treatment. Supportive psychotherapy and antidepressant medications such as bupropion helped some. Her endocrinologist put her on DHEA (dehydroepiandrosterone), which is a hormone that is a precursor for some of the sex hormones such as testosterone or progesterone. DHEA has had some trials in treating chronic fatigue syndrome. After an increase of the DHEA dose, Samantha became manic. She thought God was communicating directly to her and that she had a special mission. She was sleeping very little and talking rapidly; her mood was euphoric at times, but also irritable. Her family brought her to the emergency department and she was admitted. Stopping the DHEA and adding lithium brought her mood back to neutral. She continued to have some of the fatigue and the muscle pains even during her manic episode.

Because of her overall picture and the fact that one of her sons had a bipolar diagnosis, I recommended we continue full-dose lithium. Sam was skeptical that she truly had bipolar disorder and pushed to reduce the dose of any antimanic medications. After a number of months at a very low lithium level, she had another spell of mania, this time without any clear precipitating drug such as DHEA. Her first manic episode was considered drug-induced, but the second was clear evidence of a bipolar I disorder.

It is well known that antidepressants can trigger mania, but if the manic symptoms persist for many days after we stop the antidepressant, we consider the patient to truly have bipolar disorder. If the manic symptoms subside in a few days we consider it a drug-induced secondary mania. Studies indicate that patients who switch to a manic or hypomanic episode for the first time while on an antidepressant look more like bipolar patients than unipolar depressed patients in terms of associated features.[6]

The *DSM-5* diagnosis of "Substance/Medication-Induced Bipolar and Related Disorder" can be used with a manic, mixed, or depressive episode that follows the use of or withdrawal from a substance known to cause this effect.[7] If a bipolar or depressive mood disorder has already been present in the patient or the mood changes persist for a while after stopping the substance (they use a month as an example), then it may be most appropriate to diagnose a primary mood disorder, rather than a secondary substance-induced disorder.

DSM-5 contains the problematic statement that such switchers on antidepressants need to maintain the features of mood elevation "beyond the physiologic effect" of the antidepressant. I agree with Terao and Tanaka that this phrase is vague and prone to low reliability among clinicians.[8] Some antidepressants, for example, fluoxetine (Prozac), may continue to manifest detectable blood levels of active metabolites for several months after being discontinued. The downstream effects of antidepressants within the intracellular machinery may likewise occur many weeks after the drug is out of the bloodstream. It would not surprise me if that problematic phrase disappears from *DSM-6*.

Krauthammer and Klerman found that their series of patients with secondary mania differed in several respects from typical bipolar manias.[9] The age of onset of the first manic episode was later at forty-one years of age, compared to a median onset of about twenty-five years in typical bipolar populations. The family histories of their patients with secondary mania were often devoid of bipolar disorder, whereas in the usual bipolar population 85 percent of the probands had a positive family history of bipolar disorder. Further studies of cases of secondary mania through the years have tended to bear out these findings.

With secondary mania, treating the underlying disorder is important. Sometimes such treatment by itself may alleviate the mania. However, frequently the more standard treatments for mania such as mood stabilizers, SGAs, and occasionally FGAs are necessary to neutralize the mood. Care must be taken in elderly and medically ill patients not to cause further medical problems through drug side effects or drug interactions.

The original definition of secondary mania excluded patients with a history of any significant mood disorder, including depression. The current *DSM-5* definition lacks that exclusion and would, for example, allow a patient who had experienced major depression and now was being treated for Parkinson's disease with L-dopa and developed a manic syndrome to be diagnosed with "medication-induced bipolar disorder."

Or a patient with a previous history of depression who developed hyperthyroidism and along with that a manic syndrome would be diagnosed with "bipolar disorder due to a medical condition."

A manic syndrome can emerge out of a confusional state, for example, when a toxic delirium is clearing up. Many such cases have been reported. Some disorders that we rarely encounter today, such as general paresis (central nervous system syphilis) often displayed a presentation of euphoria, grandiosity, impulsivity, hyperactivity, and reduced sleep. These symptoms typically occurred along with impaired memory and attention. But there are some case reports of general paresis with intact cognition that would fit today's category of mania due to a medical condition.

Patients presenting with a first manic episode in later life, say beyond age fifty, also tend to lack a family history of bipolar disorder (low genetic loading), but frequently have some medical issues, especially cerebrovascular disease or risk factors such as hypertension.[10] Disorders of the brain's white matter seen on MRI and interpreted as relating to tissue ischemic changes (that is, lack of blood flow) have been described in both late-onset depression and mania. Even if a patient does not show a defined area of stroke that would qualify for a diagnosis of secondary mania (mood disorder due to medical cause), medical factors may still contribute to a primary bipolar disorder.

A continuum model of bipolarity involving genetic and environmental causes has been described by Goodwin and Jamison in their encyclopedic text, *Manic-Depressive Illness*.[11] Late-onset mania lies on such a continuum between secondary mania with clear medical causes and typical bipolar disorder with its strong genetic causation. For example, some persons with strong genetic loading for bipolar disorder might manifest mania after a very mild situational trigger. Another patient with lesser genetic loading may only manifest a manic episode when there is an additional strong etiologic factor such as a right frontal lobe infarct or hyperthyroidism.

Successful treatment of late-life mania with lithium and valproate has been described.[12] In the only randomized double-blind study of mania treatment in patients sixty years of age and older, both medications had good remission rates around 45 percent at three weeks of treatment and around 65 percent at nine weeks, although lithium reduced mania scores slightly more than valproate. Serum drug levels were targeted from 0.8–0.99 mEq/L for lithium and at 80–99 μg/mL for valproate, a bit lower than would be the case for younger patients. Both drugs were fairly well tolerated by older patients, with more tremor occurring with lithium use.

Some sources report better results with the anticonvulsants valproate or carbamazepine in treating manic patients with primary neurologic disorders.[13] SGAs can also be useful alone or along with mood stabilizers. The rule of thumb with medications in older patients is to "start low and go slow" in terms of dose increases. Older patients are more prone to side effects and likely to have other medical problems or medications that might interact with the medications targeting their mood disorder. Experts recommend starting medications one at a time at a dose 10–50 percent of the young adult dose and increasing 5–10 percent every four to seven days with a target dose about 50 percent of the young adult target dose, or in the frail elderly 25–50 percent.[14]

· 12 ·

Disorders Associated
with Bipolar Disorder

*E*d's bipolar mood disorder showed up in his twenties after he returned from the Vietnam conflict. In his manic spells he became loud
and aggressive, getting into bar fights. He drank alcohol heavily, favor-
ing whisky. Sometimes he would stay awake for days at a time. He
was jailed after one of his altercations. When he sobered up, police
could easily tell he was mentally ill. He was admitted to the first of
what would be many hospitalizations. Ed liked to drink even when in a
neutral mood or when depressed, which was a rare mood state for him.
After several hospitalizations and brushes with the law he began to see
the light. He recognized he was an alcoholic and that he had bipolar
disorder. He had an excellent response to lithium, which seemed to
prevent his manias completely. He became a faithful member of AA.
In his late fifties he was diagnosed with a carcinoma in one kidney,
which had to be removed. Given lithium's potential risk for slowly
reducing the filtration rate in the remaining kidney, it seemed prudent
to take him off lithium and try another mood stabilizer, valproate. Unfortunately, this medication and others were much less effective than
lithium. Sometimes it was hard to know if he went on a drinking binge
first and stopped taking his meds, or whether he started getting high
despite the medications and impulsively picked up the whiskey bottle.
His bipolar disorder and his alcoholism were entwined in a deadly spiral
that spun him downward into a lifestyle of homelessness, poverty, and
more physical illnesses.

Often in medicine we see diseases that cluster together. For example, hypertension and diabetes are associated with coronary artery
disease and cerebrovascular disease. Hypertension and diabetes are risk

factors for heart attack and stroke—risk factors that can be modified to reduce the chances of suffering an infarct in the heart or brain. A different type of association links psoriasis with psoriatic arthritis. Autoimmune mechanisms underlie both of those disorders.

Bipolar disorder is associated with both behavioral disorders and medical disorders. Sixty-five percent of bipolar patients have at least one such comorbid disorder and 25 percent have three or more associated or comorbid disorders.[1] Bipolar patients are more likely than not to have some associated disorder(s).

In general, having more than one psychiatric disorder leads to poorer outcomes and increased difficulties coping. For bipolar patients this means more suicide attempts, more rapid cycling, and more time spent depressed.[2]

Anxiety disorders are common in bipolar patients. One study by the Stanley Foundation found 42 percent of treated bipolar patients having an anxiety disorder. Panic disorder was most frequent, followed by social anxiety disorder, simple phobia, and generalized anxiety disorder. Obsessive-compulsive disorder, posttraumatic stress disorder, and eating disorders were also more common than in the general population.[3] For all these disorders a form of psychotherapy, frequently of the cognitive-behavioral type, has been the most effective treatment, more effective than medications. Certainly, psychotherapy is a reasonable treatment in those with comorbid anxiety disorders, along with mood stabilizing medications for the bipolar disorder.

Drugs in the antidepressant family, especially SSRIs and SNRIs, have also had success in the treatment of those comorbid behavioral disorders. If the bipolar patient is on a mood stabilizing regimen, these can often be used safely. Benzodiazepines, for example, alprazolam (Xanax) and diazepam (Valium), can also be used with many anxiety disorders, but must be used cautiously, if at all, in patients with a history of substance use disorders.

Substance abuse disorders also occurred in about 42 percent of bipolar patients in that study. Bipolar I patients had more substance abuse disorders, while bipolar II patients had more anxiety disorders.

Patients with both an anxiety disorder and bipolar disorder also have a higher risk for having a substance use disorder and higher risk for suicide attempts, more rapid cycling, more time depressed, poorer role function, poorer response to lithium, and lower quality of life.[4]

The association goes in both directions. Groups of patients with panic disorder have higher rates of bipolar disorder than the general population, both among themselves and in close relatives. It appears that both these multigene disorders share some genes in common, so that having several such genes increases one's risk for both disorders.

When Jane first came to me for treatment she was in the midst of a profound depression. Her speech and movements were noticeably slow, she had no interest in her usual hobbies and needed her husband's prompting to carry out the simplest of daily activities. She sometimes wondered if everyone would be better off without her. She had been treated elsewhere with trials of SSRIs and tricyclic antidepressants along with lithium, but to no avail—the depression had not budged. An MAOI antidepressant, phenelzine, along with lithium dramatically turned the tide. Jane reengaged with life, regaining a normal happy mood.

She did continue to manifest obsessive-compulsive disorder. One compulsion was to call in for the exact time and to then synchronize the dozen or more timepieces in her house. This happened several times each day. The bipolar depression had been a much bigger problem than the OCD, and although her compulsions took up some time, they were not extremely distressing to her. When she experienced mild hypomanic periods, the compulsions were easier to resist, but never went away completely. On the phenelzine she had no more serious depressions.

Symptoms of social anxiety disorder when associated with bipolar disorder often wax and wane with the patient's mood. During mania or hypomania, social anxiety diminishes as the patient becomes more outgoing, while social inhibition increases during episodes of depression. This waxing and waning pattern is common with other associated comorbid anxiety disorders, and with PTSD, as well as OCD.[5]

Obsessive-compulsive disorder is more often associated with bipolar II than bipolar I disorder. The severity of this OCD may vary with mood changes, worse during depression and better in euthymic and hypomanic periods when patients are more able to resist compulsive urges. The patterns of obsessive-compulsive behaviors in bipolars involve less checking and more behaviors with religious or sexual obsessions.[6]

A meta-analysis of seven studies found a prevalence of 16 percent of PTSD among bipolar patients.[7] This is about twice the prevalence in the general population. The tendency for bipolar patients to be more impulsive or less prone to exercise good judgment when manic might contribute to more trauma.[8] Symptoms of PTSD, such as insomnia, can act as triggers for mania/hypomania. As with other associated disorders, having both PTSD and bipolar disorder leads to a more difficult course, more substance abuse, higher rates of suicide, and lower functional status and quality of life.

Adult attention deficit hyperactivity disorder occurs in about 4 percent of the adult population, but in about 9 percent of bipolar adults, especially those with bipolar II.[9] ADHD tends to be a disorder manifesting itself first in childhood. Adults with bipolar disorder often show impairment in attention not only in symptomatic phases of depression and mania, but even during euthymic (normal mood) periods.[10] This impaired attention beginning after bipolar onset should be construed not as ADHD, but rather as one of those lingering symptoms of bipolar disorder that can show themselves even when the patient is not in the midst of a serious mood episode.

But youngsters with ADHD can develop bipolar disorder (it would be rare for bipolar to show up first). Studies of adolescents with both ADHD and bipolar disorder indicate that stimulants can be safely used without triggering mania when mood stabilizers are also administered.[11] In persons with a history of stimulant abuse, or even other substance abuse, stimulants may need to be avoided. Non-stimulant ADHD treatments such as atomoxetine (Straterra) or bupropion (Wellbutrin) may find a use here. I have seen many adults with both disorders in which the ADHD was a bigger factor than bipolar disorder in the person's lack of success in the working world, so treating both disorders is important.

Some but not all studies find an association between bipolar disorders and eating disorders, especially between bulimia and bipolar II disorder.[12]

Abuse of alcohol and other substances has been very strongly associated with bipolar disorder. Among psychiatric disorders, bipolar I has the highest association with alcohol use disorders, followed by bipolar II. Cocaine, opiates, and marijuana are also abused more often by bipolar patients than in the population at large.[13] In one community sample study, 46 percent of bipolar I patients had an alcohol disorder, and 39 percent of bipolar II patients did, compared with 13.5 percent in the general population.[14] The same study found a drug use disorder in 41 percent of bipolar I patients, 21 percent of bipolar II patients, and 6.2 percent of the general population. When samples of patients with alcoholism or drug abuse are studied, they have higher rates of bipolar disorder than the general population.[15]

A substance abuse disorder makes the course of bipolar disorder worse, with more suicide attempts, more rapid cycling, more mixed states, more sleep impairment, more impulsive aggression, and poorer compliance with prescribed medications.[16] Sometimes alcohol or a drug of abuse may chemically counteract the benefits of prescribed medication, or the poor compliance that goes with substance abuse may undermine treatment. In a study of patients with both bipolar disorder and substance abuse, those patients who complied well with their prescribed medications did as well as the bipolar persons with no substance abuse problems. Those who did not comply well had poorer outcomes.[17]

How much alcohol use is safe? Bipolar patients with moderate drinking of beer (2.2 beers/week) had no increased mood symptoms, but moderate drinkers of distilled spirits (2.2 drinks/week) had more manic episodes.[18] Bipolar patients with a substance abuse history who took an antidepressant and mood stabilizer had 29 percent switches into mania. Those with no substance abuse history had no such manic switches.[19] Perhaps the substance abuse causes epigenetic changes (alterations in molecules that regulate the genes) that lead to a persisting vulnerability to mood swings.[20]

Marijuana abuse has been associated with more depressive symptoms and increased suicidal ideation.[21]

What is the reason that bipolar persons have such high rates of substance abuse? One theory has been the "self-medication" hypothesis. This states that bipolar patients use alcohol or sedating substances to self-treat symptoms such as insomnia, anxiety, and excessive energy and use stimulants to counteract low moods and lack of energy. Although there may be some validity to this concept, studies find that bipolar patients abuse uppers like cocaine or amphetamines even more in the manic phase than when depressed. Often cocaine or other stimulants are used to prolong or heighten feelings of energy or euphoria.[22]

Studies that looked at the onset of bipolar symptoms and of substance abuse over the course of a patient's lifetime find that in most cases (by a factor of 1.3) the mood symptoms came first, followed by substance abuse. However, it is possible that abuse of substances may bring on mood disorders including bipolar disorder. Depressions secondary to alcohol or opiate abuse are well known. Abuse of stimulants can cause a "secondary mania," and perhaps these episodes can kindle the brain into a bipolar pattern through epigenetic mechanisms, that is, by producing substances that modulate the activity of genes.[23]

Much of the reason for the association of bipolar and substance abuse problems may lie in the genes themselves, just as we have seen in the confluence of anxiety disorders and bipolar. All these disorders seem to be multigenetic, based on a number of different genes that all contribute to the ultimate manifestation of the disorders in question. And some of those genes overlap, that is, the same gene(s) may contribute to both bipolar and to alcoholism or drug abuse problems.

Many medical disorders are also associated with bipolar disorder. Patients with bipolar disorder have nine fewer years of life expectancy. Some studies have found suicide as the most frequent cause of death among bipolar persons, followed closely by cardiovascular disease.[24] Other studies have found cardiovascular disease to account for more early deaths than suicide.[25]

Illnesses that are more frequent and begin at an earlier age in bipolar persons include diabetes mellitus, cancer, obesity, autoimmune disorders, cardiovascular conditions, hypertension, and metabolic imbalances including hypothyroidism.[26] Migraine also occurs more often in bipolar persons.[27]

Obesity increases the risk for both depressive and manic episodes and leads to longer episodes of depression, more hospitalizations, and a poorer response to lithium and valproate. Obesity in bipolar persons is associated with a higher risk for suicide and for anxiety disorders, a more severe course of illness, and more disability.[28] Thus, a healthy diet and regular exercise may help stabilize bipolar disorder, along with other health benefits.

Pronounced cognitive dysfunction, including problems of concentration and memory, occurs in 25–50 percent of bipolar persons and is associated with more psychosocial disability. This cognitive dysfunction also correlates with impaired glucose metabolism, abnormalities of lipids (such as cholesterol and triglycerides), visceral adiposity (lots of fat in internal organs), hypertension, obesity, and the metabolic syndrome. Overweight patients who lose weight improve their cognitive performance.

Bipolar disorder increases the risk for diabetes mellitus threefold. Bipolar diabetics in turn have more chronic symptoms, more rapid cycling, and more functional impairment. Insulin resistance occurs in bipolar disorder sometimes even in the absence of obesity. Obesity and bipolar disorder share an increase in inflammation, and an abnormal hypothalamic-pituitary-adrenal axis with higher levels of circulating cortisol.

Medications for treating bipolar disorder may increase weight and bring on diabetes. These include many SGAs (second-generation antipsychotics), lithium, and valproate. Some bipolar medications seem weight neutral, including lamotrigine, aripiprazole, ziprasidone, lurasidone, and asenapine.

One study looked at patients with diabetes mellitus type II and found they had 2.6 times the risk for developing bipolar disorder. Those who treated their diabetes with oral medications decreased their risk.[29] Thus, maintaining a healthy weight and normal blood sugars may be beneficial lifestyle measures that help prevent mood disorders.

An excess of thyroid disease has been found in bipolar patients, namely 26.9 percent of females and 5.7 percent of males.[30] Although both lithium and carbamazepine can cause hypothyroidism, even bipolar persons never exposed to those medications had a 9 percent rate of hypothyroidism compared with 3 percent of the general population.[31] Hypothyroidism in bipolar persons has been associated with more depressive symptoms and poorer response to treatment, and to rapid cycling. Some studies have linked mania to hyperthyroidism.[32]

Primary hypothyroidism, characterized by low levels of circulating thyroid hormones such as triiodothyronine and thyroxine, shows up with cold intolerance, lethargy and hypersomnia, weight gain, dry skin, irritability, and depression. Subclinical hypothyroidism has normal levels of circulating thyroid hormones, but elevated TSH released from the pituitary. Tertiary hypothyroidism is characterized by an excessive release of TSH in response to TRH (thyrotropin releasing hormone). All these levels of hypothyroidism can cause the problems of rapid cycling and treatment resistance described in the paragraph above.

Migraine headaches have been associated with bipolar disorder. A prevalence of 24.8 percent in bipolar persons compares with 10.3 percent in the general population. The prevalence in females is about twice that in males.[33] Valproate, which acts as a mood stabilizer, has also been used as a migraine preventative.

Besides the disorders associated with bipolar, there are some very positive associations. Artistic achievement and creativity abound in persons with bipolar disorder and in their relatives. Persons with bipolar disorder have made important contributions in the literary arts (e.g., Ernest Hemingway and Edgar Allan Poe), visual arts (e.g., Van Gogh and Edvard Munch), and music (e.g., Robert Schumann). This connection is described in detail in Jamison's book, *Touched with Fire*.[34] During hypomania and mania thoughts flow swiftly, concepts may be associated in novel ways, and senses may be more acute. In depression people may view relationships and losses in new and poignant ways that inspire artistic creation. Many memorable songs and poems have been written as a way to express and cope with profound sadness.

• 13 •

Bipolar Youth

$\mathcal{I}$n the mid-twentieth century psychiatrists thought that mood disorders such as major depression and bipolar were rare in children and youth, but research in the late twentieth and early twenty-first centuries has exploded that myth.

The median age of onset for bipolar mood disorder ranges in various studies from the late teens to the early twenties. More recent studies from 1990 to 2006 showed that the commonest age of onset for bipolar symptoms was fifteen to nineteen. The next most common were ten to fourteen and twenty to twenty-four. Most bipolar adults recall symptoms starting before age nineteen. Fifteen to 28 percent recall symptoms before age thirteen. Often these early symptoms were not recognized as being part of a bipolar syndrome at the time.[1] One recent study found that 1.8 percent of youth aged seven to eighteen had bipolar disorder.[2]

Since early in the twentieth century every generation has had a higher incidence and an earlier onset of bipolar disorder and unipolar depression. This pattern is referred to as "anticipation" in the world of genetics. We see this anticipation through successive generations in Huntington's disease, where each succeeding generation has more copies of a mutated gene leading to increased "penetrance" in geneticists' lingo. However, this does not appear to be the mechanism for anticipation in mood disorders; the cause of this anticipation eludes us.[3]

The symptoms of bipolar disorder in youth are really the same as those in adults with a few exceptions. For example, in cyclothymic disorder a youth must be symptomatic for only one year as opposed to two years for the adult diagnosis. In youth, irritability occurs much

143

more often than elation or euphoria during manic phases. Preteens with bipolar disorder often get a diagnosis of bipolar disorder, unspecified, because their illness does not meet full criteria for bipolar I or II. Often the episodes of hypomania or mania have only a few symptoms or they are of too short a duration. By the time they are teens, many of these individuals have had episodes that meet criteria for bipolar I and II. These are often accompanied by substance abuse and suicide attempts.[4]

Once it was established that bipolar disorder did occur in youth, the pendulum swung the other way with an overdiagnosis of bipolar disorder. The rate of diagnosis of bipolar disorder among youth increased fortyfold between 1994 and 2003.[5] The latest edition of the American Psychiatric Association's *Diagnostic and Statistical Manual* (*DSM-5*) contained an attempt to correct that overdiagnosis. Disruptive mood dysregulation disorder (DMDD) was a new diagnosis that attempted to capture many of the youth being misdiagnosed as bipolar. This new diagnosis was characterized by a mood state of chronic irritability punctuated by episodes of anger outbursts. DMDD starts earlier than age ten and must be present for at least one year before it can be diagnosed. Anger outbursts, verbal or physical, which are out of proportion to environmental triggers, occur an average of three times a week or more. To further differentiate it from bipolar disorder, there should be no hypomanic symptoms like euphoria or grandiosity lasting more than one day.

Symptoms of DMDD often overlap strongly with symptoms of ADHD and oppositional defiant disorder (ODD) in youth. Young people with DMDD did not tend to have the strong family history of bipolar disorder found in the truly bipolar youth. Also, as they were followed over time, they did not show clear patterns of highs and depressions interspersed among more neutral mood states that would characterize the bipolar disorder. Rather, they manifested a chronic irritability and brief episodes of anger—not the typical manic periods that would last for days to weeks in which youth might be more irritable and then return back to baseline.[6]

Making a diagnosis among youth still tends to be challenging. Disorders such as ADHD or ODD can look much like a bipolar disorder in a snapshot of time. Hyperactivity observed in speech and motor behavior, impulsivity, and increased irritability may occur in both ADHD and bipolar. The long-term picture is what differentiates these two. ADHD symptoms are chronic, while bipolar mood disorder symptoms are episodic, with any such manic or mixed periods fading away into a neutral mood or into a depression. In depression one often sees a picture opposite from mania with reduced activity, decreased speech and motor movements, and social withdrawal. Manic symptoms such as euphoria, grandiosity, and decreased need for sleep (not just insomnia) occur in the bipolar child, but not in ADHD, ODD, or DMDD.

Other disorders that may be mistaken for bipolar among youth include substance abuse and substance-induced mood disorders. As discussed in chapter 11, Secondary Mania and Late-Onset Bipolar Disorder, abuse of stimulant drugs or therapeutic doses of other drugs, such as corticosteroids, could present with a picture similar to mania.

A first psychotic episode occurring in youth and young adults can be sometimes hard to clearly classify as bipolar or schizophrenic. In a snippet of time they both manifest hallucinations, agitation, delusions, and sleeplessness. The picture over time aids diagnosis: bipolar patients recover more often to their previous baseline level of social, academic, and workplace functioning. Young people with schizophrenia retain residual symptoms of social withdrawal, apathy, and anhedonia (loss of pleasure). Schizophrenics sometimes show chronic psychotic symptoms such as hearing voices and entertaining delusional thoughts, and also may manifest a noticeable thought disorder, so that their conversations ramble and do not follow a coherent line of reasoning.

What makes matters even more complex is that bipolar youth may also have other psychiatric disorders such as ADHD, ODD, anxiety disorders, and substance abuse. Several disorders may be lived with at once. Some studies have estimated the rate of ADHD among preadolescent bipolar youth at 70–95 percent, and 50 percent among adolescent youth. Conduct disorder and ODD rates are as high as 79 percent among bipolar youth. Anxiety disorders occur along with bipolar in 77 percent of bipolar youth. Autism spectrum disorders occur in about 20 percent of bipolar youth.[7] Thirty-two percent of bipolar teens have a substance abuse problem, compared with seven percent of their nonbipolar age mates.[8] Bipolar youth who also have a conduct disorder are more likely to abuse drugs.

In bipolar disorder, as with many disorders having a strong genetic component, persons with an earlier onset of the disorder tend to have a more severe form of the disorder. Getting an accurate diagnosis for a youngster helps mobilize the right treatments to prevent the malignant progression of the disorder. Depressions that occur at an early age or have a sudden onset, a recurrent pattern, or associated psychotic symptoms are suggestive of bipolar disorder.[9] A depression occurs as the first mood episode in about twice as many bipolar youth as does a first manic episode. These young people may be mistakenly diagnosed with unipolar depression until the first manic symptoms are recognized.

Most pharmaceutical company trials of new medications are done with relatively healthy adults of young and middle age. They purposely avoid children, the elderly, and pregnant women. The FDA has incentivized pharmaceutical companies to do some studies in youth. Thus, we do have a number of FDA-approved medications for treating young people in all phases of bipolar mood disorder.

The FDA has approved lithium for treating bipolar youth over age twelve in the manic phase. Recent studies showed lithium to be effective and well tolerated in that age group, although with some bothersome nausea and vomiting. Other mood stabilizers have not fared as well. Valproate (Depakote) while showing good results in one study, failed to outperform placebo in another. Oxcarbazepine (Trileptal) also did not outperform placebo. Carbamazepine (Tegretol) had not been formally tested in acute adolescent mania.[10]

The FGA chlorpromazine and the SGAs olanzapine (Zyprexa), risperidone (Risperdal), aripiprazole (Abilify), asenapine (Saphris), and quetiapine (Seroquel) have all been FDA approved for treatment of acute mania in teens.[11] The SGAs act more rapidly than lithium and in at least one comparison study risperidone by itself was more effective than lithium. They do tend to have side effects of somnolence and sedation, headaches, dizziness, and fatigue. Increased appetite and weight gain occurred with SGAs, but was very limited with aripiprazole. Ziprasidone (Geodon), although not FDA approved in adolescents, reduced manic symptoms, but did not seem to cause weight gain in some studies. As with adults, olanzapine tended to be the worst metabolic offender, with more weight gain and elevations of fasting blood sugar and cholesterol.

The olanzapine/fluoxetine combination (OFC) is approved by the FDA for treating bipolar depression in the ten-to-seventeen age range. Possible side effects include somnolence, sedation, tremor, increased appetite, weight gain, increased cholesterol, and increased heart rate.

Lurasidone tested at doses from 20 to 80 mg/day has been recently approved by the FDA as well for treating bipolar depression in ages ten to seventeen. Side effects of nausea and somnolence were well tolerated. Lurasidone (Latuda) should be taken along with food to enhance absorption. Quetiapine (Seroquel) failed in one study to outperform placebo for bipolar depression in adolescents.

In studies of maintenance drugs for bipolar youth, lithium and valproate did similarly well. Aripiprazole was effective, but caused some weight gain. Lamotrigine, when added to other drugs in ten-to-seventeen-year-olds, did not enhance protection against relapse, although in those thirteen to seventeen it did.[12]

Psychotherapy in the form of cognitive-behavioral therapy and interpersonal and social rhythm therapy have been helpful for some youth. Family-focused psychotherapy would seem an appropriate therapy for bipolar youth, and indeed adolescent studies have indicated significant benefits from this treatment.

Family-focused therapy for bipolar adolescents was developed by two psychologists: Drs. David Miklowitz and Michael Goldstein. The goals of treatment are to help the patient and her family accept the disorder and the need for medication treatment, and to improve family functioning and avoid relapses.[13]

About twelve to twenty-one sessions are held over four to nine months. The first sessions are psychoeducational. The patient and family learn about the symptoms, course, and treatment of bipolar disorder. The learning is personalized so that patients and family identify what particular stressors may destabilize the patients and what coping strategies have helped in the past. They identify warning signs of relapse (e.g., insomnia or increased irritability). The therapist conveys information about good sleep hygiene and how to do mood charting.

Communication enhancement training characterizes the next group of sessions. Patient and family learn active listening techniques and how to communicate clearly. They learn to express positive feelings and to make requests for change in a positive fashion. They learn to express negative feelings about particular behaviors, rather than denigrating the person showing those behaviors.

A final phase involves learning problem-solving skills. The family may identify a problem and brainstorm multiple possible solutions. They then learn to focus in on a few solutions and look at the pros and cons of those solutions before making a final decision. They learn to compliment each other on their work in solving family problems.

Several formal research studies compared family-focused therapy (FFT) as described above with control conditions such as three family psychoeducational meetings. Generally, the FFT groups showed fewer relapses and faster recovery from depression. The effect was especially seen in those families that showed "high expressed emotion" coming into the study.

High expressed emotion families may show high levels of criticism, emotional overinvolvement, and/or hostility. Some such families were overprotective or highly critical. This high expressed emotion has proved to be a risk factor for faster relapse among bipolar youth. Previous research with families of schizophrenic patients had shown similar findings.

Psychotherapy in some form, whether individual, group, or family, is strongly recommended for any youth with bipolar disorder. Young people are more susceptible to drug side effects from the SGAs than adults, so keeping the number and dosage of drugs at the lowest effective level is important. Psychotherapy can give them skills to cope with what is unfortunately a lifelong disorder.

Eight Steps toward Stability

1. Accept having the disorder. If there is uncertainty, get an expert opinion.
2. Find knowledgeable providers with whom you can work comfortably. This may be just a psychiatrist or psychiatric nurse practitioner. It may include a therapist such as a psychologist or social worker. Sometimes a primary care physician may prescribe medications for bipolar disorder.
3. Scrupulously follow prescribed regimens for medications and laboratory tests. If side effects or bipolar symptoms occur between appointments, contact your prescriber before changing your regimen.
4. Avoid substance abuse, which typically leads to increased relapses. This includes alcohol, prescription drugs, street drugs like cocaine or heroin, and marijuana. It is possible some derivatives of the cannabis sativa plant may provide a benefit for bipolar patients, but current evidence finds smoking marijuana to be a risk factor for relapse.
5. Pursue a health-giving lifestyle with exercise, healthful diet and sleep patterns, and a supportive social network. This helps to minimize relapses.
6. Become knowledgeable about bipolar disorder. Books like this, websites, and support groups such as the National Alliance on Mental Illness and the Depressive and Bipolar Support Alliance can help.
7. Select at least one family member, significant other, or friend to be aware of your bipolar disorder and to help out when needed. For example, that person might call your doctor or drive you to

an emergency room when you are experiencing a severe mood episode.

8. Have a contingency plan to enact if you experience severe or suicidal depression or a manic episode when your judgment becomes impaired. This may include contacting your regular mental health provider or emergency personnel. It may include contacting trusted family members, friends, or clergy to help you to access care. Police can often help, if needed, in transport to an emergency room.

Norm (remember him from chapter 2?) did not hit it off with the first psychiatrist he consulted. He really liked the second one, who seemed both knowledgeable and easy to talk with. He, like the first psychiatrist, confirmed Norm's diagnosis of bipolar II disorder and a cluster of substance use disorders. His moods stabilized considerably on a regimen of lamotrigine and lithium. He rarely missed a dose and he got his labs drawn when the psychiatrist asked him to. He still had some noticeable mood swings, but they were much milder. He could still go to work on the depressed days. He had learned some effective coping skills to use on the days he was depressed.

He had seen a psychologist recommended by his psychiatrist for a while. Norm's treatment combined elements of interpersonal and social rhythm therapy and cognitive-behavioral therapy. He made it a point to get enough sleep, to eat regular healthy meals, and to exercise. He had even dropped a few pounds despite being on lithium. He enjoyed not only the exercise aspects of his aerobics class, but the camaraderie of the other participants. He slept great those nights that followed the exercise class. He attended biweekly meetings of a bipolar support group and a weekly Alcoholics Anonymous group just for men. Norm had read two paperback books about bipolar disorder and one about addictions. He now had a significant other, Lois, a woman who seemed understanding and supportive. Norm had brought her to a session with his psychiatrist and agreed that if he were "going off the deep end" Lois could call the psychiatrist. Accepting his disorder and working his treatment plan had made a tremendous improvement in his life.

Notes

CHAPTER 1: INTRODUCTION

1. Kenneth S. Lynn, *Hemingway* (New York: Simon & Schuster, 1987), 427, as quoted in Christopher D. Martin, "Ernest Hemingway: A Psychological Autopsy of a Suicide," *Psychiatry* 69, no. 4 (2006): 353.

2. Carlos Baker, *Hemingway: A Life Story* (New York: Charles Scribner's Sons, 1969), 137, as quoted in Christopher D. Martin, "Ernest Hemingway: A Psychological Autopsy of a Suicide," *Psychiatry* 69, no. 4 (2006): 354.

3. Michael Reynolds, *Hemingway: The Paris Years* (Oxford, UK: Basil Blackwell, 1989), 194, as quoted in Christopher D. Martin, "Ernest Hemingway: A Psychological Autopsy of a Suicide," *Psychiatry* 69, no. 4 (2006): 354.

4. Carlos Baker, ed., *Ernest Hemingway: Selected Letters: 1917–1961* (New York: Charles Scribner's Sons, 1981), 435–36, as quoted in Christopher D. Martin, "Ernest Hemingway: A Psychological Autospy of a Suicide," *Psychiatry* 68, no. 4 (2006): 354.

5. Aaron Edward Hotchner, *Papa Hemingway* (New York: Random House, 1966), 139, as quoted in Christopher D. Martin, "Ernest Hemingway: A Psychological Autopsy of a Suicide," *Psychiatry* 69, no. 4 (2006): 358–59.

6. Christopher D. Martin, "Ernest Hemingway: A Psychological Autopsy of a Suicide," *Psychiatry* 69, no.4 (2006): 360.

7. Ibid., 366.

CHAPTER 2: WHAT IS BIPOLAR DISORDER?

1. Frederick K. Goodwin and Kay Redfield Jamison, *Manic-Depressive Illness: Bipolar Disorder and Recurrent Depression*, 2nd ed. (New York: Oxford University Press, 2007), 3–4.

2. Walter A. Brown, *Lithium: A Doctor, a Drug, and a Breakthrough* (New York: Liveright, 2019), 3–4.

3. Ibid., 1–2.

4. Goodwin and Jamison, *Manic-Depressive Illness*, 5.

5. Brown, *Lithium*, 5.

6. Goodwin and Jamison, *Manic-Depressive Illness*, 7–8.

7. Ibid., 8–9.

8. *Diagnostic and Statistical Manual of Mental Disorders*, 5th ed. (Arlington, VA: American Psychiatric Association, 2013).

9. Goodwin and Jamison, *Manic-Depressive Illness*, 13.

10. Ibid., 7.

11. Ibid., 7.

12. Ibid., 95.

13. Peter Dome, Zoltan Rihmer, and Xenia Gonda, "Suicide Risk in Bipolar Disorder: A Brief Review," *Medicina (Kaunas)* 55, no. 8 (August 2019): 403, doi:10.3390/medicina55080403.

14. Terrence A. Ketter, Shefali Miller, and Po W. Wang, "Diagnosis and Treatment of Bipolar Disorder," in *Advances in Treatment of Bipolar Disorders*, ed. Terrence A. Ketter (Washington, DC: American Psychiatric Publishing, 2015), 4.

15. Goodwin and Jamison, *Manic-Depressive Illness*, 126.

16. Mary L. Phillips and David J. Kupfer, "Bipolar Disorder Diagnosis: Challenges and Future Directions," *Lancet* 381, no. 9878 (May 2013): 1664–66.

17. Goodwin and Jamison, *Manic-Depressive Illness*, 21.

18. Ibid., 134.

19. L. Lewis, "A Consumer Perspective Concerning the Diagnosis and Treatment of Bipolar Disorder," *Biological Psychiatry* 48 (2000): 442–44.

20. Goodwin and Jamison, *Manic-Depressive Illness*, 133.

21. Ibid., 128.

22. T. A. Wearne and J. L. Cornish, "A Comparison of Methamphetamine-Induced Psychosis and Schizophrenia: A Review of Positive, Negative and Cognitive Symptomatology," *Frontiers in Psychiatry* 9 (October 2018): 491, doi: 10.3389/fpsyt.2018.00491.

23. S. N. Ghaemi et al., "Bipolar or Borderline: A Clinical Overview," *Acta Psychiatrica Scandinavica* 130, no. 2 (August 2014): 99–108.

24. Goodwin and Jamison, *Manic-Depressive Illness*, 150.

25. Adauto S. Clemente et al., "Bipolar Disorder Prevalence: A Systematic Review and Meta-Analysis of the Literature," *Brazilian Journal of Psychiatry* 37, no. 2 (April–June 2015): 155, doi: 10.1590/1516-4446-2012-1693.

26. Ana Lucia R. Moreira et al., "Review and Meta-Analysis of Epidemiologic Studies of Adult Bipolar Disorder," *Journal of Clinical Psychiatry* 78, no. 9 (November–December 2017): 1259, doi: 10.4088/JCP.16r11165.

CHAPTER 3: WHAT CAUSES BIPOLAR DISORDER?

1. Keri Martinowich, Robert J. Schloesser, and Husseini K, Manji, "Bipolar Disorder: From Genes to Behavior Pathways," *Focus* 9, no. 4 (Fall 2011): 527–29; Anna Manelis, Adriane M. Soehner, and Mary L. Phillips, "Functional Brain Imaging and Neural Determinants in Bipolar II Disorder," in *Bipolar II Disorder: Recognition, Understanding, and Treatment*, ed. Holly A. Swartz and Trisha Suppes (Washington, DC: American Psychiatric Publishing, 2019), 143–45.

2. Kenneth I. Shulman, "Disinhibition Syndromes, Secondary Mania and Bipolar Disorder in Old Age," *Journal of Affective Disorders* 46, no. 3 (December 1997): 175–82.

3. Manelis, Soehner, and Phillips, "Functional Brain Imaging," 143–45.

4. Ibid., 158.

5. Husseini K. Manji et al., "The Underlying Neurobiology of Bipolar Disorder," *World Psychiatry* 2, no. 3 (October 2003): 137–41.

6. Ibid., 141–44.

7. Frederick K. Goodwin and Kay Redfield Jamison, *Manic-Depressive Illness: Bipolar Disorder and Recurrent Depression,* 2nd ed. (New York: Oxford University Press, 2007), 421–22.

8. Jennifer H. Barnett and Jordan W. Smoller, "The Genetics of Bipolar Disorder," *Neuroscience* 164, no. 1 (November 2009): 332–33.

9. Kathleen R. Merikangas et al., "Lifetime and 12-Month Prevalence of Bipolar Spectrum Disorder in the National Comorbidity Survey Replication," *Archives of General Psychiatry* 64, no. 5 (May 2007): 543.

10. Goodwin and Jamison, *Manic-Depressive Illness*, 415.

11. Melvin McInnis, "Genetics of Bipolar II Disorder," in *Bipolar II Disorder: Recognition, Understanding, and Treatment*, ed. Holly A. Swartz and Trisha Suppes (Washington, DC: American Psychiatric Publishing, 2019), 124–31.

12. Ming-Xin Tang et al., "The APOE-Epsilon4 Allele and the Risk of Alzheimer Disease among African Americans, Whites, and Hispanics," *Journal of the American Medical Association* 279, no. 10 (March 1998): 751.

13. Barnett and Smoller, "Genetics of Bipolar Disorder," 333–34.

14. Stuart Watson et al., "Childhood Trauma in Bipolar Disorder," *Australian and New Zealand Journal of Psychiatry* 48, no. 6 (June 2014): 564.

15. Jessica Agnew-Blais and Andrea Danese, "Childhood Maltreatment and Unfavourable Clinical Outcomes in Bipolar Disorder: Systematic Review and Meta-Analysis," *Lancet Psychiatry* 3, no. 4 (April 2016): 342.

16. Michael T. Compton and Ruth S. Shim, "The Social Determinants of Mental Health," *Focus* 13, no. 4 (Fall 2015): 420–23.

17. David J. Miklowitz, *The Bipolar Disorder Survival Guide*, 2nd ed. (New York: Guilford Press, 2019), 113; Sheri L. Johnson et al.,"Life Events as Predictors of Mania and Depression in Bipolar I Disorder," *Journal of Abnormal Psychology* 117, no. 2 (May 2008): 268.

18. Susan C. Sonne, Kathleen Brady, and W. Alexander Morton, "Substance Abuse and Bipolar Affective Disorder," *Journal of Nervous and Mental Disease* 182, no. 6 (June 1994): 349.

19. A. Eden Evans et al., "Does Using Marijuana Increase the Risk for Developing Schizophrenia?" *Journal of Clinical Psychiatry* 74, no. 4 (April 2013): e08.

20. Jean Lud Cadet and Mark Gold, "Methamphetamine-Induced Psychosis: Who Says All Drug Use Is Reversible?" *Current Psychiatry* 16, no. 11 (November 2017): 16–17.

21. Lin Ye et al., "Genome Editing Using CRISPR-Cas9 to Create the HPFH Genotype in HSPCs: An Approach for Treating Sickle Cell Disease and Beta-Thalassemia," *Proceedings of the National Academy of Science USA* 113, no. 38 (September 2016): 10661.

CHAPTER 4: SETTING A HEALTHY BASELINE

1. Thomas A. Wehr, David A. Sack, and Norman E. Rosenthal, "Sleep Reduction as a Final Common Pathway in the Genesis of Mania," *American Journal of Psychiatry* 144, no. 2 (February 1987): 201.

2. David J. Miklowitz and Michel J. Gitlin, "Psychosocial Approaches to the Treatment of Bipolar Disorder," *Focus* 13, no. 1 (Winter 2015): 42.

3. Gregg D. Jacobs, *Say Good Night to Insomnia* (New York: Henry Holt and Company, 2009).

4. Simon Evans and Paul Burghardt, "Exercise, Nutrition, and Treatment Resistant Depression," in *Treatment Resistant Depression*, ed. John F. Greden, Michelle B. Riba, and Melvin G. McInnis (Washington, DC: American Psychiatric Publishing, 2011), 240–43; Mirko Wegner et al., "Effects of Exercise on Anxiety and Depression Disorders: Review of Meta-Analyses and Neuro-

biological Mechanisms," *CNS & Neurological Disorders—Drug Targets* 13, no. 6 (2014): 1002.

5. World Health Organization Guidelines at https://www.who.int/diet physicalactivity/physical-activity-recommendations-18-64years.pdf.

6. Katrina L. Piercy et al., "The Physical Activity Guidelines for Americans," *Journal of the American Medical Association* 320, no. 19 (November 2018): 2020.

7. John L. Beyer and Martha E. Payne, "Nutrition and Bipolar Depression," *Psychiatric Clinics of North America* 39, no. 1 (March 2016): 75.

8. Ibid., 77–79.

9. Pedro L. Delgado et al., "Serotonin Function and the Mechanism of Antidepressant Action: Reversal of Antidepressant-Induced Remission by Rapid Depletion of Plasma Tryptophan," *Archives of General Psychiatry* 47 (1990): 411.

10. Rodrigo B. Mansur and Roger S. McIntyre, "Metabolic Comorbidity and Physical Health Implications for Bipolar Disorder," *Focus* 13, no. 1 (Winter 2015): 12.

11. Evans and Burghardt, "Exercise, Nutrition, and Treatment," 245–46.

12. Simona Noaghiul and Joseph R. Hibbein, "Cross-National Comparisons of Seafood Consumption and Rates of Bipolar Disorders," *American Journal of Psychiatry* 160, no. 2 (December 2003): 2222.

13. Evans and Burghardt, "Exercise, Nutrition, and Treatment," 247.

14. Jerome Sarris, David Mischoulon, and Isaac Schweitzer, "Omega-3 for Bipolar Disorder: Meta-Analysis of Use in Mania and Bipolar Depression," *Journal of Clinical Psychiatry* 73, no. 1 (2012): 81.

15. Paul Montgomery and Alexandra J. Richardson, "Omega-3 Fatty Acids for Bipolar Disorder," *Cochrane Database for Systematic Reviews* 16, no. 2 (April 2008): CD005169.

16. Beyer and Payne, "Nutrition and Bipolar Depression," 80–81.

17. Isabelle E. Bauer et al., "A Double-Blind, Randomized, Placebo-Controlled Study of Aspirin and N-Acetylcysteine as Adjunctive Treatments for Bipolar Depression," *Journal of Clinical Psychiatry* 80, no. 1 (2013): pii: 18m12200.

18. David Perlmutter and K. Loberg, *Grain Brain: The Surprising Truth about Wheat, Carbs and Sugar—Your Brain's Silent Killers* (New York: Little, Brown, 2013).

19. Maciej Gasior, Michael A. Rogawski, and Adam L. Hartman, "Neuro-Protective and Disease-Modifying Effects of the Ketogenic Diet," *Behavioral Pharmacology* 17, no. 5–6 (September 2006): 431.

20. James R. Phelps, Susan V. Siemers, and Rif S. El-Mallakh, "The Ketogenic Diet for Type II Bipolar Disorder," *Neurocase* 19, no. 5 (2013): 4323.

21. Martha Clare Morris et al., "MIND Diet Slows Cognitive Decline with Aging," *Alzheimers and Dementia* 11, no. 9 (June 2015): 1015.

22. Frederick K. Goodwin and Kay Redfield Jamison, *Manic-Depressive Illness: Bipolar Disorder and Recurrent Depression*, 2nd ed. (New York: Oxford University Press, 2007), 225–27.

23. Jean Lud Cadet and Mark Gold, "Methamphetamine-Induced Psychosis: Who Says All Drug Use Is Reversible?" *Current Psychiatry* 16, no. 11 (November 2017): 16–18.

24. Stephen T. Chermack, John M. Wyrobeck, and Frederick C. Blow, "Substance Abuse among Older Adults with Bipolar Disorder," in *Bipolar Disorder in Late Life*, ed. Martha Sajatovic and Frederick C. Blow (Baltimore: Johns Hopkins University Press, 2007), 148–51; Michael J. Ostacher, "Bipolar and Substance Use Disorder Comorbidity: Diagnostic and Treatment Considerations," *Focus* 9, no. 4 (Fall 2011): 429–30.

25. Susan L. McElroy et al., "Axis I Psychiatric Comorbidity and Its Relationship to Historical Illness Variables in 288 Patients with Bipolar Disorder," *American Journal of Psychiatry* 158, no. 3 (March 2001): 420–26.

26. Goodwin and Jamison, *Manic-Depressive Illness*, 230–31.

27. Melanie Gibbs et al., "Cannabis Use and Mania Symptoms: A Systematic Review and Meta-Analysis," *Journal of Affective Disorders* 171, no. 15 (January 2015): 39.

28. I. Zorilla et al., "Cannabis and Bipolar Disorder: Does Quitting Cannabis Use during Manic/Mixed Episode Improve Clinical/Functional Outcomes?" *Acta Psychiatrica Scandinavica* 131, no. 2 (February 2015): 100.

29. S. Van Gerpen, T. Vik, and T. J. Soundy, "Medicinal and Recreational Marijuana: What Are the Risks?" *South Dakota Medicine* (2015): 58.

30. Samuel T. Wilkinson, Elina Stefanovics, and Robert A. Rosenheck, "Marijuana Use Is Associated with Worse Outcomes in Symptom Severity and Violent Behavior in Patients with PTSD," *Journal of Clinical Psychiatry* 76, no. 9 (September 2015): 1174.

31. Marja Kaunonen, Marja-Terttu Tarrka, Marita Paunonen, and Pekka Laippala, "Grief and Social Support after the Death of a Spouse," *Journal of Advanced Nursing* 30, no. 6 (December 2001): 1304.

CHAPTER 5: TREATMENT OF
MANIA AND MIXED STATES

1. Susan G. Simpson and Corinne L. Reid, "Therapeutic Alliance in Video-Conferencing Psychotherapy: A Review," *Australian Journal of Rural Health* 22, no. 6 (December 2014): 280.

2. Kevin M. McKay, Zac E. Imel, and Bruce E. Wampold, "Psychiatrist Effects in the Psychopharmacological Treatment of Depression," *Journal of Affective Disorders* 92, no. 2–3 (June 2006): 287; Philip Kaminstein, "Importance of the Transference and Therapeutic Alliance in Pharmacotherapy," *American Journal of Psychiatry* 78, no. 4 (March 1989): 404–5.

3. John Cade, "Lithium Salts in the Treatment of Psychotic Excitement," *Bulletin of the World Health Organization* 78, no. 4 (1949): 518–20.

4. Walter A. Brown, *Lithium: A Doctor, a Drug, and a Breakthrough* (New York: Liveright),14–22.

5. Ibid., 49–53.

6. Ibid., 53–55.

7. Ibid., 55–56.

8. Ibid., 56–59.

9. Francesco Bartoli, "Allopurinol as Add-On Treatment for Mania Symptoms in Bipolar Disorder: Systematic Review and Meta-Analysis of Randomized Controlled Trials," *British Journal of Psychiatry* 210, no. 1 (January 2017): 10.

10. Brown, *Lithium*, 32–33.

11. Ibid., 40–44.

12. Ibid., 61–64, 72–73.

13. Ibid., 72.

14. Ibid., 90–92.

15. Ibid., 93–95.

16. Ibid., 101–104.

17. Ibid., 105–11.

18. Ibid., 112.

19. Alan F. Schatzberg and Charles DeBattista, *Manual of Clinical Psychopharmacology*, 8th ed. (Washington, DC: American Psychiatric Publishing, 2015), 346.

20. Ibid., 335–36.

21. Ibid., 329–36.

22. Charles Bowden, "Valproate in Mania," in *Bipolar Medications: Mechanisms of Action*, ed. Husseini K. Manji, Charles L. Bowden, and Robert H. Belmaker (Washington, DC: American Psychiatric Publishing, 2000), 357–65.

23. Robert G. Fawcett, "Dose-Related Thrombocytopenia and Macrocytic Anemia Associated with Valproate Use in Bipolar Disorder," *Journal of Clinical Psychiatry* 58, no. 3 (March 1997): 125.

24. Robert G. Fawcett, "Erythema Multiforme Major in a Patient Treated with Carbamazepine," *Journal of Clinical Psychiatry* 48, no. 10 (October 1987): 416–17.

25. Terence A. Ketter and Po W. Wang, "Mood Stabilizers and Antipsychotics: Pharmacokinetics, Drug Interactions, Adverse Effects, and Administration,"

in *Handbook of Diagnosis and Treatment of Bipolar Disorders,* ed. Terence A. Ketter (Washington, DC: American Psychiatric Publishing, 2010): 533–35.

26. Ibid., 526–33.

27. Schatzberg and DeBattista, *Manual of Clinical Psychopharmacology,* 379–80.

28. Terence A. Ketter and Po W. Wang, "Overview of Pharmacotherapy for Bipolar Disorders," in *Handbook of Diagnosis and Treatment of Bipolar Disorders,* ed. Terence A. Ketter (Washington, DC: American Psychiatric Publishing, 2010): 90–92.

29. Ibid., 262–74.

30. Christopher U. Correll, "Epidemiology and Prevention of Tardive Dyskinesia," *Journal of Clinical Psychiatry* 78, no. 9 (November–December 2017): e1426, doi: 10.4088/JCPO.tv17016x1c.

31. Robert A. Hauser et al., "KINECT 3: A Phase 3 Randomized, Double-Blind, Placebo-Controlled Trial of Valbenazine for Tardive Dyskinesia," *American Journal of Psychiatry* 174, no. 5 (May 2017): 476.

32. Richard C. Josiassen et al., "Long-Term Safety and Tolerability of Valbenazine (NBI-98854) in Subjects with Tardive Dyskinesia and a Diagnosis of Schizophrenia or Mood Disorder," *Psychopharmacology Bulletin* 47, no. 3 (August 2017): 61.

33. Schatzberg and DeBattista, *Manual of Clinical Psychopharmacology,* 269.

34. Vladimir Lerner et al., "Vitamin B6 Treatment for Tardive Dyskinesia: A Randomized, Double-Blind, Placebo-Controlled, Crossover Study," *Journal of Clinical Psychiatry* 68, no 11 (2007): 1648; Adegoke Oloruntoba Adelufosi, Olukayode Abayomi, and Tunde Massey-Ferguson Ojo, "Pyridoxal 5 Phosphate for Neuroleptic-Induced Tardive Dyskinesia," *Cochrane Database of Systematic Reviews* (April 2015), https://doi.org/10.1002/14651858.CD010501.pub2.

35. Karla Soares-Weiser, Nicola Maayan, and Hanna Bergman, "Vitamin E for Antipsychotic-Induced Tardive Dyskinesia," *Cochrane Database of Systematic Reviews* (January 2018), https://doi:10.1002/14651858.CD000209.pub3.

36. Schatzberg and DeBattista, *Manual of Clinical Psychopharmacology,* 272–74.

37. Dan L. Longo et al., *Harrison's Manual of Medicine,* 18th ed. (New York: McGraw-Hill Medical, 2013), 1329.

38. Terence A. Ketter and Shefali Miller, "Treatment of Acute Manic and Mixed Episodes," in *Advances in Treatment of Bipolar Disorders,* ed. Terence A. Ketter (Washington, DC: American Psychiatric Publishing, 2015), 93.

39. Terence A. Ketter, "Mood Stabilizers and Second-Generation Antipsychotics: Pharmacology, Drug Interactions, Adverse Effects, and Dosing," in *Advances in Treatment of Bipolar Disorders,* ed. Terence A. Ketter (Washington, DC: American Psychiatric Publishing, 2015), 281–82.

40. Ibid., 280–83.

41. Ibid., 283–85.

42. Sukdeb Mukherjee, Harold A. Sackeim, and David B. Schnur, "Electro-convulsive Therapy of Acute Manic Episodes: A Review of 50 Years' Experience," *American Journal of Psychiatry* 151, no. 2 (February 1994): 169.

CHAPTER 6: TREATMENT OF BIPOLAR DEPRESSION

1. Frederick K. Goodwin and Kay Redfield Jamison, *Manic-Depressive Illness: Bipolar Disorder and Recurrent Depression*, 2nd ed. (New York: Oxford University Press, 2007), 145; Lewis L. Judd et al., "The Comparative Clinical Phenotype and Long Term Longitudinal Episode Course of Bipolar I and II: A Clinical Spectrum or Distinct Disorders?" *Journal of Affective Disorders* 73, no. 1–2 (January 2003): 19.

2. Goodwin and Jamison, *Manic-Depressive Illness*, 749–50.

3. Po W. Wang and Terence A. Ketter, "Management of Acute Major Depressive Episodes in Bipolar Disorders," in *Handbook of Diagnosis and Treatment of Bipolar Disorders*, ed. Terence A. Ketter (Washington, DC: American Psychiatric Publishing, 2010), 173–75.

4. Ibid., 175–77.

5. Terence A. Ketter et al., "Treatment of Acute Bipolar Depression," in *Advances in Treatment of Bipolar Disorders*, ed. Terence A. Ketter (Washington, DC: American Psychiatric Publishing, 2015), 32–33.

6. Ibid., 35–38.

7. Martha Sajatovic et al., "Efficacy of Lurasidone in Adults Aged 55 Years and Older with Bipolar Depression," *Journal of Clinical Psychiatry* 77, no. 10 (October 2016): 1324.

8. Suresh Durgam et al., "An 8-Week Randomized, Double-Blind, Placebo-Controlled Evaluation of the Safety and Efficacy of Cariprazine in Patients with Bipolar I Depression," *American Journal of Psychiatry* 173, no. 3 (March 2016): 271–81.

9. Ketter et al., "Treatment of Acute Bipolar Depression," 40.

10. Michelle M. Sidor and Glenda M. MacQueen, "Antidepressants for the Acute Treatment of Bipolar Depression: A Systematic Review and Meta-Analysis," *Journal of Clinical Psychiatry* 72, no. 2 (February 2011): 156.

11. Gustavo H. Vazquez et al.,"Overview of Antidepressant Treatment of Bipolar Depression," *International Journal of Neuropsychopharmacology* 16, no. 7 (August 2013): 1673.

12. Isabella Pacchiarotti et al., "The International Society for Bipolar Disorders (ISBD) Task Force Report on Antidepressant Use in Bipolar Disorders," *American Journal of Psychiatry* 170, no. 11 (November 2013): 1249.

13. Alan F. Schatzberg and Charles DeBattista, *Manual of Clinical Psychopharmacology*, 8th ed. (Washington, DC: American Psychiatric Publishing, 2015), 68–74.

14. Ibid., 146–50.

15. Ketter et al., "Treatment of Acute Bipolar Depression," 44–46.

16. Robert M. Post, "Treatment of Bipolar Depression: Evolving Recommendations," *Psychiatric Clinics of North America* 39, no. 1 (March 2016): 22–23.

17. Jerome Sarris, David Mischoulon, and Isaac Schweitzer, "Omega-3 for Bipolar Disorder: Meta-Analysis of Use in Mania and Bipolar Depression," *Journal of Clinical Psychiatry* 73, no. 1 (January 2012): 81.

18. E. Sherwood Brown and Barry Gabrielson, "A Randomized, Double-Blind, Placebo-Controlled Trial of Citicoline for Bipolar and Unipolar Depression and Methamphetamine Dependance," *Journal of Affective Disorders* 143, no. 1–3 (December 2012): 257–58.

19. Post, "Treatment of Bipolar Depression," 19.

20. Ibid., 21.

21. Ibid., 19.

22. Ellen E. Lee et al., "Ketamine as a Novel Treatment for Major Depressive Disorder and Bipolar Depression: A Systematic Review and Quantitative Meta-Analysis," *General Hospital Psychiatry* 37, no. 2 (March–April 2015): 178.

23. Chittaranjan Andrade, "Ketamine for Depression, 1: Clinical Summary of Issues Related to Efficacy, Adverse Effects, and Mechanisms of Action," *Journal of Clinical Psychiatry* 78, no. 4 (2017): e415-19.

24. Tayla McCloud et al., "Ketamine and Other Glutamate Receptor Modulators for Depression in Bipolar Disorder in Adults," *Cochrane Database of Systematic Reviews* (September 2015), doi: 10.1002/14651858.CD011611.pub2.

25. Michael F. Grunebaum et al., "Ketamine vs. Midazolam in Bipolar Depression with Suicidal Thoughts: A Pilot Midazolam-Controlled Randomized Clinical Trial," *Bipolar Disorders* 19, no. 3 (April 2017): 176.

26. Carla M. Canuso et al., "Efficacy and Safety of Intranasal Esketamine for the Rapid Reduction of Symptoms of Depression and Suicidality in Patients at Imminent Risk for Suicide: Results of a Double-Blind, Randomized, Placebo-Controlled Study," *American Journal of Psychiatry* 175, no. 7 (February 2018): 131.

27. Francesco Benedetti et al., "Rapid Treatment Response of Suicidal Symptoms to Lithium, Sleep Deprivation, and Light Therapy (Chronotherapeutics) in Drug-Resistant Bipolar Depression," *Journal of Clinical Psychiatry* 75, no. 2 (February 2014): 133.

28. Dorothy K. Sit et al., "Adjunctive Bright Light Therapy for Bipolar Depression: A Randomized Double-Blind Placebo-Controlled Trial," *American Journal of Psychiatry* 175, no. 2 (February 2018): 131.

29. Joseph C. Wu et al., "Rapid and Sustained Antidepressant Response with Sleep Deprivation and Chronotherapy in Bipolar Disorder," *Biological Psychiatry* 66, no. 3 (August 2009): 298.

30. Stephan F. Taylor et al., "Device-Related Neuromodulation in Treatment Resistant Depression," in *Treatment Resistant Depression*, ed. John F. Greden, Michelle B. Riba, and Melvin G. McInnis (Washington, DC: American Psychiatric Publishing, 2011), 226–28.

31. Alexander McGirr et al., "Clinical Efficacy and Safety of Repetitive Transcranial Magnetic Stimulation in Acute Bipolar Depression," *World Psychiatry* 15, no. 1 (February 2016): 85–86.

32. Clement Donde et al., "Transcranial Direct-Current Stimulation (tDCS) for Bipolar Depression: A Systematic Review and Meta-Analysis," *Progress in Neuro-Psychopharmacology and Biological Psychiatry* 78, no. 1 (August 2017): 123.

33. Bernardo Sampaio-Junior et al., "Efficacy and Safety of Transcranial Direct Current Stimulation as an Add-On Treatment for Bipolar Depression," *JAMA Psychiatry* 75, no. 2 (February 2018): 158.

34. Wang and Ketter, "Management of Acute Major Depressive Episodes," 212–14.

35. Taylor et al., "Device-Related Neuromodulation," 217–19.

36. Helle K. Schoeyen et al., "Treatment-Resistant Bipolar Depression: A Randomized Controlled Trial of Electroconvulsive Therapy versus Algorithm-Based Pharmacological Treatment," *American Journal of Psychiatry* 172, no. 1 (January 2015): 41.

37. Taylor et al., "Device-Related Neuromodulation," 221–22.

38. Ibid., 222–26.

39. Ibid., 226.

40. David J. Miklowitz et al., "Intensive Psychosocial Intervention Enhances Functioning in Inpatients with Bipolar Depression: Results from a 9-Month Randomized Controlled Trial," *American Journal of Psychiatry* 164, no. 9 (2007): 1340.

CHAPTER 7: MAINTENANCE TREATMENT FOR BIPOLAR DISORDER

1. Terence A. Ketter, Po W. Wang, and Jenifer L. Culver, "Multiphase Treatment Strategy for Bipolar Disorder," in *Handbook of Diagnosis and*

Treatment of Bipolar Disorders, ed. Terence A. Ketter (Washington, DC: American Psychiatric Publishing, 2010): 75–77.

2. Martin B. Keller et al., "Bipolar I: A Five-Year Prospective Follow-Up," *Journal of Nervous and Mental Disease* 81, no. 4 (April 1993): 238–45.

3. Emil Kraepelin, *Manic-Depressive Insanity and Paranoia* (Edinburgh: E. & S. Livingstone, 1921), 123.

4. Robert M. Post, "Preventing the Malignant Transformation of Bipolar Disorder," *Journal of the American Medical Association* 319, no. 12 (2018): 1197–98.

5. Robert M. Post and S. R. Weiss, "Sensitization, Kindling, and Anticonvulsants in Mania," *Journal of Clinical Psychiatry* 50, Suppl. (December 1989): 23–30.

6. Robert M. Post, "Epigenetic Basis of Sensitization to Stress, Affective Episodes, and Stimulants: Implications for Illness Progression and Prevention," *Bipolar Disorders* 18, no. 4 (June 2016): 315.

7. Lewis L. Judd et al., "The Long-Term Natural History of the Weekly Symptomatic Status of Bipolar I Disorder," *Archives of General Psychiatry* 59, no. 6 (2002): 530.

8. Frederick K. Goodwin and Kay Redfield Jamison, *Manic-Depressive Illness: Bipolar Disorder and Recurrent Depression,* 2nd ed. (New York: Oxford University Press, 2007), 150.

9. Terence A. Ketter, Shefali Miller, and Jenifer Culver, "Bipolar Disorder Preventative Treatment," in *Advances in Treatment of Bipolar Disorders,* ed. Terence A. Ketter (Washington, DC: American Psychiatric Publishing, 2015), 145–48.

10. Guy M. Goodwin et al., "A Pooled Analysis of 2 Placebo-Controlled 18-Month Trials of Lamotrigine and Lithium Maintenance in Bipolar I Disorder," *Journal of Clinical Psychiatry* 65, no. 3 (2004): 432.

11. Terence A. Ketter and Po W. Wang, "Longer-Term Management of Bipolar Disorders," in *Handbook of Diagnosis and Treatment of Bipolar Disorders,* ed. Terence A. Ketter (Washington, DC: American Psychiatric Publishing, 2010), 251.

12. Ibid., 273–75.

13. Chien-Hsiun Chen et al., "Variant GADL1 and Response to Lithium Therapy in Bipolar I Disorder," *New England Journal of Medicine* 370, no. 2 (January 2014): 119.

14. Alan F. Schatzberg and Charles DeBattista, *Manual of Clinical Psychopharmacology,* 8th ed. (Washington, DC: American Psychiatric Publishing, 2015), 329–36.

15. Alan J. Gelenberg et al., "Comparison of Standard and Low Serum Levels of Lithium for Maintenance Treatment of Bipolar Disorder," *New England Journal of Medicine* 321, no. 22 (November 1989): 1489.

16. Terence A. Ketter, "Mood Stabilizers and Second Generation Antipsychotics: Pharmacology, Drug Interactions, Adverse Effects and Dosing," in *Advances in Treatment of Bipolar Disorders*, ed. Terence A. Ketter (Washington, DC: American Psychiatric Publishing, 2015), 251–58.

17. Andrea Cipriani et al., "Lithium in the Prevention of Suicide in Mood Disorders: Updated Systematic Review and Meta-Analysis," *British Medical Journal* 346 (June 2013): f3646.

18. Ross J. Baldessarini et al., "Effects of the Rate of Discontinuing Lithium Maintenance Treatment in Bipolar Disorders," *Journal of Clinical Psychiatry* 57, no. 10 (1996): 441.

19. Ketter, "Mood Stabilizers and Second Generation Antipsychotics," 277–78.

20. Ketter, Miller, and Culver, "Bipolar Disorder Preventative Treatment," 141–45.

21. American Diabetes Association et al., "Consensus Development Conference on Antipsychotic Drugs and Obesity and Diabetes," *Diabetes Care* 27, no. 2 (February 2004): 596–601.

22. Ketter, Miller, and Culver, "Bipolar Disorder Preventative Treatment," 144–45.

23. American Diabetes Association et al., "Consensus Development Conference," 600.

24. Ketter, Miller, and Culver, "Bipolar Disorder Preventative Treatment," 142–44.

25. Ibid., 143–44.

26. Ibid., 145–46.

27. J. R. Geddes et al., "Lithium Plus Valproate Combination Therapy versus Monotherapy for Relapse Prevention in Bipolar I Disorder (BALANCE): A Randomized Open-Label Trial," *Lancet* 375, no. 9712 (January 2010): 385.

28. Ketter, Miller, and Culver, "Bipolar Disorder Preventative Treatment," 145–46.

29. Schatzberg and DeBattista, *Manual of Clinical Psychopharmacology*, 351–53.

30. Ibid., 356–63.

31. Robert G. Fawcett, "Erythema Multiforme Major in a Patient Treated with Carbamazepine," *Journal of Clinical Psychiatry* 48, no. 10 (October 1987): 416–17.

32. S. N. Ghaemi et al., "Long-Term Antidepressant Treatment in Bipolar Disorder: Meta-Analysis of Benefits and Risks," *Acta Psychiatrica Scandinavica* 118, no. 5 (November 2008): 347.

33. Lori Altshuler et al., "Impact of Antidepressant Discontinuation after Acute Bipolar Depression Remission on Rates of Depressive Relapse at 1-Year Follow-Up," *American Journal of Psychiatry* 160, no. 7 (July 2003): 1252.

34. Isabella Pacchiarotti et al., "The International Society for Bipolar Disorders (ISBD) Task Force Report on Antidepressant Use in Bipolar Disorders," *American Journal of Psychiatry* 170, no. 11 (November 2013): 1249–62.

35. Baldessarini et al., "Effects of the Rate of Discontinuing Lithium," 441.

36. Rasmus W. Licht et al., "Lamotrigine versus Lithium as Maintenance Treatment in Bipolar I Disorder: An Open, Randomized Effectiveness Study Mimicking Clinical Practice. The 6th Trial of the Danish University Antidepressant Group (DUAG-6)," *Bipolar Disorders* 12, no. 5 (August 2010): 483.

37. Ketter, Miller, and Culver, "Bipolar Disorder Preventative Treatment," 158–59.

CHAPTER 8: PSYCHOTHERAPY
FOR BIPOLAR DISORDER

1. Frederick K. Goodwin and Kay Redfield Jamison, *Manic-Depressive Illness: Bipolar Disorder and Recurrent Depression*, 2nd ed. (New York: Oxford University Press, 2007), 871.

2. David J. Miklowitz and Michael J. Gitlin, "Psychosocial Approaches to the Treatment of Bipolar Disorder," *Focus* 13, no. 1 (Winter 2015): 38.

3. Gerald L. Klerman and Myrna M. Weissman, *Interpersonal Psychotherapy of Depression* (New York: Basic Books, 1984).

4. Ellen Frank et al., "Two-Year Outcomes for Interpersonal and Social Rhythm Therapy in Individuals with Bipolar I Disorder," *Archives of General Psychiatry* 62 (2005): 996.

5. Miklowitz and Gitlin, "Psychosocial Approaches," 40.

6. Aaron T. Beck et al., *Cognitive Therapy of Depression* (New York: Guilford Press, 1979).

7. Peter McLean, "Behavioral Therapy: Theory and Research," in *Short-Term Psychotherapies for Depression*, ed. A. John Rush (New York: Guilford Press, 1982), 19–45.

8. Miklowitz and Gitlin, "Psychosocial Approaches," 38–39.

9. Ibid., 42.

10. Holly A. Swartz et al., "Psychotherapy Alone and Combined with Medication as Treatments for Bipolar II Depression: A Randomized Controlled Trial," *Journal of Clinical Psychiatry* 79, no. 2 (March–April 2018): 16m11027.

11. T. D. Meyer and M. Hautzinger, "Cognitive Behaviour Therapy and Supportive Therapy for Bipolar Disorders: Relapse Rates for Treatment Period and 2-Year Follow-Up," *Psychological Medicine* 42, no. 7 (July 2012): 1429.

12. Maree L. Inder et al., "Randomized, Controlled Trial of Interpersonal and Social Rhythm Therapy for Young People with Bipolar Disorder," *Bipolar Disorders* 17, no. 2 (October 2014): 128; Maree L. Inder et al., "Three-Year

Follow-Up after Psychotherapy for Young People with Bipolar Disorder," *Bipolar Disorders* (December 2017): 441–47, doi: 10.1111/bdi.12582.

CHAPTER 9: PREGNANCY AND BIPOLAR DISORDER

1. Sabrina J. Kahn et al., "Bipolar Disorder in Pregnancy and Postpartum: Principles of Management, " *Current Psychiatry Reports* 18, no. 2 (February 2016): 13; Adele C. Viguera et al., "Risk of Recurrence in Women with Bipolar Disorder during Pregnancy: Prospective Study of Mood Stabilizer Discontinuation," *American Journal of Psychiatry* 164, no. 12 (December 2007): 1817.

2. Kimberly A. Yonkers et al., "Management of Bipolar Disorder during Pregnancy and the Postpartum Period," *American Journal of Psychiatry* 161, no. 4 (April 2004): 608.

3. Kimberly A. Yonkers, Simone Vigod, and Lori E. Ross, "Diagnosis, Pathophysiology, and Management of Mood Disorders in Pregnant and Postpartum Women," *Obstetrics and Gynecology* 117, no. 4 (April 2011): 961.

4. Robert Boden et al., "Risks of Adverse Pregnancy and Birth Outcomes in Women Treated or Not Treated with Mood Stabilizers for Bipolar Disorder: Population Based Cohort Study," *British Medical Journal* 345 (November 2012): e7085; Marie Rusner, Marie M. Berg, and Cecily C. Begley, "Bipolar Disorder in Pregnancy and Childbirth: A Systematic Review of Outcomes," *BMC Pregnancy Childbirth* 16, no. 1 (October 2016): 331.

5. Terence A. Ketter, Natalie L. Rasgon, and Mytilee Vemuri, "Treatment of Women with Bipolar Disorder," in *Advances in Treatment of Bipolar Disorders*, ed. Terence A. Ketter (Washington, DC: American Psychiatric Publishing, 2015), 204–8.

6. Eydie L. Moses-Kolko et al., "Reproductive-Age Women with Bipolar II Disorder," in *Bipolar II Disorder: Recognition, Understanding, and Treatment*, ed. Holly A. Swartz and Trisha Suppes (Washington, DC: American Psychiatric Publishing, 2019), 276–77.

7. Ketter, Rasgon, and Vemuri, "Treatment of Women with Bipolar Disorder," 204.

8. Lee S. Cohen et al., "A Reevaluation of Risk of in Utero Exposure to Lithium," *Journal of the American Medical Association* 271, no. 2 (January 1994): 146.

9. Yonkers et al., "Management of Bipolar Disorder during Pregnancy," 608–20.

10. Sarah Yacobi and Asher Ornoy, "Is Lithium a Real Teratogen? What Can We Conclude from the Prospective versus Retrospective Studies? A Review," *Israeli Journal of Psychiatry and Related Sciences* 45, no. 2 (2008): 95.

11. Yonkers et al., "Management of Bipolar Disorder during Pregnancy," 608–20.

12. Mogens Schou, "What Happened Later to the Lithium Babies? A Follow-Up Study of Children Born without Malformations," *Acta Psychiatrica Scandinavica* 54, no. 3 (September 1976): 193; N. Margreth van der Lugt et al., "Fetal, Neonatal and Developmental Outcomes of Lithium-Exposed Pregnancies," *Early Human Development* 88, no. 6 (June 2012): 375.

13. L. Forsberg et al., "Maternal Mood Disorders and Lithium Exposure *in Utero* Were Not Associated with Poor Cognitive Development during Childhood," *Acta Paediatrica* 107, no. 8 (November 2017): 1379.

14. Ketter, Rasgon, and Vemuri, "Treatment of Women with Bipolar Disorder," 205–6.

15. Moses-Kolko et al., "Reproductive-Age Women with Bipolar II Disorder," 274.

16. Kenneth Lyons Jones et al., "Pattern of Malformations in the Children of Women Treated with Carbamazepine during Pregnancy," *New England Journal of Medicine* 320 (June 1989): 1661; Franz W. Rosa, "Spina Bifida in Infants of Women Treated with Carbamazepine during Pregnancy," *New England Journal of Medicine* 324 (March 1991): 674.

17. Laurel N. Zappert and Natalie L. Rasgon, "Management of Bipolar Disorders in Women," in *Handbook of Diagnosis and Treatment of Bipolar Disorder*, ed. Terence A. Ketter (Washington, DC: American Psychiatric Publishing, 2010), 440.

18. Ketter, Rasgon, and Vemuri, "Treatment of Women with Bipolar Disorder," 206.

19. Ibid., 205.

20. Chittaranjan Andrade, "Valproate in Pregnancy: Recent Research and Regulatory Responses," *Journal of Clinical Psychiatry* 79, no. 3 (May 2018): pii: 18f12351

21. Moses-Kolko et al., "Reproductive-Age Women with Bipolar II Disorder," 265.

22. Ketter, Rasgon, and Vemuri, "Treatment of Women with Bipolar Disorder," 206.

23. Elizabeth Albertini, Carrie L. Ernst, and Rachel S. Tamaroff, "Psychopharmacological Decision Making in Bipolar Disorder during Pregnancy and Lactation: A Case-by-Case Approach to Using Current Evidence," *Focus* 17, no. 3 (Summer 2019): 251–52.

24. S. X. Poo and M. Agius, "Atypical Antipsychotics for Schizophrenia and/or Bipolar Disorder in Pregnancy: Current Recommendations and Updates in the NICE Guidelines," *Psychiatria Danubina* 27, Suppl. 1 (2015): S255–60.

25. Sarah Tosato et al., "A Systematized Review of Atypical Antipsychotics in Pregnant Women: Balancing Between Risks of Untreated Illness and Risks of Drug-Related Adverse Effects," *Journal of Clinical Psychiatry* 78, no. 5 (May 2017): e477.

26. Krista F. Huybrechts et al., "Antipsychotic Use in Pregnancy and the Risk of Congenital Malformations," *JAMA Psychiatry* 73, no. 9 (September 2016): 938.

27. Yoonyoung Park, et al., "Continuation of Atypical Antipsychotic Medication during Early Pregnancy and the Risk of Gestational Diabetes," *American Journal of Psychiatry* 175, no. 6 (June 2018): 564.

28. Jennifer L. Payne et al., "Familial Aggregation of Postpartum Mood Symptoms in Bipolar Disorder Pedigrees," *Bipolar Disorders* 10, no. 1 (February 2008): 38.

29. Salvatore Gentile, "Prophylactic Treatment of Bipolar Disorder in Pregnancy and Breastfeeding: Focus on Emerging Mood Stabilizers," *Bipolar Disorders* 8, no. 3 (May 2006): 207–20.

30. From the *Medical Letter on Drugs and Therapeutics* quoted in *Journal of the American Medical Association* 322, no. 1 (July 2019): 73.

31. Sophie Grigoriadis et al., "The Effect of Prenatal Antidepressant Exposure on Neonatal Adaptation: A Systematic Review and Meta-Analysis," *Journal of Clinical Psychiatry* 74, no. 4 (April 2013): e309.

32. Keele E. Wurst et al., "First Trimester Paroxetine Use and the Prevalence of Congenital, Specifically Cardiac, Defects: A Meta-Analysis of Epidemiological Studies," *Birth Defects Research Part A: Clinical and Molecular Teratology* 88, no. 3 (September 2009): 159.

33. Ketter, Rasgon, and Vemuri, "Treatment of Women with Bipolar Disorder," 207–8.

34. Moses-Kolko et al., "Reproductive-Age Women with Bipolar II Disorder," 267.

CHAPTER 10: SUICIDE AND BIPOLAR DISORDER

1. Ayal Schaffer and Mark Sinyor, "Suicide and Bipolar II Disorder," in *Bipolar II Disorder: Recognition, Understanding, and Treatment*, ed. Holly A. Swartz and Trisha Suppes (Washington, DC: American Psychiatric Publishing, 2019), 100–101.

2. Kay Redfield Jamison, "Suicide and Manic-Depressive Illness: An Overview and Personal Account," in *The Harvard Medical School Guide to Suicide Assessment and Intervention*, ed. Douglas G. Jacobs (San Francisco: Jossey-Bass, 1999), 252–54.

3. Ayal Schaffer et al., "Epidemiology, Neurobiology and Pharmacological Interventions Related to Suicide Deaths and Suicide Attempts in Bipolar Disorder: Part I of a Report of the International Society for Bipolar Disorders Task Force on Suicide in Bipolar Disorder," *Australia and New Zealand Journal of Psychiatry* 49, no. 9 (September 2015): 785–86.

4. Peter Dome, Zoltan Rihmer, and Xenia Gonda, "Suicide Risk in Bipolar Disorder: A Brief Review," *Medicina (Kaunas)* 55, no. 8 (August 2019): 403.

5. Frederick K. Goodwin and Kay Redfield Jamison, *Manic-Depressive Illness: Bipolar Disorder and Recurrent Depression*, 2nd ed. (New York: Oxford University Press, 2007), 971–75.

6. Terence A. Ketter and Po W. Wang, "Mood Stabilizers and Antipsychotics: Pharmacokinetics, Drug Interactions, Adverse Effects and Administration," in *Handbook of Diagnosis and Treatment of Bipolar Disorders*, ed. Terence A. Ketter (Washington, DC: American Psychiatric Publishing, 2010), 524–25.

7. John L. Beyer and Richard H. Weisler, "Suicide Behaviors in Bipolar Disorder: A Review and Update for the Clinician," *Psychiatric Clinics of North America* 39, no. 1 (March 2016): 117.

8. Ibid., 114–15.

9. Jan Fawcett et al., "Time-Related Predictors of Suicide in Major Affective Disorders," *American Journal of Psychiatry* 147, no. 9 (September 1990): 1189–94.

10. Beyer and Weisler, "Suicide Behaviors in Bipolar Disorder," 113–16.

11. Ibid., 113.

12. Goodwin and Jamison, *Manic-Depressive Illness*, 958.

13. N. Kreitman, "The Coal Gas Story: United Kingdom Suicide Rates," *British Journal of Preventive and Social Medicine* 30, no. 2 (June 1976): 86.

14. David A. Brent et al., "The Presence and Accessibility of Firearms in the Homes of Adolescent Suicides," *Journal of the American Medical Association* 266, no. 21 (December 1991): 2989.

15. Goodwin and Jamison, *Manic-Depressive Illness*, 954.

16. Ibid., 956.

17. Ross J. Baldessarini, Leonardo Tondo, and John Hennen, "Lithium Treatment and Suicide Risk in Major Affective Disorders," *Journal of Clinical Psychiatry* 64, Suppl. 5 (2003): 44.

18. Ross J. Baldessarini and Leonardo Tondo, "Antisuicidal Effect of Lithium Treatment in Major Mood Disorders," in *The Harvard Medical School Guide to Suicide Assessment and Intervention*, ed. Douglas G. Jacobs (San Francisco: Jossey-Bass, 1999), 361–67.

19. Ross J. Baldessarini et al., "Reduced Morbidity after Gradual Discontinuation of Lithium Treatment for Bipolar I and II Disorders: A Replication Study," *American Journal of Psychiatry* 154, no. 4 (April 1997): 551.

20. Frederick K. Goodwin et al., "Suicide Risk in Bipolar Disorder during Treatment with Lithium and Divalproex," *Journal of the American Medical Association* 290, no. 11 (September 2003): 1467.

21. Andrea Cipriani et al., "Lithium in the Prevention of Suicidal Behavior and All-Cause Mortality in Patients with Mood Disorders: A Systematic Review of Randomized Trials," *American Journal of Psychiatry* 162, no. 10 (October 2005): 1805.

22. Alexander M. Walker et al., "Mortality in Current and Former Users of Clozapine," *Epidemiology* 8, no. 6 (November 1997): 671.

23. Antonio Ciapparelli et al., "Clozapine for Treatment-Refractory Schizophrenia, Schizoaffective Disorder, and Psychotic Bipolar Disorder: A 24-Month Naturalistic Study," *Journal of Clinical Psychiatry* 61, no. 5 (May 2000): 329.

CHAPTER 11: SECONDARY MANIA AND LATE-ONSET BIPOLAR DISORDER

1. Robert G. Fawcett, "Cerebral Infarct Presenting as Mania," *Journal of Clinical Psychiatry* 52, no. 8 (August 1991): 352–53.

2. Charles Krauthammer and Gerald L. Klerman, "Secondary Mania: Manic Syndromes Associated with Antecedent Physical Illness or Drugs," *Archives of General Psychiatry* 35, no. 11 (1978): 1333–39.

3. American Psychiatric Association, *Desk Reference to the Diagnostic Criteria from DSM-5* (Washington, DC: American Psychiatric Publishing, 2013), 80.

4. Chris Stasiek and Mark Zetin, "Organic Manic Disorders," *Psychosomatics* 26, no. 5 (May 1985): 394–96; Eric W. Larson and Elliot Richelson, "Organic Causes of Mania," *Mayo Clinic Proceedings* 63, no. 9 (September 1988): 906–12.

5. Frederick K. Goodwin and Kay Redfield Jamison, *Manic-Depressive Illness: Bipolar Disorder and Recurrent Depression*, 2nd ed. (New York: Oxford University Press, 2007), 139–40.

6. Kemal Dumlu et al., "Treatment-Induced Manic Switch in the Course of Unipolar Depression Can Predict Bipolarity: Cluster Analysis Based Evidence," *Journal of Affective Disorders* 134, no. 1–3 (November 2011): 91.

7. American Psychiatric Association, *Desk Reference*, 76-77.

8. Takeshi Terao and Teruaki Tanaka, "Antidepressant-Induced Mania or Hypomania in *DSM-5*," *Psychopharmacology* 231, no. 1 (January 2014): 315.

9. Krauthammer and Klerman, "Secondary Mania," 1333–39.

10. Paul E. Holtzheimer III and William M. McDonald, "Late-Onset Bipolar Disorder and Secondary Mania," in *Bipolar Disorder in Late Life*, ed.

Martha Sajatovic and Frederick C. Blow (Baltimore: Johns Hopkins University Press, 2007), 58–59.

11. Goodwin and Jamison, *Manic-Depressive Illness*, 135–41.

12. Robert C. Young et al., "Geri-BD: A Randomized Double-Blind Controlled Trial of Lithium and Divalproex in the Treatment of Mania in Older Patients with Bipolar Disorder," *American Journal of Psychiatry* 174, no. 11 (November 2017): 1086.

13. Holtzheimer and McDonald, "Late-Onset Bipolar Disorder," 62.

14. John O. Brooks III, Barbara R. Sommer, and Terence A. Ketter, "Management of Bipolar Disorder in Older Adults," in *Handbook of Diagnosis and Treatment of Bipolar Disorders*, ed. Ternce A. Ketter (Washington, DC: American Psychiatric Publishing, 2010), 458–59.

CHAPTER 12: DISORDERS ASSOCIATED WITH BIPOLAR DISORDER

1. Frederick K. Goodwin and Kay Redfield Jamison, *Manic-Depressive Illness: Bipolar Disorder and Recurrent Depression*, 2nd ed. (New York: Oxford University Press, 2007), 223–25.

2. Susan McElroy et al., "Axis I Psychiatric Comorbidity and Its Relationship to Historical Illness Variables in 288 Patients with Bipolar Disorder," *American Journal of Psychiatry* 158, no. 3 (March 2001): 420.

3. Ibid.

4. Goodwin and Jamison, *Manic-Depressive Illness*, 224–25; McElroy et al., "Axis I Psychiatric Comorbidity," 420–26.

5. Goodwin and Jamison, *Manic-Depressive Illness*, 239.

6. Ibid. 237–38.

7. Michel W. Otto et al., "Posttraumatic Stress Disorder in Patients with Bipolar Disorder: A Review of Prevalence, Correlates and Treatment Strategies," *Bipolar Disorders* 6, no. 6 (November 2004): 470.

8. Goodwin and Jamison, *Manic-Depressive Illness*, 238–39.

9. Timothy E. Wilens et al., "Can Adults with Attention Deficit/Hyperactivity Disorder Be Distinguished from Those with Comorbid Bipolar Disorder? Findings from a Sample of Clinically Referred Adults," *Biological Psychiatry* 54, no. 1 (July 2003): 1.

10. Goodwin and Jamison, *Manic-Depressive Illness*, 289–91.

11. Luis R. Patino et al., "Management of Bipolar Disorder in Children and Adolescents," *Focus* 13, no. 1 (Winter 2015): 32.

12. Goodwin and Jamison, *Manic-Depressive Illness*, 239–40.

13. Ibid., 225–29.

14. Darrel A. Reiger et al., "Comorbidity of Mental Disorders with Alcohol and Other Drug Abuse: Results from the Epidemiologic Catchment Area (ECA) Study," *Journal of the American Medical Association* 264, no. 19 (November 1990): 2511.

15. Goodwin and Jamison, *Manic-Depressive Illness*, 225–29.

16. Ibid., 232–33.

17. Joseph R. Calabrese and Gustavo A. Delucchi, "Spectrum of Efficacy of Valproate in 55 Patients with Rapid-Cycling Bipolar Disorder," *American Journal of Psychiatry* 147, no. 4 (April 1990): 431–34.

18. Goodwin and Jamison, *Manic-Depressive Illness*, 232–33.

19. Joseph F. Goldberg and Joyce E. Whiteside, "The Association between Substance Abuse and Antidepressant-Induced Mania in Bipolar Disorder: A Preliminary Study," *Journal of Clinical Psychiatry* 63, no. 9 (2002): 791.

20. Robert M. Post, "Epigenetic Basis of Sensitization to Stress, Affective Episodes, and Stimulants: Implications for Illness Progression and Prevention," *Bipolar Disorder* 18, no. 4 (June 2016): 315.

21. Gregory B. Bovasso, "Cannabis Abuse as a Risk Factor for Depressive Symptoms," *American Journal of Psychiatry* 158, no. 12 (December 2001): 2033.

22. Goodwin and Jamison, *Manic-Depressive Illness*, 230–33.

23. Post, "Epigenetic Basis of Sensitization to Stress," 315.

24. F. Angst et al., "Mortality of Patients with Mood Disorders: Follow-Up over 34–38 Years," *Journal of Affective Disorders* 68, no. 2–3 (April 2002): 167.

25. Urban Osby et al., "Excess Mortality in Bipolar and Unipolar Disorder in Sweden," *Archives of General Psychiatry* 58, no. 9 (September 2001): 844.

26. Rodrigo B. Mansur and Roger S. McIntyre, "Metabolic Comorbidity and Physical Health Implications for Bipolar Disorder: Data from the First 500 STEP-BD Participants," *Focus* 13, no. 1 (Winter 2015): 12.

27. Goodwin and Jamison, *Manic-Depressive Illness*, 244.

28. Mansur and McIntyre, "Metabolic Comorbidity and Physical Health Implications," 12–15.

29. Ibid., 14.

30. Claudia F. Baldassano et al., "Gender Differences in Bipolar Disorder: Retrospective Data from the First 500 STEP-BD Participants," *Bipolar Disorder* 7, no. 5 (September 2005): 465.

31. J. Valle et al., "Evaluation of Thyroid Function in Lithium-Naïve Bipolar Patients," *European Psychiatry* 14, no. 6 (October 1999): 341.

32. Goodwin and Jamison, *Manic-Depressive Illness*, 241–42.

33. Ibid., 244.

34. Kay Redfield Jamison, *Touched with Fire: Manic-Depressive Illness and the Artistic Temperament*, 2nd ed. (New York: Free Press, 1993).

CHAPTER 13: BIPOLAR YOUTH

1. Robert L. Findling and Kiki D. Chang, "Improving the Diagnosis and Treatment of Pediatric Bipolar Disorder," *Journal of Clinical Psychiatry* 79, no. 2 (2018): su17023ah3c.

2. Robert A. Kowatch, "Diagnosis, Phenomenology, Differential Diagnosis and Comorbidity of Pediatric Bipolar Disorder," *Journal of Clinical Psychiatry* 77, Suppl. E1 (2016): e1.

3. Kezia J. Lange and Melvin G. McInnis, "Studies of Anticipation in Bipolar Affective Disorder," *CNS Spectrums* 7, no. 3 (March 2002): 196.

4. Gabrielle A. Carlson and Caroly Pataki, "Bipolar Disorder among Children and Adolescents," *Focus* 14, no. 1 (Winter 2016): 15–19.

5. Findling and Chang, "Improving the Diagnosis and Treatment."

6. Gabrielle A. Carlson and Caroly Pataki, "Disruptive Mood Dysregulation Disorder among Children and Adolescents," *Focus* 14, no. 1 (Winter 2016): 20–25.

7. Carlson and Pataki, "Bipolar Disorder among Children and Adolescents," 15–19.

8. Kowatch, "Diagnosis, Phenomenology," e1.

9. Kowatch, "Diagnosis, Phenomenology"; Findling and Chang, "Improving the Diagnosis and Treatment."

10. Robert L. Findling, "Evidence-Based Pharmacologic Treatment of Pediatric Bipolar Disorder," *Journal of Clinical Psychiatry* 77, Suppl. E1 (2016): e02.

11. Ibid.

12. Findling and Chang, "Improving the Diagnosis and Treatment."

13. David J. Miklowitz, "Evidence-Based Family Interventions for Adolescents and Young Adults with Bipolar Disorder," *Journal of Clinical Psychiatry* 77, Suppl. E1 (2016): e05.

Resources for Further Study

BOOKS

Bauer, M., E. Ludman, et al. *Overcoming Bipolar Disorder: A Comprehensive Workbook for Managing Your Symptoms and Achieving Your Life Goals.* Oakland, CA: New Harbinger Publications, 2008.

Brown, W. A. *Lithium: A Doctor, a Drug, and a Breakthrough.* New York: Liveright, 2019. An engrossing history of the discovery of lithium's benefits for bipolar disorder and its slow acceptance into the mainstream of psychiatry.

Goodwin, F. K., and K. R. Jamison. *Manic-Depressive Illness: Bipolar Disorders and Recurrent Depression.* 2nd ed. New York: Oxford University Press, 2007. A definitive and encyclopedic text with more than 1,200 pages.

Jamison, K. R. *Touched with Fire: Manic-Depressive Illness and the Artistic Temperament.* New York: Vintage Press, 1993. A discussion of bipolar disorder among literary, visual, and musical artists including some personal histories and reviews of research studies.

Jamison, K. R. *An Unquiet Mind: A Memoir of Moods and Madness.* New York: Vintage Books, 1996. An autobiographical account of bipolar disorder by a bipolar psychologist who is also one of the world's leading authorities on bipolar disorder.

Miklowitz, D. J. *The Bipolar Survival Guide: What You and Your Family Need to Know.* 3rd ed. New York: Guilford Press, 2019. A highly readable book with lots of information on coping with bipolar disorder, written by one of the foremost experts on psychotherapy for bipolar disorder.

Mondimore, F. M. *Bipolar Disorder: A Guide for Patients and Families.* 3rd ed. Baltimore: Johns Hopkins University Press, 2014. Another highly readable overview of bipolar disorder.

INTERNET RESOURCES

American Psychiatric Association www.psychiatry.org
Depression and Bipolar Support Alliance (DBSA) www.dbsalliance.org
Esperanza (a magazine, paper or online); subscribe at www.hopetocope.com
International Bipolar Foundation www.ibpf.org
International Society for Bipolar Disorders www.isbd.org
National Alliance on Mental Illness (NAMI) www.nami.org
National Institute of Mental Health https://www.nimh.nih.gov/index.shtml
National Suicide Prevention Lifeline 1-800-273-8255

Bibliography

Adelufosi, Adegoke Oloruntoba, Olukayode Abayomi, and Tunde Massey-Ferguson Ojo. "Pyridoxal 5 Phosphate for Neuroleptic-Induced Tardive Dyskinesia." *Cochrane Database of Systematic Reviews* (April 2015). https://doi.org/10.1002/14651858.CD010501.pub2.

Agnew-Blais, Jessica, and Andrea Danese. "Childhood Maltreatment and Unfavourable Clinical Outcomes in Bipolar Disorder: Systematic Review and Meta-Analysis." *Lancet Psychiatry* 3, no. 4 (April 2016): 342–49. doi: 10.1016/S2215-0366(15)00544-1.

Albertini, Elizabeth, Carrie L. Ernst, and Rachel S. Tamaroff. "Psychopharmacological Decision Making in Bipolar Disorder during Pregnancy and Lactation: A Case-by-Case Approach to Using Current Evidence." *Focus* 17, no. 3 (Summer 2019): 251–52.

Altshuler, Lori, Trisha Suppes, David Black, Willem A. Nolen, Paul E. Keck, Mark A. Frye, Susan McElroy, et al. "Impact of Antidepressant Discontinuation after Acute Bipolar Depression Remission on Rates of Depressive Relapse at 1-Year Followup." *American Journal of Psychiatry* 160, no. 7 (July 2003): 1252–62. https://doi.org/10.1176/appi.ajp.160.7.1252.

American Diabetes Association, American Psychiatric Association, American Association of Clinical Endocrinologists, and North American Association for the Study of Obesity. "Consensus Development Conference on Antipsychotic Drugs and Obesity and Diabetes." *Diabetes Care* 27, no. 2 (February 2004): 596–601 https://doi.org/10.2337/diacare.27.2.596.

American Psychiatric Association. *Desk Reference to the Diagnostic Criteria from DSM-5.* Washington, DC: American Psychiatric Publishing, 2013.

Andrade, Chittaranjan. "Ketamine for Depression, 1: Clinical Summary of Issues Related to Efficacy, Adverse Effects, and Mechanisms of Action." *Journal of Clinical Psychiatry* 78, no. 4 (2017): e415-19.

————. "Valproate in Pregnancy: Recent Research and Regulatory Responses." *Journal of Clinical Psychiatry* 79, no. 3 (May 2018): pii: 18f12351. doi: 10.4088/JCP.18f12351.

Angst, F., H. H. Stassen, Paula J. Clayton, and J. Angst. "Mortality of Patients with Mood Disorders: Follow-Up over 34–38 Years." *Journal of Affective Disorders* 68, no. 2–3 (April 2002): 167–81. https://doi.org/10.1016/S0165-0327(01)00377-9.

Baldassano, Claudia F., Lauren B. Marangell, Laszlo Gyulai, S. Nassir Ghaemi, Hadine Joffe, Deborah R. Kim, Kemal Sagduyu, et al. "Gender Differences in Bipolar Disorder: Retrospective Data from the First 500 STEP-BD Participants." *Bipolar Disorder* 7, no. 5 (September 2005): 465–70. https://doi.org/10.1111/j.1399-5618.2005.00237.x.

Baldessarini, Ross J., Leonardo Tondo, Gianni L. Faedda, Trisha Suppes, Gianfranco Floris, and Nereide Rudas. "Effects of the Rate of Discontinuing Lithium Maintenance Treatment in Bipolar Disorders." *Journal of Clinical Psychiatry* 57, no. 10 (1996): 441–48.

Baldessarini, Ross J., Leonardo Tondo, Gianfranco Floris, and Nereide Rudas. "Reduced Morbidity after Gradual Discontinuation of Lithium Treatment for Bipolar I and II Disorders: A Replication Study." *American Journal of Psychiatry* 154, no. 4 (April 1997): 551–53.

Baldessarini, Ross J., Leonardo Tondo, and John Hennen. "Lithium Treatment and Suicide Risk in Major Affective Disorders." *Journal of Clinical Psychiatry* 64, Suppl. 5 (2003): 44–52.

Barnett, Jennifer H., and Jordan W. Smoller. "The Genetics of Bipolar Disorder." *Neuroscience* 164, no. 1 (November 2009): 331–43.

Bartoli, Francesco. "Allopurinol as Add-On Treatment for Mania Symptoms in Bipolar Disorder: Systematic Review and Meta-Analysis of Randomized Controlled Trials." *British Journal of Psychiatry* 210, no. 1 (January 2017): 10–15. doi: 10.1192/bjp.bp 115.180281.

Bauer, Isabella E., Charles Green, Gabriela D. Colpo, Antonio L. Teixeira, Sudhakar Selvaraj, Katherine Durkin, Giovana B. Zunta-Soares, and Jair C. Soares. "A Double-Blind, Randomized, Placebo-Controlled Study of Aspirin and N-Acetylcysteine as Adjunctive Treatments for Bipolar Depression." *Journal of Clinical Psychiatry* 80, no. 1 (2013): pii: 18m12200.

Beck, Aaron T., A. John Rush, Brian F. Shaw, and Gary Emery. *Cognitive Therapy of Depression*. New York: Guilford Press, 1979.

Benedetti, Francesco, Roberta Riccaboni, Clara Locatelli, Sara Poletti, Sara Dallaspezia, and Cristina Colombo. "Rapid Treatment Response of Suicidal Symptoms to Lithium, Sleep Deprivation, and Light Therapy (Chronotherapeutics) in Drug-Resistant Bipolar Depression." *Journal of Clinical Psychiatry* 75, no. 2 (February 2014): 133–40. https://doi.org/10.4088/JCP.13m08455.

Beyer, John L., and Martha E. Payne. "Nutrition and Bipolar Depression." *Psychiatric Clinics of North America* 39, no. 1 (March 2016): 75–86.

Beyer, John L., and Richard H. Weisler. "Suicide Behaviors in Bipolar Disorder: A Review and Update for the Clinician." *Psychiatric Clinics of North America* 39, no. 1 (March 2016): 111–23.

Boden, Robert, Maria Lundgren, Lena Brandt, Johan Reutfors, Morten Andersen, and Helle Kieler. "Risks of Adverse Pregnancy and Birth Outcomes in Women Treated or Not Treated with Mood Stabilizers for Bipolar Disorder: Population Based Cohort Study." *British Medical Journal* 345 (November 2012): e7085. doi: 10.1136/bmj.e7085.

Bovasso, Gregory B. "Cannabis Abuse as a Risk Factor for Depressive Symptoms." *American Journal of Psychiatry* 158, no. 12 (December 2001): 2033–37. https://doi.org/10.1176/appi.ajp.158.12.2033.

Brent, David A., Joshua A. Perper, Christopher J. Allman, Grace M. Moritz, Mary E. Wartella, and Janice P. Zelenak. "The Presence and Accessibility of Firearms in the Homes of Adolescent Suicides." *Journal of the American Medical Association* 266, no. 21 (December 1991): 2989–95. doi: 10.1001/jama.1991.03470210057032.

Brown, E. Sherwood, and Barry Gabrielson. "A Randomized, Double-Blind, Placebo-Controlled Trial of Citicoline for Bipolar and Unipolar Depression and Methamphetamine Dependence." *Journal of Affective Disorders* 143, no. 1–3 (December 2012): 257–58.

Brown, Walter A. *Lithium: A Doctor, a Drug, and a Breakthrough.* New York: Liveright, 2019.

Cade, John. "Lithium Salts in the Treatment of Psychotic Excitement." *Bulletin of the World Health Organization* 78, no. 4 (1949): 518–20.

Cadet, Jean Lud, and Mark Gold. "Methamphetamine-Induced Psychosis: Who Says All Drug Use Is Reversible?" *Current Psychiatry* 16, no. 11 (November 2017): 15–20.

Calabrese, Joseph R., and Gustavo A. Delucchi. "Spectrum of Efficacy of Valproate in 55 Patients with Rapid-Cycling Bipolar Disorder." *American Journal of Psychiatry* 147, no. 4 (April 1990): 431–34.

Canuso, Carla M., Jaskaran B. Singh, Maggie Fedgchin, Larry Alphs, Rosanne Lane, Pilar Lim, Christine Pinter, et al. "Efficacy and Safety of Intranasal Esketamine for the Rapid Reduction of Symptoms of Depression and Suicidality in Patients at Imminent Risk for Suicide: Results of a Double-Blind, Randomized, Placebo-Controlled Study." *American Journal of Psychiatry* 175, no. 7 (February 2018): 620–30.

Carlson, Gabrielle A., and Caroly Pataki. "Disruptive Mood Dysregulation Disorder among Children and Adolescents." *Focus* 14, no. 1 (Winter 2016): 20–25.

———. "Bipolar Disorder among Children and Adolescents." *Focus* 14, no. 1 (Winter 2016): 15–19.

Chen, Chien-Hsiun, Chau-Shoun Lee, Ming-Ta Michael Lee, Wen-Chen Ouyang, Chiao-Chicy Chen, Mian-Yoon Chong, Jer-Yuarn Wu, et al. "Variant GADL1 and Response to Lithium Therapy in Bipolar I Disorder." *New England Journal of Medicine* 370, no. 2 (January 2014): 119–128. doi: 10.1056/NEJMoa1212444.

Ciapparelli, Antonio, Liliana dell'Osso, Stefano Pini, Maria Cristina Chiavacci, Melania Fenzi, and Giovanni B. Cassano. "Clozapine for Treatment-Refractory Schizophrenia, Schizoaffective Disorder, and Psychotic Bipolar Disorder: A 24-Month Naturalistic Study." *Journal of Clinical Psychiatry* 61, no. 5 (May 2000): 329–34. doi: 10.4088/jcp.v61n0502.

Cipriani, Andrea, Keith Hawton, Sarah Stockton, and John R. Geddes. "Lithium in the Prevention of Suicide in Mood Disorders: Updated Systematic Review and Meta-Analysis." *British Medical Journal* 346 (June 2013): f3646. https://doi.org/10.1136/bmj.f3646.

Cipriani, Andrea, Heather Pretty, Keith Hawton, and John R. Geddes. "Lithium in the Prevention of Suicidal Behavior and All-Cause Mortality in Patients with Mood Disorders: A Systematic Review of Randomized Trials." *American Journal of Psychiatry* 162, no. 10 (October 2005):1805–19.

Clemente, A. S., B. S. Diniz, R. Nicolato, F. P. Kapczinski, J. C. Soares, J. O. Firmo, and E. Castro-Costa. "Bipolar Disorder Prevalence: A Systematic Review and Meta-Analysis of the Literature." *Brazilian Journal of Psychiatry* 37, no. 2 (April–June 2015): 155–61. doi: 10.1590/1516-4446-2012-1693.

Cohen, Lee S., J. M. Friedman, James W. Jefferson, E. Marshall Johnson, and Myrna L. Weiner. "A Reevaluation of Risk of in Utero Exposure to Lithium." *Journal of the American Medical Association* 271, no. 2 (January 1994): 146–50.

Compton, Michael T., and Ruth S. Shim. "The Social Determinants of Mental Health." *Focus* 13, no. 4 (Fall 2015): 419–25.

Correll, Christopher U. "Epidemiology and Prevention of Tardive Dyskinesia." *Journal of Clinical Psychiatry* 78, no. 9 (November–December 2017): e1426. doi: 10.4088/JCPO.tv17016x1c.

Delgado, Pedro L., Dennis S. Charney, Lawrence H. Price, George K. Aghajanian, Harold Landis, and George R. Heninger. "Serotonin Function and the Mechanism of Antidepressant Action: Reversal of Antidepressant-Induced Remission by Rapid Depletion of Plasma Tryptophan." *Archives of General Psychiatry* 47 (1990): 411–18.

Dome, Peter, Zoltan Rihmer, and Xenia Gonda. "Suicide Risk in Bipolar Disorder: A Brief Review." *Medicina (Kaunas)* 55, no. 8 (August 2019): 403. doi: 10.3390/medicina55080403.

Donde, Clement, Ali Amad, Isabel Nieto, Andre Russowsky Brunoni, Nicholas H. Neufeld, Frank Bellivier, Emmanuel Poulet, and Pierre-Alexis Geoffroy. "Transcranial Direct-Current Stimulation (tDCS) for Bipolar Depression: A Systematic Review and Meta-Analysis." *Progress in Neuro-Psychopharmacology and Biological Psychiatry* 78, no. 1 (August 2017): 123–31. https://doi.org/10.1016/j.pnpbp.2017.05.021.

Dumlu, Kemal, Zahide Orhon, Aysegul Ozerdem, Umit Tural, Halis Ulas, and Zeliha Tunca. "Treatment-Induced Manic Switch in the Course of Unipolar Depression Can Predict Bipolarity: Cluster Analysis Based Evidence." *Journal of Affective Disorders* 134, no. 1–3 (November 2011): 91–101. https://doi.org/10.1016/j.jad.2011.06.019.

Durgam, Suresh, Willie Earley, Alan Lipschitz, Hua Guo, Istvan Laszlovzky, Gyorgy Nemeth, Eduard Vieta, Joseph Calabrese, and Lakshmi N. Yatham. "An 8-Week Randomized, Double-Blind, Placebo-Controlled Evaluation of the Safety and Efficacy of Cariprazine in Patients with Bipolar I Depression." *American Journal of Psychiatry* 173, no. 3 (March 2016): 271–81. doi: 10.1176/appi.ajp.2015. 15020164.

Evans, A. Eden, Alan I. Green, John M. Kane, and Sir Robin M. Murray. "Does Using Marijuana Increase the Risk for Developing Schizophrenia?" *Journal of Clinical Psychiatry* 74, no. 4 (April 2013): e08. https://doi.org/10.4088/JCP.12012tx2c.

Fawcett, Jan, William A. Scheftner, Louis Fogg, David C. Clark, Michael A. Young, Don Hedeker, and Robert Gibbons. "Time-Related Predictors of Suicide in Major Affective Disorders." *American Journal of Psychiatry* 147, no. 9 (September 1990): 1189–94.

Fawcett, Robert G. "Cerebral Infarct Presenting as Mania." *Journal of Clinical Psychiatry* 52, no. 8 (August 1991): 352–53.

———. "Dose-Related Thrombocytopenia and Macrocytic Anemia Associated with Valproate Use in Bipolar Disorder." *Journal of Clinical Psychiatry* 58, no. 3 (March 1997): 125.

———. "Erythema Multiforme Major in a Patient Treated with Carbamazepine." *Journal of Clinical Psychiatry* 48, no. 10 (October 1987): 416–17.

Forsberg, L., M. Adler, I. Romer Ek, M. Ljungdahl, L. Naver, L. L. Gustafsson, G. Berglund, et al. "Maternal Mood Disorders and Lithium Exposure *in Utero* Were Not Associated with Poor Cognitive Development during Childhood." *Acta Paediatrica* 107, no. 8 (November 2017): 1379–88. https://doi.org/10.1111/apa.14152.

Findling, Robert L. "Evidence-Based Pharmacologic Treatment of Pediatric Bipolar Disorder." *Journal of Clinical Psychiatry* 77, Suppl. E1 (2016): e02. https://doi.org/10.4988/JCP.15017su1c.02.

Findling, Robert L., and Kiki D. Chang. "Improving the Diagnosis and Treatment of Pediatric Bipolar Disorder." *Journal of Clinical Psychiatry* 79, no. 2 (2018): su17023ah3c.

Frank, Ellen, David J. Kupfer, Michael Thase, Alan G. Mallinger, Holly A. Swatz, Andrea M. Fagiolini, Victoria Grochocinski, et al. "Two-Year Outcomes for Interpersonal and Social Rhythm Therapy in Individuals with Bipolar I Disorder." *Archives of General Psychiatry* 62 (2005): 996–1004. doi: 10.1001/archpsyc.62.9.996.

Gasior, Maciej, Michael A. Rogawski, and Adam L. Hartman. "Neuroprotective and Disease-Modifying Effects of the Ketogenic Diet." *Behavioral Pharmacology* 17, no. 5–6 (September 2006): 431–39.

Geddes, John R., G. M. Goodwin, J. Rendell, J. M. Azorin, Andrea Cipriani, M. J. Ostacher, R. Morriss, N. Alder, and E. Juszczak. "Lithium Plus Valproate Combination Therapy versus Monotherapy for Relapse Prevention in Bipolar I Disorder (BALANCE): A Randomized Open-Label Trial." *Lancet* 375, no. 9712 (January 2010): 385–95. doi: 10.1016/S0140-6736(09)61828-6.

Gelenberg, Alan J., John M. Kane, Martin B. Keller, Philip Lavori, Jerrold F. Rosenbaum, Karyl Cole, Janet Lavelle, et al. "Comparison of Standard and Low Serum Levels of Lithium for Maintenance Treatment of Bipolar Disorder." *New England Journal of Medicine* 321, no. 22 (November 1989): 1489–93. doi: 10.1056/NEJM198911303212201.

Gentile, Salvatore. "Prophylactic Treatment of Bipolar Disorder in Pregnancy and Breastfeeding: Focus on Emerging Mood Stabilizers." *Bipolar Disorders* 8, no. 3 (May 2006): 207–20. https://doi.org/j.1399-5618.2006.00295.x.

Ghaemi, S. N., S. Dalley, C. Catania, and S. Barroilhet. "Bipolar or Borderline: A Clinical Overview." *Acta Psychiatrica Scandinavica* 130, no. 2 (August 2014): 99–108.

Ghaemi, S. N., A. P. Wingo, M. A. Filkowski, and Ross J. Baldessarini. "Long-Term Antidepressant Treatment in Bipolar Disorder: Meta-Analysis of Benefits and Risks." *Acta Psychiatrica Scandinavica* 118, no. 5 (November 2008): 347–56. doi: 10.1111/j.1600-0447.2008.01257.x.

Gibbs, Melanie, Catherine Winsper, Steven Marwaha, Eleanor Gilbert, Matthew Broome, and Swaran P. Singh. "Cannabis Use and Mania Symptoms: A Systematic Review and Meta-Analysis." *Journal of Affective Disorders* 171, no. 15 (January 2015): 39–47. doi: 10.10165/j.jad.2014.09.016.

Goldberg, Joseph F., and Joyce E. Whiteside. "The Association between Substance Abuse and Antidepressant-Induced Mania in Bipolar Disorder: A Preliminary Study." *Journal of Clinical Psychiatry* 63, no. 9 (2002): 791–95.

Goodwin, Frederick K., Bruce Fireman, Gregory E. Simon, Enid M. Hunkeler, Janelle Lee, and Dennis Revicki. "Suicide Risk in Bipolar Disorder during Treatment with Lithium and Divalproex." *Journal of the American*

Medical Association 290, no. 11 (September 2003): 1467–73. doi: 10.1001 /jama.290.11.1467.

Goodwin, Frederick K., and Kay Redfield Jamison. *Manic-Depressive Illness: Bipolar Disorder and Recurrent Depression.* 2nd ed. New York: Oxford University Press, 2007.

Goodwin, Guy M., Charles Bowden, Joseph R. Calabrese, Heinz Grunze, Siegfried Kasper, Robin White, Paul Greene, and Robert Leadbetter. "A Pooled Analysis of 2 Placebo-Controlled 18-Month Trials of Lamotrigine and Lithium Maintenance in Bipolar I Disorder." *Journal of Clinical Psychiatry* 65, no. 3 (2004): 432–41.

Greden, John R., Michelle B. Riba, and Melvin G. McInnis, eds. *Treatment Resistant Depression.* Washington, DC: American Psychiatric Publishing, 2011.

Grigoriadis, Sophie, Emily H. VonderPorten, Lana Mamishavilli, Allison Eady, George Tomlinson, Cindy-Lee Dennis, Gideon Koren, et al. "The Effect of Prenatal Antidepressant Exposure on Neonatal Adaptation: A Systematic Review and Meta-Analysis." *Journal of Clinical Psychiatry* 74, no. 4 (April 2013): e309-e20. https://doi.org/10.4088/JCP.12r07967.

Grunebaum, Michael F., Steven P. Ellis, John G. Keilp, Vivek K. Moitra, Thomas B. Cooper, Julia E. Marver, Ainsley K. Burke, et al. "Ketamine vs. Midazolam in Bipolar Depression with Suicidal Thoughts: A Pilot Midazolam-Controlled Randomized Clinical Trial." *Bipolar Disorders* 19, no. 3 (April 2017): 176–83.

Hauser, Robert A., Stewart A. Factor, Stephen R. Marder, Mary Ann Knesevich, Paul M. Ramirez, Roland Jimenez, Joshua Burke, Grace S. Liang, and Christopher F. O'Brien. "KINECT 3: A Phase 3 Randomized, Double-Blind, Placebo-Controlled Trial of Valbenazine for Tardive Dyskinesia." *American Journal of Psychiatry* 174, no. 5 (May 2017): 476–84. https://doi .org/10.1176/appi.ajp.2017.16091037.

Huybrechts, Krista F., Sonia Hernandez-Diaz, Elisabetta Patorno, Rishi J. Desai, Helen Mogun, Sara Z. Dejene, Jacqueline M. Cohen, Alice Panchaud, Lee Cohen, and Brian Bateman. "Antipsychotic Use in Pregnancy and the Risk of Congenital Malformations." *JAMA Psychiatry* 73, no. 9 (September 2016): 938–46. doi: 10.1001/jamapsychiatry.2016.1250.

Inder, Maree L., Marie T. Crowe, Suzanne E. Luty, Janet D. Carver, Stephanie Moor, Christopher M. Frampton, and Peter R. Joyce. "Randomized, Controlled Trial of Interpersonal and Social Rhythm Therapy for Young People with Bipolar Disorder." *Bipolar Disorders* 17, no. 2 (October 2014): 128–38. doi: 10.1111/bdi. 12273.

Inder, Maree L., Marie T. Crowe, Stephanie Moor, Janet D. Carter, Suzanne E. Luby, Christopher M. Frampton, and Peter R. Joyce. "Three-Year Follow-Up after Psychotherapy for Young People with Bipolar Disorder." *Bipolar Disorders* (December 2017). doi: 10.1111/bdi.12582.

Jacobs, Douglas G., ed. *The Harvard Medical School Guide to Suicide Assessment and Intervention.* San Francisco: Jossey-Bass, 1999.

Jacobs, Gregg D. *Say Good Night to Insomnia.* New York: Henry Holt and Company, 2009.

Jamison, Kay Redfield. *Touched with Fire: Manic-Depressive Illness and the Artistic Temperament.* New York: Free Press, 1993.

Johnson, Sheri L., Amy K. Cuellar, Camillo Ruggero, Carol Winett-Perlman, Paul Goodnick, Richard White, and Ivan Miller. "Life Events as Predictors of Mania and Depression in Bipolar I Disorder." *Journal of Abnormal Psychology* 117, no. 2 (May 2008): 268–77.

Jones, Kenneth Lyons, Ronald V. Lacro, Kathleen A. Johnson, and Jane Adams. "Pattern of Malformations in the Children of Women Treated with Carbamazepine during Pregnancy." *New England Journal of Medicine* 320 (June 1989): 1661–66. doi: 10.1056/NEJM198906223202505.

Josiassen, Richard C., John M. Kane, Grace S. Liang, Joshua Burke, and Christopher F. O'Brien. "Long-Term Safety and Tolerability of Valbenazine (NBI-98854) in Subjects with Tardive Dyskinesia and a Diagnosis of Schizophrenia or Mood Disorder." *Psychopharmacology Bulletin* 47, no. 3 (August 2017): 61–68.

Judd, Lewis L., Hagop S. Akiskal, Pamela J. Schettler, William Coryell, Jack Maser, John A. Rice, David A. Solomon, and Martin Keller. "The Comparative Clinical Phenotype and Long-Term Longitudinal Episode Course of Bipolar I and II: A Clinical Spectrum or Distinct Disorders?" *Journal of Affective Disorders* 73, no. 1–2 (January 2003): 19–32.

Judd, Lewis L., Hagop S. Akiskal, Pamela J. Schettler, Jean Endicott, Jack Maser, David A. Solomon, Andrew C. Leon, John A. Rice, and Martin B. Keller. "The Long-Term Natural History of the Weekly Symptomatic Status of Bipolar I Disorder." *Archives of General Psychiatry* 59, no. 6 (2002): 530–37. doi: 10.1001/archpsyc.59.6.530.

Kahn, Sabrina, Madeline E. Fersh, Carrie Ernst, Kim Klipstein, Elizabeth Streicker Albertini, Shari Lusskin, et al. "Bipolar Disorder in Pregnancy and Postpartum: Principles of Management." *Current Psychiatry Reports* 18, no. 2 (February 2016): 13. doi: 10.1007/s11920-015-0658-x.

Kaminstein, Philip. "Importance of the Transference and Therapeutic Alliance in Pharmacotherapy." *American Journal of Psychiatry* 78, no. 4 (March 1989): 404–5.

Kaunonen, Marja, Marja-Terttu Tarrka, Marita Paunonen, and Pekka Laippala. "Grief and Social Support after the Death of a Spouse." *Journal of Advanced Nursing* 30, no. 6 (December 2001): 1304–11.

Keller, Martin B., Philip Lavori, William Corytell, Jean Endicott, and Timothy Mueller. "Bipolar I: A Five-Year Prospective Follow-Up." *Journal of Nervous and Mental Disease* 81, no. 4 (April 1993): 238–45.

Ketter, Terence A., ed. *Advances in Treatment of Bipolar Disorders.* Washington, DC: American Psychiatric Publishing, 2015.

———, ed. *Handbook of Diagnosis and Treatment of Bipolar Disorders.* Washington, DC: American Psychiatric Publishing, 2010.

Klerman, Gerald L., and Myrna M. Weissman. *Interpersonal Psychotherapy of Depression.* New York: Basic Books, 1984.

Kowatch, Robert A. "Diagnosis, Phenomenology, Differential Diagnosis and Comorbidity of Pediatric Bipolar Disorder." *Journal of Clinical Psychiatry* 77, Suppl. E1 (2016): e01. https://doi.org/10.4088/JCP.15017su1c.01.

Kraepelin, Emil. *Manic-Depressive Insanity and Paranoia.* Edinburgh: E. & S. Livingstone, 1921.

Krauthammer, Charles, and Gerald L. Klerman. "Secondary Mania: Manic Syndromes Associated with Antecedent Physical Illness or Drugs." *Archives of General Psychiatry* 35, no. 11 (1978): 1333–39.

Kreitman, N. "The Coal Gas Story: United Kingdom Suicide Rates." *British Journal of Preventive and Social Medicine* 30, no. 2 (June 1976): 86–93. doi: 10.1136/jech.30.2.86.

Lange, Kezia J., and Melvin G. McInnis. "Studies of Anticipation in Bipolar Affective Disorder." *CNS Spectrums* 7, no. 3 (March 2002): 196–202.

Larson, Eric W., and Elliot Richelson. "Organic Causes of Mania." *Mayo Clinic Proceedings* 63, no. 9 (September 1988): 906–12.

Lee, Ellen E., Megan P. Della Selva, Anson Liu, and Seth Himelhoch. "Ketamine as a Novel Treatment for Major Depressive Disorder and Bipolar Depression: A Systematic Review and Quantitative Meta-Analysis." *General Hospital Psychiatry* 37, no. 2 (March–April 2015): 178–84. https://doi.org/j.genhosppsych.2015.01.003.

Lerner, Vladimir, Chanoch Miodownik, Alexander Kapstan, Yuly Bersudsky, Igor Libov, Ben-Ami Sela, and Ellezer Witztum. "Vitamin B6 Treatment for Tardive Dyskinesia: A Randomized, Double-Blind, Placebo-Controlled, Crossover Study." *Journal of Clinical Psychiatry* 68, no. 11 (2007): 1648–54.

Lewis, L. "A Consumer Perspective Concerning the Diagnosis and Treatment of Bipolar Disorder." *Biological Psychiatry* 48 (2000):442–44.

Licht, Rasmus W., Jannie N. Nielsen, Lars F. Gram, Per Vestergaard, and Hans Bendz. "Lamotrigine versus Lithium as Maintenance Treatment in Bipolar I Disorder: An Open, Randomized Effectiveness Study Mimicking Clinical Practice. The 6th Trial of the Danish University Antidepressant Group (DUAG-6)." *Bipolar Disorders* 12, no. 5 (August 2010): 483–93. https://dpi.org/10.1111/j.1399-5618.2010.00836.x.

Longo, Dan L., Anthony S. Fauci, Dennis L. Kasper, Stephen L. Hauser, J. Larry Jameson, and Joseph Loscalzo, eds. *Harrison's Manual of Medicine.* 18th ed. New York: McGraw-Hill Medical, 2013.

Manji, Husseini K., Charles L. Bowden, and Robert H. Belmaker, eds. *Bipolar Medications: Mechanisms of Action.* Washington, DC: American Psychiatric Publishing, 2000.

Manji, Husseini K., Jorge A. Quiroz, Jennifer L. Payne, Jaskaran Singh, Barbara P. Lopes, Jenilee S. Viegas, and Carlos A. Zarate. "The Underlying Neurobiology of Bipolar Disorder." *World Psychiatry* 2, no. 3 (October 2003): 136–46.

Mansur, Rodrigo B., and Roger S. McIntyre. "Metabolic Comorbidity and Physical Health Implications for Bipolar Disorder: Data from the First 500 STEP-BD Participants." *Focus* 13, no. 1 (Winter 2015): 12–18.

Martin, Christopher D. "Ernest Hemingway: A Psychological Autopsy of a Suicide." *Psychiatry* 69, no 4 (2006): 351–61.

Martinowich, Keri, Robert J. Schloesser, and Husseini K. Manji. "Bipolar Disorder: From Genes to Behavior Pathways." *Focus* 9, no. 4 (Fall 2011): 526–39.

McCloud, Tayla L., Caroline Caddy, Janina Jochim, Jennifer M. Rendell, Peter R. Diamond, Claire Shuttleworth, Daniel Brett, et al. "Ketamine and Other Glutamate Receptor Modulators for Depression in Bipolar Disorder in Adults." *Cochrane Database of Systematic Reviews* (September 2015). doi: 10.1002/14651858.CD011611.pub2.

McElroy, Susan L., Lori L. Altshuler, Trisha Suppes, Paul E. Keck, Mark A. Frye, Kirk D. Denicoff, Willem A. Nolen, et al. "Axis I Psychiatric Comorbidity and Its Relationship to Historical Illness Variables in 288 Patients with Bipolar Disorder." *American Journal of Psychiatry* 158, no. 3 (March 2001): 420–26.

McGirr, Alexander, Sneha Karmani, Rashmi Arsappa, Marcelo T. Berlim, Jagadisha Thirthalli, Kesavan Muralidharan, and Lakshmi N. Yatham. "Clinical Efficacy and Safety of Repetitive Transcranial Magnetic Stimulation in Acute Bipolar Depression." *World Psychiatry* 15, no. 1 (February 2016): 85–86. doi: 10. 1002/wps.20300.

McKay, Kevin M., Zac E. Imel, and Bruce E. Wampold. "Psychiatrist Effects in the Psychopharmacological Treatment of Depression." *Journal of Affective Disorders* 92, no. 2–3 (June 2006): 287.

Medical Letter on Drugs and Therapeutics quoted in *Journal of the American Medical Association* 322, no. 1 (July 2019): 73.

Merikangas, Kathleen R., Hagop S. Akiskal, Jules Angst, Paul E. Geenberg, Robert M. A. Hirschfeld, Maria Petukhova, and Ronald C. Kessler. "Lifetime and 12-Month Prevalence of Bipolar Spectrum Disorder in the National Comorbidity Survey Replication." *Archives of General Psychiatry* 64, no. 5 (May 2007): 543–52.

Meyer, T. D., and M. Hautzinger. "Cognitive Behaviour Therapy and Supportive Therapy for Bipolar Disorders: Relapse Rates for Treatment Period and 2-Year Follow-Up." *Psychological Medicine* 42, no. 7 (July 2012): 1429.

Miklowitz, David J. *The Bipolar Disorder Survival Guide*. 2nd ed. New York: Guilford Press, 2019.

———. "Evidence-Based Family Interventions for Adolescents and Young Adults with Bipolar Disorder." *Journal of Clinical Psychiatry* 77, Suppl. E1 (2016): e05. https://doi.org/10.4088/JCP.15017su1c.05.

Miklowitz, David J., and Michel J. Gitlin. "Psychosocial Approaches to the Treatment of Bipolar Disorder." *Focus* 13, no. 1 (Winter 2015): 37–46.

Miklowitz, David J., Michael W. Otto, Ellen Frank, Noreen A. Reilly-Harrington, Jane N. Kogan, Gary S. Sachs, Michael E. Thase, et al. "Intensive Psychosocial Intervention Enhances Functioning in Inpatients with Bipolar Depression: Results from a 9-Month Randomized Controlled Trial." *American Journal of Psychiatry* 164, no. 9 (2007): 1340–47. doi: 10.1176/appi.ajp.2007.07020311.

Montgomery, Paul, and Alexandra J. Richardson. "Omega-3 Fatty Acids for Bipolar Disorder." *Cochrane Database for Systematic Reviews* 16, no. 2 (April 2008). doi: 10.1002/14651858.CD005169.pub2.

Moreira, Ana Lucia R., Anna Van Meter, Jacquelynne Genzlinger, and Eric A. Youngstrom. "Review and Meta-Analysis of Epidemiologic Studies of Adult Bipolar Disorder." *Journal of Clinical Psychiatry* 78, no. 9 (November–December 2017): e1259-e69. doi: 10.4088/JCP.16r11165.

Morris, Martha Clare, Christy C. Tangney, Yamin Wang, Frank M. Sacks, Lisa L. Barnes, David A. Bennet, and Neelum T. Aggarwai. "MIND Diet Slows Cognitive Decline with Aging." *Alzheimers and Dementia* 11, no. 9 (June 2015): 1015–22. doi: 10.1016/j.alz.2015.04.011.

Mukherjee, Sukdeb, Harold A. Sackeim, and David B. Schnur. "Electroconvulsive Therapy of Acute Manic Episodes: A Review of 50 Years' Experience." *American Journal of Psychiatry* 151, no. 2 (February 1994): 169–76.

Noaghiul, Simona, and Joseph R. Hibbein. "Cross-National Comparisons of Seafood Consumption and Rates of Bipolar Disorders." *American Journal of Psychiatry* 160, no. 2 (December 2003): 2222–27.

Osby, Urban, Lena Brandt, Nestor Correia, Anders Ekbom, and Par Sparen. "Excess Mortality in Bipolar and Unipolar Disorder in Sweden." *Archives of General Psychiatry* 58, no. 9 (September 2001): 844–50. doi: 10.1001/archpsyc.58.9.844.

Ostacher, Michael J. "Bipolar and Substance Use Disorder Comorbidity: Diagnostic and Treatment Considerations." *Focus* 9, no. 4 (Fall 2011): 428–34.

Otto, Michael W., Carol A. Perlman, Rachel Wernicke, Hannah E. Reese, Mark S. Bauer, and Mark H. Pollack. "Posttraumatic Stress Disorder in Patients with Bipolar Disorder: A Review of Prevalence, Correlates and Treatment Strategies." *Bipolar Disorders* 6, no. 6 (November 2004): 470–79. https://doi.org/10.1111/j.1399-5618.2004.00151.x.

Pacchiarotti, Isabella, David J. Bond, Ross J. Baldessarini, Willem A. Nolen, Heinz Grunze, Rasmus W. Licht, Robert M. Post, et al. "The International Society for Bipolar Disorders (ISBD) Task Force Report on Antidepressant Use in Bipolar Disorders." *American Journal of Psychiatry* 170, no. 11 (November 2013): 1249–62. doi: 10.1176/appi.ajp.2013.13020185.

Park, Yoonyoung, Sonia Hernandez-Diaz, Brian Bateman, Jacqueline M. Cohen, Rishi J. Desai, Elisabetta Patorno, Robert J. Glynn, Lee S. Cohen, Helen Mogun, and Krista F. Huybrechts. "Continuation of Atypical Antipsychotic Medication during Early Pregnancy and the Risk of Gestational Diabetes." *American Journal of Psychiatry* 175, no. 6 (June 2018): 564–74. doi: 10.1176/appi.ajp.2018.17040393.

Patino, Luis R., Kaitlyn M. Bruns, Natalie M. Witt, Nina R. McCune, and Melissa P. DelBello. "Management of Bipolar Disorder in Children and Adolescents." *Focus* 13, no. 1 (Winter 2015): 25–36.

Payne, Jennifer L., Dean F. MacKinnon, Francis M. Mondimore, Melvin G. McInnis, Barbara Schweitzer, Rachel B. Zamoiski, Francis J. McMahon, et al. "Familial Aggregation of Postpartum Mood Symptoms in Bipolar Disorder Pedigrees." *Bipolar Disorders* 10, no. 1 (February 2008): 38–44. doi: 10.1111/j.1399-5618.2008.00455.x.

Perlmutter, David, and K. Loberg. *Grain Brain: The Surprising Truth about Wheat, Carbs and Sugar—Your Brain's Silent Killers.* New York: Little, Brown, 2013.

Phelps, James R., Susan V. Siemers, and Rif S. El-Mallakh. "The Ketogenic Diet for Type II Bipolar Disorder." *Neurocase* 19, no. 5 (2013): 4323–26. doi: 10.1080/13554794.2012.690421.

Phillips, Mary L., and David J. Kupfer. "Bipolar Disorder Diagnosis: Challenges and Future Directions." *Lancet* 381, no. 9878 (May 2013): 1663–71. doi: 10.1016/S0140-6736(13)60989-7.

Piercy, Katrina L., Richard P. Troiano, Rachel M. Ballard, S. A. Carlson, J. E. Fulton, D. A. Galuska, S. M. George, and R. D. Olson. "The Physical Activity Guidelines for Americans." *Journal of the American Medical Association* 320, no. 19 (November 2018): 2020–28.

Poo, S. X., and M. Agius. "Atypical Antipsychotics for Schizophrenia and/or Bipolar Disorder in Pregnancy: Current Recommendations and Updates in the NICE Guidelines." *Psychiatria Danubina* 27, Suppl. E1 (2015): S255-60.

Post, Robert M. "Epigenetic Basis of Sensitization to Stress, Affective Episodes, and Stimulants: Implications for Illness Progression and Prevention." *Bipolar Disorders* 18, no. 4 (June 2016): 315–24. doi: 10.1111/bdi.12401.

———. "Preventing the Malignant Transformation of Bipolar Disorder." *Journal of the American Medical Association* 319, no. 12 (2018): 1197–1202.

———. "Treatment of Bipolar Depression: Evolving Recommendations." *Psychiatric Clinics of North America* 39, no. 1 (March 2016): 11–35.

Post, Robert M., and S. R. Weiss. "Sensitization, Kindling, and Anticonvulsants in Mania." *Journal of Clinical Psychiatry* 50, Suppl. (December 1989): 23–30.

Reiger, Darrel A., Mary E. Farmer, Donald S. Rae, Ben Z. Locke, Samuel J. Keith, Lewis L. Judd, and Frederick K. Goodwin. "Comorbidity of Mental Disorders with Alcohol and Other Drug Abuse: Results from the Epidemiologic Catchment Area (ECA) Study." *Journal of the American Medical Association* 264, no. 19 (November 1990): 2511–18. doi: 10.1001 /jama.1990.03450190043026.

Rosa, Franz W. "Spina Bifida in Infants of Women Treated with Carbamazepine during Pregnancy." *New England Journal of Medicine* 324 (March 1991): 674–77. doi: 10.1056/NEJM199103073241006.

Rush, A. John, ed. *Short-Term Psychotherapies for Depression.* New York: Guilford Press, 1982.

Rusner, Marie, Marie M. Berg, and Cecily C. Begley. "Bipolar Disorder in Pregnancy and Childbirth: A Systematic Review of Outcomes." *BMC Pregnancy Childbirth* 16, no. 1 (October 2016): 331.

Sajatovic, Martha, and Frederick C. Blow, ed. *Bipolar Disorder in Late Life.* Baltimore: Johns Hopkins University Press, 2007.

Sajatovic, Martha, Brent Forrester, Joyce Tsai, Hans Kroger, Andrei Pikalov, Josephine Cucchiaro, and Anthony Loebel. "Efficacy of Lurasidone in Adults Aged 55 Years and Older with Bipolar Depression." *Journal of Clinical Psychiatry* 77, no. 10 (October 2016): e1324-e1331. https://doi.org /10.4088/JCP.15m10261.

Sampaio-Junior, Bernardo, Gabriel Tortella, Lucas Borrione, Adriano H. Moffa, Rodrigo Machado-Viera, Eric Cretaz, Adriano Fernandes da Silva, et al. "Efficacy and Safety of Transcranial Direct Current Stimulation as an Add-On Treatment for Bipolar Depression." *JAMA Psychiatry* 75, no. 2 (February 2018): 158–66. doi: 10.1001/lamapsychiatry.2017.4040.

Sarris, Jerome, David Mischoulon, and Isaac Schweitzer. "Omega-3 for Bipolar Disorder: Meta-Analysis of Use in Mania and Bipolar Depression." *Journal of Clinical Psychiatry* 73, no. 1 (2012): 81–86.

Schaffer, Ayal, Erkki T. Isometsa, Leonardo Tondo, Doris H. Moreno, Mark Sinyor, Lars Vedel Kessing, Gustavo Turecki, et al. "Epidemiology, Neurobiology and Pharmacological Interventions Related to Suicide Deaths and Suicide Attempts in Bipolar Disorder: Part I of a Report of the International Society for Bipolar Disorders Task Force on Suicide in Bipolar Disorder." *Australia and New Zealand Journal of Psychiatry* 49, no. 9 (September 2015): 785–802. doi: 10.1177/0004867415594427.

Schatzberg, Alan F., and Charles DeBattista. *Manual of Clinical Psychopharmacology.* 8th ed. Washington, DC: American Psychiatric Publishing, 2015.

Schoeyen, Helle K., Ute Kessler, Ole A. Andreassen, Bjoern H. Auestad, Per Bergsholm, Ulrik F. Malt, Gunnar Murken, Ketil J. Oedegaard, and Arne

Vaaler. "Treatment-Resistant Bipolar Depression: A Randomized Controlled Trial of Electroconvulsive Therapy versus Algorithm-Based Pharmacological Treatment." *American Journal of Psychiatry* 172, no. 1 (January 2015): 41–51. https://doi.org/10.1176/appi.ajp.2014.13111517.

Schou, Mogens. "What Happened Later to the Lithium Babies? A Follow-Up Study of Children Born without Malformations." *Acta Psychiatrica Scandinavica* 54, no. 3 (September 1976): 193–97. doi: 10.1111/j.1600-0447.1976.tb00112.x.

Shulman, Kenneth I. "Disinhibition Syndromes, Secondary Mania and Bipolar Disorder in Old Age." *Journal of Affective Disorders* 46, no. 3 (December 1997): 175–82.

Sidor, Michelle M., and Glenda M. MacQueen. "Antidepressants for the Acute Treatment of Bipolar Depression: A Systematic Review and Meta-Analysis." *Journal of Clinical Psychiatry* 72, no. 2 (February 2011): 156–67. https://doi.org/10.4088/JCP.09r05385gre.

Simpson, Susan G., and Corinne L. Reid. "Therapeutic Alliance in Videoconferencing Psychotherapy: A Review." *Australian Journal of Rural Health* 22, no. 6 (December 2014): 280–99. doi: 10.1111/ajr.12149.

Sit, Dorothy K., James McGowan, Christopher Wiltrout, Rasim Somer Diler, John (Jesse) Dills, James Luther, Amy Yang, et al. "Adjunctive Bright Light Therapy for Bipolar Depression: A Randomized Double-Blind Placebo-Controlled Trial." *American Journal of Psychiatry* 175, no. 2 (February 2018): 131–39. https://doi.org/10.1176/appi.ajp.2017.16101200.

Soares-Weiser, Karla, Nicola Maayan, and Hanna Bergman. "Vitamin E for Antipsychotic-Induced Tardive Dyskinesia." *Cochrane Database of Systematic Reviews* (January 2018). https://doi: 10.1002/14651858.CD000209.pub3.

Sonne, Susan C., Kathleen Brady, and W. Alexander Morton. "Substance Abuse and Bipolar Affective Disorder." *Journal of Nervous and Mental Disease* 182, no. 6 (June 1994): 349–52.

Stasiek, Chris, and Mark Zetin. "Organic Manic Disorders." *Psychosomatics* 26, no. 5 (May 1985): 394–96, 399, 402.

Swartz, Holly, Paola Rucci, Michael E. Thase, Meredith Wallace, Elisa Carretta, Karen L. Celedonia, and Ellen Frank. "Psychotherapy Alone and Combined with Medication as Treatments for Bipolar II Depression: A Randomized Controlled Trial." *Journal of Clinical Psychiatry* 79, no. 2 (March–April 2018): 16m11027.

Swartz, Holly A., and Trisha Suppes, eds. *Bipolar II Disorder: Recognition, Understanding, and Treatment.* Washington, DC: American Psychiatric Publishing, 2019.

Tang, Ming-Xin, Yaakov Stern, Karen Marder, Karen Bell, Barry Gurland, Rafael Lantigua, Howard Andrews, Lin Feng, Benjamin Tycko, and Richard Mayeux. "The APOE-Epsilon4 Allele and the Risk of Alzheimer

Disease among African Americans, Whites, and Hispanics." *Journal of the American Medical Association* 279, no. 10 (March 1998): 751–55.

Terao, Takeshi, and Teruaki Tanaka. "Antidepressant-Induced Mania or Hypomania in *DSM-5*." *Psychopharmacology* 231, no. 1 (January 2014): 315.

Tosato, Sarah, Umberto Albert, Simona Tomassi, Felice Iasevoli, Claudia Carmassi, Silvia Ferrari, Maria Giulia Nanni, et al. "A Systematized Review of Atypical Antipsychotics in Pregnant Women: Balancing between Risks of Untreated Illness and Risks of Drug-Related Adverse Effects." *Journal of Clinical Psychiatry* 78, no. 5 (May 2017): e477-e89. https://doi.org/10.4088 /JCP.15r10483.

Valle, J., J. L. Ayuso-Gutierrez, A. Abril, and J. L. Ayuso-Mateos. "Evaluation of Thyroid Function in Lithium-Naïve Bipolar Patients." *European Psychiatry* 14, no. 6 (October 1999): 341–45. doi: 10.1016/s0924-9338(99)00158-3.

Van der Lugt, N. Margreth, Josephine S. van de Maat, Inge L. van Kamp, Elise A. M. Knoppert-van der Klein, Jacqueline G. F. M. Hovens, and Frans J. Walther. "Fetal, Neonatal and Developmental Outcomes of Lithium-Exposed Pregnancies." *Early Human Development* 88, no. 6 (June 2012): 375–78. https://doi.org/j.earlhumdev.2011.09.013.

Van Gerpen, S., T. Vik, and T. J. Soundy, "Medicinal and Recreational Marijuana: What Are the Risks?" *South Dakota Medicine* (2015): 58–62.

Vazquez, Gustavo H., Leonardo Tondo, Juan Undurraga, and Ross J. Baldessarini. "Overview of Antidepressant Treatment of Bipolar Depression." *International Journal of Neuropsychopharmacology* 16, no. 7 (August 2013): 1673–85. https://doi.org/10/1017/S1461145713000023.

Viguera, Adele C., Theodore Whitfield, Ross J. Baldessarini, Jeffrey Newport, Zachary Stowe, Alison Reminick, Amanda Zurick, and Lee S. Cohen. "Risk of Recurrence in Women with Bipolar Disorder during Pregnancy: Prospective Study of Mood Stabilizer Discontinuation." *American Journal of Psychiatry* 164, no. 12 (December 2007): 1817–24. https://doi.org/10.1176 /appi.ajp.2007.06101639.

Walker, Alexander M., Lee L. Lanza, Felix Arellano, and Kenneth J. Rothman. "Mortality in Current and Former Users of Clozapine." *Epidemiology* 8, no. 6 (November 1997): 671–77. doi: 10.1097/00001648-199710000 -00010.

Watson, Stuart, Peter Gallagher, Dominic Dougall, Richard Porter, Joanna Moncrieff, I. Nicole Ferrier, and Allan H. Young. "Childhood Trauma in Bipolar Disorder." *Australian and New Zealand Journal of Psychiatry* 48, no. 6 (June 2014): 564–70.

Wearne, T. A., and J. L. Cornish. "A Comparison of Methamphetamine-Induced Psychosis and Schizophrenia: A Review of Positive, Negative and Cognitive Symptomatology." *Frontiers in Psychiatry* 9 (October 2018): 491. doi: 10.3389/fpsyt.2018.00491.

Wegner, Mirko, Ingo Helmich, Sergio Machado, Antonio E. Nardi, Oscar Arias-Carrion, and Henning Budde. "Effects of Exercise on Anxiety and Depression Disorders: Review of Meta-Analyses and Neurobiological Mechanisms." *CNS & Neurological Disorders—Drug Targets* 13, no. 6 (2014): 1002–14.

Wehr, Thomas A., David A. Sack, and Norman Rosenthal. "Sleep Reduction as a Final Common Pathway in the Genesis of Mania." *American Journal of Psychiatry* 144, no. 2 (February 1987): 201–4.

Wilens, Timothy E., Joseph Biederman, Janet Wozniak, Samantha Gunawardene, Jocelyn Wong, and Michael Monuteaux. "Can Adults with Attention Deficit/Hyperactivity Disorder Be Distinguished from Those with Comorbid Bipolar Disorder? Findings from a Sample of Clinically Referred Adults." *Biological Psychiatry* 54, no. 1 (July 2003): 1–8. https://doi.org/10.1016/S0006-3223(02)01666-9.

Wilkinson, Samuel T., Elina Stefanovics, and Robert A. Rosenheck. "Marijuana Use Is Associated with Worse Outcomes in Symptom Severity and Violent Behavior in Patients with PTSD." *Journal of Clinical Psychiatry* 76, no. 9 (September 2015): 1174–80. doi: 10.4088/cjp.14m09475.

World Health Organization. "Global Recommendations on Physical Activity for Health: 18–64 years old." 2011. https://www.who.int/dietphysicalactivity/physical-activity-recommendations-18-64years.pdf?ua=1.

Wu, Joseph C., John R. Kelsoe, Carol Schachat, Blynn G. Bunney, Anna DeModena, Shahrokh Golshan, J. Christian Gillin, Steven G. Potkin, and William E. Bunney. "Rapid and Sustained Antidepressant Response with Sleep Deprivation and Chronotherapy in Bipolar Disorder." *Biological Psychiatry* 66, no. 3 (August 2009): 298–301. https://doi.org/10.1016/j.biopsych.2009.02.018.

Wurst, Keele E., Charles Poole, Sara A. Ephross, and Andrew F. Olshan. "First Trimester Paroxetine Use and the Prevalence of Congenital, Specifically Cardiac, Defects: A Meta-Analysis of Epidemiological Studies." *Birth Defects Research Part A: Clinical and Molecular Teratology* 88, no. 3 (September 2009): 159–70. https://doi.org/10.1002/bdra.20627.

Yacobi, Sarah, and Asher Ornoy. "Is Lithium a Real Teratogen? What Can We Conclude from the Prospective Versus Retrospective Studies? A Review." *Israeli Journal of Psychiatry and Related Sciences* 45, no. 2 (2008): 95–106.

Ye, Lin, Jiaming Wang, Yuting Tan, Ashley I. Beyer, Fei Xie, Marcus O. Muench, and Yuet Wai Kan. "Genome Editing Using CRISPR-Cas9 to Create the HPFH Genotype in HSPCs: An Approach for Treating Sickle Cell Disease and Beta-Thalassemia." *Proceedings of the National Academy of Science USA* 113, no. 38 (September 2016): 10661–65.

Yonkers, Kimberly, Simone Vigod, and Lori E. Ross. "Diagnosis, Pathophysiology, and Management of Mood Disorders in Pregnant and Postpartum

Women." *Obstetrics and Gynecology* 117, no. 4 (April 2011): 961–77. doi: 10.1097/AOG.0b013e31821187a7.

Yonkers, Kimberly, Katherine Wisner, Zachary Stowe, Ellen Leibenluft, Lee Cohen, Laura Miller, Rachel Manber, Adele Viguera, Trisha Suppes, and Lori Altshuler. "Management of Bipolar Disorder during Pregnancy and the Postpartum Period." *American Journal of Psychiatry* 161, no. 4 (April 2004): 608–20. https://doi.org/10.1176/appi.ajp.161.4.608.

Young, Robert C., Benoit Mulsant, Martha Sajatovic, Ariel G. Gildengers, Laszlo Gyulai, Rayan K. Al Jurdi, John Beyer, et al. "Geri-BD: A Randomized Double-Blind Controlled Trial of Lithium and Divalproex in the Treatment of Mania in Older Patients with Bipolar Disorder." *American Journal of Psychiatry* 174, no. 11 (November 2017): 1086–93. doi: 10.1176 /appi.ajp.2017.15050657.

Zorilla, I., J. Aquado, J. M. Haro, S. Barbeito, Zurbano S. Lopez, A. Ortiz, P. Lopez, and A. Gonzalez-Pinto. "Cannabis and Bipolar Disorder: Does Quitting Cannabis Use during Manic/Mixed Episode Improve Clinical/ Functional Outcomes?" *Acta Psychiatrica Scandinavica* 131, no. 2 (February 2015): 100–10. doi: 10.111/acps.12366.

Index

Note: all drugs are listed by their generic name only

About the Author

Robert G. Fawcett, MD, graduated with honors from Michigan State University and was elected to Phi Beta Kappa. He majored in psychology and then pursued studies in that field at Duke University until he realized he wanted to be a clinical psychiatrist and use both psychotherapy and the growing number of medications and biologic treatments to help persons with emotional disorders. He obtained his MD from Wayne State University School of Medicine, interned at the Maine Medical Center, and completed his residency in psychiatry at the University of Michigan.

Settling in Petoskey, Michigan, he joined the Burns Clinic, a large multispecialty clinic, later serving on its board of directors. Dr. Fawcett served as medical director of a fourteen-bed acute inpatient unit and treated private outpatients, as well as working at several community mental health centers. He has treated some individual bipolar patients for more than thirty years and members of three generations in several families. He served as president of the Northern Michigan Medical Society, and was designated a Distinguished Life Fellow of the American Psychiatric Association. He has had publications in several prominent psychiatric journals and given scores of lectures to clinical colleagues.

In his leisure hours he enjoys spending time with family and friends, bicycling, skiing, and fishing, performing as a singer-songwriter, writing poems such as his collection in *Limericks and Poems from County Emmet*, and being continually amazed by his granddaughter.